Technology and Productivity

Technology and Productivity

The Korean Way of
Learning and Catching Up

Youngil Lim

The MIT Press
Cambridge, Massachusetts
London, England

This book was set in Palatino on the Miles System by Achorn Graphic Services, Inc.

Printed and bound in the United States of America.

Library of Congress Cataloging-in-Publication Data

Lim, Youngil.
    Technology and productivity : the Korean way of learning and catching up / Youngil Lim.
        p.   cm.
    Includes bibliographical references and index.
    ISBN 0-262-12221-9 (alk. paper)
    1. Industrial productivity—Korea (South) 2. Industrial policy—Korea (South) 3. Technology—Korea (South) 4. Technology and state—Korea (South) 5. Human capital—Korea (South) 6. Business enterprises—Korea (South) 7. Industrial organization—Korea (South) 8. Free enterprise—Korea (South) I. Title.
    HC470.I52 L56   1999
    338.95195—dc21   99-28634
                                                                          CIP

to Helen

Contents

Figures

Tables

Boxed Articles

Acknowledgments

I would like to thank Lewis M. Branscomb of Kennedy School of Government (Harvard University) who guided my work, read every page of the manuscript, and suggested better ways to think and write. He was a scrupulous mentor and congenial colleague during my tenure (1996–97) as visiting scholar at the Kennedy School. Alice H. Amsden at the Massachusetts Institute of Technology has given me valuable advice and comments. Kenneth Oye and Philip S. Khoury arranged to make my stay at the Institute (1997–99) as visitor most comfortable. I have benefited from exchanging preliminary ideas with students and researchers at seminars arranged by my colleagues, notably, Peter de Valk at the Institute of Social Studies (The Hague, The Netherlands), Charles Cooper and Nagesh Kumar at INTECH (United Nations University Institute of New Technologies, Maastricht, The Netherlands), Mike Gregory, Engineering Department, Cambridge University, Choong-Young Ahn, Joong-Ang University Institute of Economic Research (Seoul, Korea), Kwang-Doo Kim, Sogang University (Seoul, Korea), Se-Joong Yong (Ajou University), KunMo Chung (former Minister of Science and Technology) Ajou University (Suwon, Korea), and George Hazelrig (National Science Foundation).

The researchers and scholars to whom I owe much for exchanging ideas, or receiving help in collecting hard-to-get information, include: Robert Barro (Harvard University), Sung-Nak Cho (Korea Industrial Technology Association), Ki-Ryun Choi (Ajou University), Sung-Chul Chung (Science and Technology Policy Institute), Byeong-Ho Gong (Korea Economic Research Institute), Hyun-Hwai Hur (Korea Industrial Technology Association), Jin-Hwa Jung (Korea Institute of Industrial Economics and Trade), Linsu Kim (Science and Technology Policy Institute), Hahn-Been Lee (former Deputy Prime Minister, Republic of Korea), JinJoo Lee (KAIST), Jong-Wha Lee (Korea University), another

Jong-Hwa Lee (Institute for Advanced Engineering), Kyu-Sik Lee (World Bank), Gerhart Margreiter (UNIDO), Duck-Woo Nam (former Prime Minister, Republic of Korea), Kee-Yung Nam (UNIDO), Se-Ki Oh (Ajou University), Woong-Suh Park (Samsung Institute of Economic Research), Yang-Ki Park (Korea Foreign Traders Association), Lucien Randazzese (Kennedy School of Government), Sang-Chul Shim (KAIST), and Hee-Yul Yu (Director-General of Technical Manpower Bureau, Ministry of Science and Technology).

For the able research assistance I received, I thank Shin-Kyu Yang who co-authored section 5.6 on U.S. information technology, Keonbeom Lee, and Ji-Yong Kim. For editing my English, I owe much to Kenneth Kronenberg, Anna Lim and to two anonymous referees whose comments have helped improve readability and correct errors.

The idea of this book was conceived as a response to questions that visitors (diplomats, journalists, businessmen, researchers, and students) asked during my stint at UNIDO. I thank them all for provoking me to search for the answers. I have tested the basic themes in seminars, particularly in a course I taught in the Systems Engineering Department of Ajou University Graduate School. I thank the discussants and students whose challenging comments led me to revise mistakes and rash statements.

Finally I thank Ajou University Graduate School and Chul Kim for providing financial assistance. This volume is an outgrowth of a project carried out under the Special Research and Development Program of the Ministry of Science and Technology.

Acronyms

ARPANET	Advanced Research Project Agency Network
ASEAN	Association of Southeast Asian Nations
ASIC	Application Specific Integrated Circuit (custom-made chips)
CALS	Computer-aided acquisition and logistics system
CIS	Confederation of Independent States (former USSR)
CSIA	Center for Science and International Affairs (Harvard University)
DARPA	Defense Advanced Research Projects Agency (USA)
DRAM	Dynamic Random Access Memory
EPB	Economic Planning Board
ERC	Engineering Research Center
ETRI	Electronics and Telecommunication Research Institute
GDP	Gross domestic product
GFRI	Government Financed Research Institute
GNP	Gross national product
GTD	General Technology Development (Program)
HCI	Heavy and Chemical Industries (Program)
HP	Hewlett-Packard (Company Inc.)
IBM	International Business Machines (Company Inc.)
IEEE	Institute of Electrical and Electronic Engineers
KAIST	Korea Advanced Institute of Science and Technology
KDI	Korea Development Institute
KERI	Korea Economic Research Institute

KIET   Korea Institute of Industrial Economics and Trade
KIST   Korea Institute of Science and Technology
KITA   Korea Industrial Technology Association
KORDIC   Korea Research and Development Information Center
KOSEF   Korea Science and Engineering Foundation
L-G   Lucky-Goldstar (Company Inc.)
MIC   Ministry of Information and Communications
MOAF   Ministry of Agriculture and Forestry
MOC   Ministry of Construction
MOF   Ministry of Finance
MOST   Ministry of Science and Technology
MOTIE   Ministry of Trade, Industry, and Energy
MVA   Manufacturing value added
NIEs   Newly industrializing economies
NSF   National Science Foundation
NTC   National Telecommunication (Program)
OECD   Organization for Economic Cooperation and Develop-
            ment
OEM   Original equipment manufacturer
POSCO   Pohang Iron and Steel Company
S&T   Science and technology
SME   Small and medium enterprise
SRC   Science Research Center
STEPI   Science and Technology Policy Institute
TCP/IP   Transmission control protocol/internet protocol
TFP   Total factor productivity
TFT   Task force team
TNC   Trans National Corporation
UNIDO   United Nations Industrial Development Organization
U.S. AID   United States Agency for International Development
WTO   World Trade Organization

Technology and Productivity

Out of such unpromising materials the new nation has to be constructed, by education, by protecting the producing classes, by punishing dishonest officials, and by the imposition of a labor test in all Government offices, i.e. by paying only for work actually done.

Isabella Bird Bishop (1897)
Korea and Her Neighbours

1   Introduction

This book explains the process by which poverty-stricken, agrarian South Korea was transformed in the last three decades into an urban semi-industrial country. Today South Korea exports major technologically sophisticated items like semiconductors, automobiles, television sets, personal computers, numerically controlled machines, ships, excavators, and cranes. From the existing data on labor productivity growth and total factor productivity growth, it is evident that a significant measure of technological learning has been achieved. The questions addressed in this book include:

1. Where did this technological competence come from?

2. What did the government and market do to nurture such capabilities?

3. Will a continuation of the current policy enable Korea to catch up more rapidly with other OECD countries?

4. What is the appropriate role of the National Research and Development Program within the framework of the National System of Innovation?

It is hypothesized here that the Korean experience in technological upgrading can be explained by a combination of (1) knowledge assets, (2) human capital assets, and (3) institutional-organization assets (or capabilities). These factors complement each other and collectively determine the pace of "technological ladder climbing" at the enterprise (micro) level as well as at the national (macro) level with large externality effects. It is argued that the accumulation of the three types of assets has led to a continuous rise in productivity growth and competitiveness. This analysis provides a basis for discussing some possible policy options and also for speculating on future technological progress in Korean industries.

1.1 Purpose of the Study and Issues Raised

Readers interested in the literature on Korean development will immediately find that the above perspective differs from existing explanations. I will review briefly some of the common existing views of the
Korean case. These include the author's own view that a synthesis of
diverse explanations is necessary in order to make the resulting hypothesis useful, particularly for policy makers. The author believes that
quantitative analysis using econometric methods should be combined
with historical-institutional analysis to yield valuable policy lessons
with practical insights.

The traditional World Bank view asserts that the Korean experience
can be explained by the neoclassical logic of outward-looking, free-
trade philosophy. This school of thought is represented by Bela Balassa,
Anne O. Krueger, and Deepak Lal, among others.[1] Their argument is
based on the Walrasian general equilibrium theory. Free-trade policy
has led the Korean economy to achieve higher values from given limited resources, thereby facilitating more rapid economic growth. This
argument is also thought to be applicable to other Asian NICs (i.e.,
Taiwan, Hong Kong, and Singapore). In addition Latin American and
South Asian import-substitution approaches (e.g., in Brazil and Mexico
during the 1980s) would seem to provide a broad confirmation of the
free-trade argument, as their growth rates faltered under inward-
looking trade regimes. It follows, according to this argument, that less
government intervention and the opening up of the economy to world
trade provide the best development policy. This, in simplified form,
has been the World Bank position until very recently.[2]

Theoretical elegance notwithstanding, the neoclassical position, as
traditionally advocated, seems inadequate to explain some real on-the-
ground observations. Among others, the rapid shift of Korean industry
from an unskilled, labor-intensive structure toward a capital-intensive,
skill-intensive, and (in the near future) information-intensive structure,
would seem to require some supplementary explanation. It is true that
initially the export orientation of unskilled, labor-intensive goods provided the major driving force for rapid industrialization à la comparative advantage theory, which is consistent with the neoclassical theory.
But, it is also true that the government followed a "selective import-
substitution policy," though with varying emphasis and intensity,
throughout the last three decades.[3]

Recent revisions to the neoclassical approach are exemplified by
those who believe that technology-mastering is a crucial factor in ex-

plaining rapid industrialization and productivity growth. Prominent writers in this school include Howard Pack, Larry Westphal, Christopher Freeman, Henry Bruton, Giovanni Dosi, Linsu Kim, and Jinjoo Lee.[4] They argue that technology learning and diffusion can be promoted by a set of policy measures, including temporary protection such as quotas on a selective basis. By taking this approach, the productivity of labor and capital can be raised, and consequently existing comparative advantage structures can be changed.

Acquiring technological capabilities is a complex matter, often defying operational conceptualization and measurement. Major difficulties include tacitness, sequentiality, cumulativeness, nonreversibility, externalities, and information asymmetry. The skill and effectiveness with which these complexities are mastered seems to provide an important determinant of technology-mastering and diffusion, leading to productivity growth. Differences in learning speeds would appear to determine the superiority of excellent Japanese companies such as Toyota, Sony, and NEC, as well as the U.S. companies such as GM, IBM, AT&T, and Hewlett-Packard. In South Korea, excellent companies include Samsung, Hyundai, L-G (Lucky Goldstar), and Daewoo. Having studied the Korean experience, Pack and Westphal argue that "trade considerations are secondary to technological ones in searching for an understanding of industrialization that is relevant to policy making."[5]

There is still another school of dissent to the neoclassical interpretation, a group emphasizing the institutional aspects of industrialization. This group includes Alice Amsden, Shahid Alam, Chalmers Johnson, Chung H. Lee, and Douglas North.[6] They discard the assumption of the perfect market and embrace instead the notion that government has an important role to play in constructing institutional-organizational devices. And the market is nothing but an edifice of millions of such devices. One can take the interpretational position that these devices collectively can repair market failures and imperfections with continuous calibration of institutional-organizational devices. Often makeshift arrangements can be crafted and experimentally calibrated. For example, Amsden states that "getting prices wrong" served as a device for providing an incentive for private enterprises to take risks (e.g., subsidized interest loans to reduce risk burdens of learning automobile technology).

In the author's view, there is some truth to each of these interpretations, although only a partial truth. They can be synthesized, and by doing so, useful policy implications can be extracted. The major factors, namely technological knowledge accumulation, human skills, and

institution building, are complementary. Structural changes in industry with productivity growth can be explained fully only when the
interactions of the major factors are analyzed together.

1.2   Conceptual Framework

This section attempts to provide a broad framework to explain structural or compositional changes in industry, as driven by technological
learning. Three factors are assumed to be important determinants of
technological learning, namely technological knowledge, human capital accumulation, and organizational, or more broadly, institutional
capabilities.

The conventional theory has assumed that output is a function of
capital and labor such that

$$Q = F(K, L), \tag{1.1}$$

where Q is output; K, physical capital; and L, labor. A specific form
of this function is often represented by the Cobb-Douglas production
function:

$$Q = AK^a L^{(1-a)}, \tag{1.2}$$

where A is a coefficient indicating a level of technology capabilities
and a is the capital share of output.

Equation (1.2) implies that

$$\frac{dQ}{Q} = \left(\frac{dA}{A}\right) + a\left(\frac{dK}{K}\right) + (1-a)\left(\frac{dL}{L}\right) \tag{1.3}$$

as expressed in growth rate of inputs and output. Applying time series
data, one could estimate the growth rates of the technology level index,
dA/A.[7]

The hypothesis advanced in this research project can be expressed as

$$Q = F(K, L, T, H, O), \tag{1.4}$$

where T is technological knowledge; H, human capital; and O, organizational (institutional) skills or devices. The last three factors determine
the technological capabilities, A. In addition the secondary hypothesis
can be specified as

$$A = \frac{Q}{K^a L^{(1-a)}} = F(T, H, O). \tag{1.5}$$

In other words, the progress of technical advance, A (or a learning indicator) in the catching-up process, depends on the amount of knowledge capital (e.g., engineering, knowledge), human capital (e.g., educated line-workers, engineers, and managers capable of exploiting the knowledge for production and marketing), and organizational skills. These factors are capable of shifting the production function upward (i.e., dynamic increasing returns). The chief questions addressed to the Korean experience are therefore as follows:

1. Where did technological knowledge come from?

2. How was human capital accumulated so quickly?

3. What institutional devices were crafted that facilitated rapid learning?

1.3   Structure of the Book

The conceptual framework noted above informs the organization of the following chapters. Chapter 2 reviews a set of indicators representing technological capability development in relation to the growth of productivity indexes measured in various ways. The period covers the last three decades since the early 1960s when Korean industrialization began. Central to the review is the estimate of total factor productivity (TFP), now a popular tool of analysis for gauging progress in technological learning. Despite ongoing debates concerning its usefulness and limitations, the TFP approach helps researchers to gain insights about the pace of learning if used judiciously along with other learning indicators. The chapter thus attempts to bring together indicators of human capital formation, R&D capital assets, and the like to explain changes in TFP levels. An estimate of subsectoral TFPs reveals diverse rates of technological learning across the manufacturing sector. High TFP growth has been recorded, for example, in electronics-related subsectors, automobiles, shipbuilding, and office machines, which are industries to which a high level of human and R&D capital have been devoted.

Chapter 3 addresses the question: How was human capital accumulated so quickly? What role did human capital play in enhancing industrial productivity? The review of human capital indicators, particularly formal education, aims to evaluate its productivity-enhancing effect. Although increasing numbers of studies have reported estimates of the internal rate of returns to investment in education and positive coefficients of the education factor in wages and salaries function, there has been precious little analysis of the direct connection between TFP and educated manpower stock. This chapter reports on this aspect of regression analysis conducted by the author. This chapter also reviews the role that universities played in Korea as critical institutions contributing to the formation of human capital. Positive contributions include an abundant supply of college and university graduates especially since the 1980s, from which Korean enterprises, more specifically the large ones and *chaebols,* could pick and choose their new recruits. On the negative side, the universities have often contributed to a mismatch between skills needed by expanding enterprises and those supplied, leading to excess manpower in certain skill categories and shortages in high-tech-related skills. The deterioration in the quality of graduates remains yet another problem. The chapter concludes with recommendations for ways to improve the quality of graduates as well as the quality of research-oriented universities, specifically with respect to the need of private enterprises to upgrade their technology capabilities in the next century.

Chapter 4 turns to the issue of corporate organizations as learning institutions. The importance of enterprise organization as a strategic learning tool has been increasingly recognized in recent years. The growing literature on this issue bears witness to its importance. The primary researchers writing on this issue are Richard R. Nelson (1991), William Lazonick (1990), Masahiko Aoki and Ronald Dore (1994), Giovanni Dosi, David Teece, and Sidney Winter (1992), among others.[8] These works bring to the center of analysis the creativity and uncertainty-bearing required for organizational changes in order to accommodate technological innovation and thereby to enhance competitiveness of the enterprise. This chapter goes on to examine the *chaebols* as a learning institution and examines their strategies of innovation, since they have emerged as the leader in upgrading Korean manufacturing technology from its virtual nonexistent level in the 1950s. They started out using the Japanese *zaibatsu* as a benchmark target but developed into an organization with a cultural mix of American management techniques, a militaristic mind-set, and Confucian ethics. This mix served the industry well as an institutional device facilitating the rapid pace of learning new techniques advancing rapidly from imitative learning to inventive learning. This is illustrated by the development of Samsung's innovative capability in the semiconductor business, providing a model of excellence to be emulated by other Korean enterprises. The chapter concludes with comments on future roles that may be played by *chaebols* in helping small-and-medium enterprises (SMEs) to advance their technological capability. Further it is emphasized that the *chaebols* should contribute to the process of national-technology policy formulation in a more positive way by suggesting their own preferences and priorities rather than just following governmental dictates.

Chapter 5 delves into the roles played by the government in designing institutional devices to provide infrastructure for implementing and managing policy decisions. The major devices reviewed in this chapter include five-year plans for industrial development (as they affect the technological progress of industries), national R&D programs, government-financed research institutes (particularly those under the Ministry of Science and Technology, MOST), trade regimes (functioning as an infrastructure to enhance innovation of firms), and cooperation between university, industry, and government agencies. The reviews of these instruments lead to the conclusion that the catalytic and infrastructure-design roles played by the government deserve greater appreciation than they have received. The chapter ends with a set of policy options that could strengthen the morale and leadership of researchers at the government-financed research institutes.

Chapter 6 concludes by summarizing the major findings and interpreting them to draw lessons for policy makers who will be looking toward the twenty-first century. The proper roles of the three major actors are projected into the future, namely academe, industry, and government. Finally the broader significance of the Korean experience in technology accumulation is considered, particularly with respect to utilizing it as a tool for S&T diplomacy. A specific question addressed is: Can Korea play a role in "bridging" the interests of developed countries and those of developing countries?

In each chapter as outlined above, an overarching theme recurs with respect to the importance of institutional and organizational devices invented to motivate the actors and to bring out the best of their latent abilities. Thus the structure of incentive devices are illustrated with examples in each chapter. For instance, the center-of-excellence program (e.g., science research center, SRC, and engineering research center, ERC) as well as the Korea Advanced Institute of Science and Technology (KAIST) are selected for discussion in chapter 3, Samsung Electronics in chapter 4, and the Korea Institute of Science and Technology (KIST) in chapter 5.

Institutional and organizational skills defy measurement and are therefore often neglected in mainstream economic analysis. Fortunately, however, economists have begun to realize that incentive systems put in place in institutions and organizations make a difference in terms of creating systemic efficiency. Thus Douglass North, one of the foremost institutional advocates, asserts, "Incentives are the underlying determinants of economic performance. . . . Bringing incentives up front focuses attention where it belongs, on the key to the performance of economies. The central argument advanced . . . is that incentives have varied immensely over time and still do. Integrating institutional analysis into economics and economic history is redirecting emphasis, but not abandoning the theoretical tools already developed."[9] In this study, a formal analysis is melded with "appreciative theory" as advocated by Richard Nelson.[10]

Furthermore the edifice (or matrix) of various institutions in an economy defines not only (1) the incentive structure but also (2) the information-flow structure, (3) uncertainty levels that firms face, (4) transaction costs, and (5) effective rules of competition and cooperation. Some arrangements of institutional devices turn out to be more efficient than others, as observed between different economic regimes as well as between different firms.

The institutional difference between North Korea and South Korea provides an apt example of explaining the growing gaps in productivity and technological capability during the last three decades.[11] The former Federal Republic of Germany and German Democratic Republic provide another example. China under Chairman Mao versus Taiwan provides still another example. Even mainland China under Paramount Leader Deng Shao Ping's revolution (e.g., the family responsibility system in agriculture and the factory manager's responsibility system in industry) furnish telling evidence of the proposition that institution matters.[12]

Comparative studies on patterns of enterprise-level organization in the United States, Japan, and Western Europe have uncovered significant differences in institutional instruments in use among industrial countries. These differences are regarded as determining risk-taking behavior and learning behavior of individual firms. Thus, for example, the Japanese practice of maintaining a horizontal flow of information, job rotation, autonomy on the shop floor, company loyalty (or trust), life-long employment, and consensus-oriented industrial relations and decision making have been recognized as contributing to innovation and productivity.[13]

General risk-taking activities are affected by these five factors mentioned above. Technological risk-taking activities such as R&D effort, quality control, and learning are even more crucially governed by them. This is especially the case because the markets for technologies and human capital are imperfect or even nonexistent in developing economies. This means that some institutional devices must be crafted to overcome or manage such market failures. The Korean experience provides fertile ground for exploring ways of managing externalities, complementarities, lumpiness, cumulativeness, tacitness, path-dependence, fundamental uncertainties, and asymmetric information which distinguish technology and its capabilities from other goods and services. This work will hopefully serve as a catalyst for the research needed to understand the Korean experience.[14]

Box 1.1

Financial Crisis, IMF Rescue Package, and Institutional Reform

The current (1997–98) financial crisis in Korea has brought an opportunity to accelerate the reform process that Korea has initiated with its application for OECD membership (granted, September 30, 1996). The Korean government agreed with the OECD to open the financial market, to place more reliance on market competition rather than industrial policies, and to liberalize the labor market. The implementation process of the agreement, however, has been slow mainly due to the political maneuvering of interest groups, namely the Blue House (Presidential Office), labor unions, chaebol groups, bureaucrats, bankers, and political parties.

The onset of the 1997–98 financial crisis has wholly changed Korea's circumstances, with the IMF reform package as the centerpiece of economic survival. The package consists of not only short-term measures, such as $55 billion in standby loans, but also structural changes with profound long-term implications. This includes measures to redesign (1) the government-business alliance, (2) corporate governance, (3) the labor market, and (4) the banking industry. In short, new institutional devices are to replace old ones under unprecedented political pressure coming from international organizations (e.g., IBRD, IMF, OECD, and WTO) and foreign creditor banks.[15] The Kim Dae Jung government inherited from the earlier government of Kim Young Sam the crisis and the task of implementing the IMF package. A brief review follows focusing on the major institutional changes being negotiated between the interest groups. The remaining pages of this chapter were written in order to update the final draft of the book. The reader familiar with the 1997–98 episode of the financial crisis may wish to skip reading these pages.

Government-Business Alliance

The practice of government nurturing and protecting business needs to be overhauled. The government has operated as the *de facto* risk-sharing partner with *chaebols* during the 1960s and 1970s when Korean industry was preparing for economic take off. (See chapter 5 for details.) "Policy loans" provided the major policy instrument (i.e., subsidized interest loans channeled to preferred industrial sectors). This practice has been the target of criticism from many quarters because it has been accompanied by "unfair disadvantages" given to a certain group of competitors in addition to moral harzard problems and corruption (patronage, kickbacks, slush funds, cover-ups of illegal activities, secretive rent-seeking activities, etc.). Recall that the two former presidents have served jail terms on such corruption charges. (Kim Dae Jung pardoned them on the occasion of his inauguration as president.)

Under the new arrangement the government would not come to rescue faltering enterprises, *chaebol* or not. Market competition would determine the entry and exit of enterprises according to the rules of Kong-Jung-Ko-Rae-Pob (or Fair Transaction Law). Several *chaebols*, having lost government aid of any kind, have already fallen including Hanbo and Kia.

Furthermore, under the new regime, the government will attempt to reach broad social consensus on important issues through the institution of a Government-Business-Labor Deliberation Council. President Kim Dae Jung experimented with this Council (much like the German model) during the first several months of his administration in 1998. He used the experiment to arrive at a tripartite agreement regarding "fair share of adjustment costs." This provides a sharp contrast to the earlier dictatorial enforcement mode. Whether this experiment will evolve into a well-crafted institutional device remains to be seen.

Corporate Sector Restructuring

The dominant perception in Korea is that the financial crisis has come as a result of the *chaebols'* reckless borrowing in domestic as well as in international money markets. Many of the *chaebols* borrowed money in the form of short-term loans and invested in long-term assets like equity or real estate. When foreign creditors felt increasing uncertainty in Asia (subsequent to the crisis in Thailand), they called back their loans. The creditors refused refinancing and the "herd instinct" bunched their exodus from the Korean market. Individual borrowers as well as the entire economy unexpectedly encountered a severe shortage of foreign exchange. The country was unable to service its debt. By the time the policy makers realized the severity of the crisis, it was too late for an easy solution because of the lack of information (e.g., how much Korea owed to foreign bankers). Borrowers had concealed their real financial status often by keeping double accounting books (a book for tax purposes and another for internal use). When an IMF team visited Korea at the beginning of the crisis, the team members could not believe that neither the government nor the banking industry had been collecting relevant data. This disaster reflected the rare combination of both market and government failure.

Such behavior of the *chaebols* prompted the government to call for a "fair share of restructuring costs" to be born by the *chaebol* sector. The latter was urged by the government to downsize by selling inefficient subsidiaries. Sales revenue could be used to lower abnormally high debt / equity ratios (e.g., from over 500 to 200 percent). This means less diversification than in earlier days, although the diversification strategy has served well as an opportunity to learn new technologies. (See chapter 4 for details.) It also means more specialization than before. To twist the *chaebols'* arms further, the government has been pressuring *chaebols* to engage in "big deals," meaning the swapping of businesses between *chaebol* groups. Only three or four major industrial activities should be retained and consolidated by each *chaebol*, rather than the 30 or 40 activities as in earlier days. But, so far, the reaction of the *chaebol* sector has been slow and tepid, owing in part to the lack of clear rules or precedence of factory swapping in Korea. The *chaebol* sector has been insisting that a specific law should be enacted to govern and assist transactions involved with such factory swapping.

The reform package includes also a new provision that will allow not only freer foreign direct investment (FDI) but hostile takeover bids from foreign companies. This, if well implemented, will enhance competition and render effective pressure for *chaebols* to become more efficient. The inflow of FDI has been the smallest (as a proportion of total investment) in Korea compared to other newly industrializing countries in Asia. It behooves Korea to increase the ratio of FDI as she aspires to become a world player in trade and finance. More important, inflows of FDI can provide an efficient policy tool to alleviate the shortage of foreign exchange.

In addition new accounting laws will be enacted to require *chaebols* to enhance accountability and transparency. Starting in fiscal year 1999, the 30 largest *chaebols* must submit to the Security Supervision Board consolidated financial statements involving all subsidiary companies. The report must include details of intersubsidiary transactions such as mortgages and debt/credit offered among subsidiaries even including their own insurance companies and overseas corporations.

Furthermore the mutual guaranteeing of loans between *chaebol* group members has been banned as of April 1998. The sum of the 30 largest *chaebols'* mutual loan guarantees is estimated at 23 trillion won (approximately $17 billion), and this will be liquidated by the year 2003. This requirement limits the maneuvering room of the *chaebols,* and it is an additional cause for the slow response to restructuring.

In return, employers in general will have greater freedom to hire and fire laborers. The practice of lifetime employment will be discontinued. Since the beginning of the financial crisis, unemployment has been rising, already heading toward 2 million unemployed workers (about 10 percent of the economically active population) by the beginning of 1999. This in part owes to the severe contractionary measures implemented under IMF programs. It also marks record unemployment in the Korean history of industrialization.

Labor Market Reforms

Union activities were severely suppressed during the Park Chung Hee era (1961–79) and also the Chun Doo Hwan government (1979–87). Since then labor unions have won a measure of progress in restoring labor's rights (e.g., the right to strike), and today labor unions constitute a legitimate political force (and voice). The Kim Dae Jung government has adopted a "pro-labor policy" involving institution building. High on the agenda are the issues of strengthening the social safety-net, especially providing unemployment compensation at an affordable level, and a generous provision for retraining facilities. The crafting of these institutions must dovetail with the current effort to overhaul the corporate governance structure. But the extent to which the social safety-net will be strengthened is still uncertain. It is also unclear whether labor unions will accept a new social compact as the "fair sharing of adjustment costs" incurred in meeting the IMF conditions.

Reform of the Financial Sector

As noted earlier, the government controlled the banking sector in order to allocate financial resources to targeted industrial sectors. This meant the banking sector remained as a weak spot in the edifice of economic institutions of the nation. Little effort was made to develop a venture-capital market, risk management skills, credibility control, or an early warning system. The banking industry remained "primitive" and weak in competitiveness. Liberalizing inflows of foreign capital (short and long term) without built-in monitoring and warning devices wrought havoc triggering the "financial meltdown." There is not yet complete agreement among policy makers, scholars, and bankers regarding the true size of nonperforming loans. Some estimates put the figure at 200 to 300 trillion won (approximately $150 to $220 billion) as of June 1998.

Furthermore the crisis of insolvency has brought down, so far, 5 banks, 16 merchant banking corporations, 4 securities, and 2 investment trust companies. In addition two large national banks—Seoul Bank and Cheil Bank—have been "nationalized" to be sold to foreign banks after restructuring. Allegedly, the sale would help restore the confidence of foreign bankers. This situation calls for wholesale over-hauling of the rules of the game in banking and other financial markets.

Under the new rules the government will have little influence in commercial bank lending and in selecting the chief managers of banks. (Earlier, retired bureaucrats, national assemblymen [the Korean equivalent of congressmen], and army generals, were often chosen, on government recommendation, to occupy CEO positions in banks.) Stockholders will now have a greater voice in decision making on important matters including the appointment of bank managers. Hostile takeovers (even by foreign banks) will be allowed as well as mergers and acquisitions (M&As).

Furthermore bank supervision will be strengthened. Autonomy will be given to the Financial Supervision Commission, which will report directly to the President. The Commission will require banks to report all lending and borrowing transactions so as to enhance transparency. The Commission will have the power to issue warnings and shut down delinquent banks and other financial institutions.

The definition of "credit lines" will be changed. The new definition will include lines of credit extended through banks' trust accounts, and corporate bonds and commercial papers. Currently the term is defined as lending through banks' own accounts and payment guarantees, excluding corporate bonds and commercial papers.

In sum, the Korean economic system is facing a defining moment involving fundamental institutional reforms in major markets (new rules of competition and cooperation in capital markets, labor markets, and rules for mergers and acquisitions, etc.). This could result in great strides toward integrating the economy more fully into the global system, making Korea ready to become a major economic player.

2   Indicators of Technological Capability and Productivity Growth

This chapter reviews a set of selected quantitative indicators of technological capability development and productivity growth in the manufacturing sector. Various indicators are available, permitting a broad-based assessment of industry's capacity to learn and absorb new technologies. Such learning, taking place in an enterprise or an industry, enables it to raise its productivity to a higher level. As will be shown, Korea has achieved some significant progress in climbing the "technological ladder," starting from a very low level after being devastated by the Korean War (1950–53). But yet, Korea has a long way to go if it is to catch up with the so-called G-7 countries in technological-capability building. Korea has reached a turning point in learning high-tech industries, having lost its competitiveness in labor-intensive industries.[1] It behooves Korea to ask: How far have we come? How far must we go before Korea catches up with the industrial powers?

The indicators collected for review include some basic time series such as the capital–labor ratio (an index useful for studying the capital-deepening phenomenon), R&D capital stock, number of R&D personnel, number of engineers and technicians, and educated human resources. These represent the input side necessary to raise productivity through technology-based innovation. Some regression analyses from various sources are also reviewed regarding the relationship between technology-related input variables and productivity growth, the output side. Further, where possible, an international comparison of these indicators is attempted in order to provide a broad perspective on the Korean performance.

2.1 Growth of Capital–Labor Ratio and Labor Productivity

Capital per unit of labor is a time-honored approach to measuring the degree of capital intensiveness. Over time, the ratio measures the capital-deepening phenomenon, reflecting the extent of technological upgrading in an industry. Table 2.1 shows the degree of capital deepening achieved in the 28 manufacturing subsectors during the last three decades. Normally capital is measured by summing up investment purchases of land, buildings, structures, machines and equipment, and transport equipment. Subsequently the component items of capital are adjusted each year by a depreciation factor. But the figures presented in the table are for machines and equipment only, since the technological content of capital is thought to be better measured by this approach. The manufacturing sector as a whole has increased its capital–labor ratio more than threefold from 3,916 thousand won in 1963 to 12,132 thousand won in 1990 (all figures calculated in 1985 constant prices).[2]

Virtually all 28 subsectors have increased their respective ratios, but it should be noted that heavy industry subsectors have exceeded the manufacturing average. Take for instance, the iron and steel subsector. The ratio has grown over tenfold. This reflects the fact that the Pohang steel complex (with state-of-the-art technology) came into being in 1973. In fact many modern enterprises producing new goods (meaning goods that were not produced in Korea previously) emerged in Korea after the Heavy and Chemical Industry Program (1973–79) was launched.

It is also noteworthy that between 1963 and 1970, many subsectors lowered their capital–labor ratio, reflecting a significant entry of firms with below average levels of the ratio. This seems to have taken place in food, apparel, wood products, industrial chemicals, plastic products, nonmetallic minerals, fabricated metals, electric machinery, professional equipment, and the "other" category. For the manufacturing sector as a whole, this period saw a slight decline from 3,916 thousand won to 3,499 thousand won. But between 1970 and 1980, virtually all subsectors jumped in terms of capital–labor ratio. The fast pace of capital formation continued during the years 1980–90, reflecting fast shifts in technology. It should be noted that the capital-deepening phenomenon occurred in footwear (an over twenty-fold jump in the capital per labor ratio between 1970 and 1990), in the beverage industry (over 15 times), in pottery (over 11 times), and so on. This indicator suggests that the acquisition of new (capital-intensive) methods of production has been taking place ubiquitously, though to varying degrees, and not just in the heavy industry sectors. If the technology shifts are taken together with the record of productivity gains, the extent of technological learning that must have taken place can be easily inferred.

Table 2.1
Machinery and equipment stock per worker (unit: 1985 constant thousand won)

Sector	1963	1970	1980	1990
Food	1,978	1,707	3,851	9,889
Beverage	1,360	1,342	5,938	21,262
Tobacco	2,139	2,645	2,803	24,872
Textile	2,362	2,394	5,400	12,710
Apparels	853	511	857	1,137
Leather	941	1,606	3,145	4,205
Footwear	680	804	2,986	16,141
Wood	2,991	1,696	2,945	4,433
Furniture	375	400	760	1,994
Paper	3,942	4,250	7,027	14,506
Publishing	2,149	2,110	4,927	7,133
Industrial chemicals	30,688	17,340	19,204	59,378
Other chemicals	1,005	1,437	4,886	13,147
Petroleum refining		21,937	80,375	53,268
Petroleum and coal	911	1,805	3,613	9,588
Rubber	1,303	1,896	2,692	2,997
Plastic	7,789	2,034	3,452	5,772
Pottery	143	369	1,668	4,319
Glass	162	908	4,792	8,783
Nonmetal minerals	7,839	6,298	12,220	33,867
Iron and steel	5,880	6,644	28,665	61,688
Nonferrous metal	3,679	5,791	12,719	19,091
Fabricated metal	1,421	1,377	4,128	5,874
Machinery	1,706	2,618	10,000	15,371
Electronic machinery	2,100	1,648	5,267	12,417
Transport equipment	2,645	3,356	9,699	17,994
Professional equipment	1,779	1,036	1,243	4,136
Other	840	350	1,726	3,040
Total	3,916	3,499	7,525	12,132

Source: Computed from basic data provided by Hak K. Pyo, "A Synthetic Estimate of the National Wealth of Korea, 1953–1990," Korea Development Institute (KDI Working Paper 9212), May 1992, and employment data by sector UNIDO databank.

Growth of Labor Productivity

Labor productivity is defined as value added divided by the number of workers (for a firm, an industry, or the national economy in the aggregate), or divided by the number of work-hours. For our purpose the former data are more useful than the latter because of their broader availability and because they cover more countries for the purpose of international comparison. (See table 2.2 for data on a set of countries including Korea.)

During the 1970s, the Korean manufacturing sector showed a value-added growth of 13.8 percent annually, and a 9.1 percent annual growth in employment. The difference between these two figures, namely 4.7 percent, represents approximately the annual growth rate of labor productivity. Similarly, during the 1980s, manufacturing value added (MVA) grew by 12.9 percent annually and employment by 4.0 percent annually. Thus labor productivity grew by 8.9 percent annually, not a mean achievement. In terms of productivity growth performance, the Asian NIEs (newly industrializing economies in Asia, i.e., Korea, Singapore, Hong Kong, and Taiwan) appear to have done exceptionally well. There seems to be a consensus emerging with regard to the ultimate source of industrial growth among these countries, namely that an abundant, well-trained and well-educated labor force offset the relative disadvantage of poor natural resource endowment.[3]

Nevertheless, the controversy remains as to how education enters into a production function; that is, how precisely does it raise the productivity of labor. For example, does the productive role of education derive more from cognitive knowledge or behavioral characteristics? Further, does education enhance labor productivity or just screen talents? These questions will be touched upon in the next chapter. Here it suffices to point out that the issues are alive, and the Korean experience appears to offer a fertile ground for research.

The figures in table 2.2 also reveal that Korea has a long way to go if she is to catch up with Japan's level of labor productivity. Assuming that Korea's labor productivity grows at 7.0 percent per year and Japan's labor productivity at 3.5 percent per year, Korea could catch up with Japan in approximately fifteen years. This means that by the year 2010, both Korea and Japan would converge at a labor-productivity level of about $140,000 (in 1990 constant U.S.$). Considering the recorded growth of labor productivity in Korea and Japan during the

Table 2.2
Annual average growth rates of manufacturing value added (MVA), employment, and labor productivity, selected countries, 1970–1995

Country	1970–1980			1980–1990			1990–1995			MVA, 1995 (1990 U.S.$)
	Value added	Employment	Labor productivity	Value added	Employment	Labor productivity	Value added	Employment	Labor productivity	
United States	2.74	0.53	2.20	1.21	−0.93	2.16	2.23	−0.26	2.50	85,460
Japan	3.35	−0.66	4.03	3.61	0.18	3.42	−0.46	−1.24	0.79	83,043
Korea	13.83	9.11	4.33	12.87	3.97	8.56	9.59	0.30	9.26	51,673
Singapore	15.04	8.66	5.87	6.89	2.05	4.74	7.61	1.66	5.85	45,041
Hong Kong	10.42	5.49	4.68	1.26	−2.03	3.37	−5.20	−8.68	3.81	19,021
Taiwan	7.18	4.40	2.67	7.24	1.27	5.90	4.08	−0.74	4.86	29,625
Malaysia	13.25	9.76	3.18	7.72	6.37	1.28	14.57	9.13	4.99	13,880
Thailand	8.69	6.83	1.74	8.81	2.10	6.57	9.13	6.26	2.70	15,719
Indonesia	12.26	7.20	4.72	15.57	10.64	4.46	12.12	8.75	3.10	6,484
Philippines	5.34	10.21	−4.42	5.33	1.41	3.87	3.20	−2.37	5.70	9,513
India	3.02	3.95	−0.90	7.24	0.43	6.78	5.65	2.91	1.84	3,767
Pakistan	4.80	1.57	3.18	8.58	2.46	5.98	4.66	0.38	4.27	10,112
Bangladesh	3.08	7.15	−3.80	5.94	11.70	−5.15	8.18	4.44	3.58	1,683
Brazil	11.77	10.41	1.23	−1.20	−1.60	0.40	3.77	−0.58	4.37	22,282
Mexico	6.50	3.42	2.98	2.27	−1.19	3.49	−0.65	−5.22	4.83	24,437
Chile	0.13	−1.85	2.01	6.27	3.72	2.45	4.03	2.91	1.09	30,902

Source: Compiled from the UNIDO database.

1970s and 1980s, the assumptions adopted for the calculation do not seem totally out of place.

It should be born in mind, however, that these observations concern the manufacturing sectors as a whole. There could be a leading sector or two in which Korea could reach the Japanese level much sooner. One is tempted to speculate on some segments of the electronics industry that might lead the way. The current would-be champions in productivity growth appear to be semiconductor and related businesses. Their record of labor productivity supports such speculation.

Table 2.3 presents the labor productivity index prepared by the Korea Productivity Center for 27 manufacturing subsectors. It is to be noted that the electrical and electronic machinery subsector ranks first with the highest growth rate in labor productivity, followed by fabricated metal products, other chemical products, nonferrous metal, scientific measuring and controlling equipment, miscellaneous manufacturing products, and so forth. Most of these represent an assembly type of processing where incremental technological progress can be most effective, as Japanese industries have well demonstrated. Korean firms seem to be following the footsteps of the Japanese firms. More will be said on Japanese tutelage in chapter 4.

2.2   Growth of Total Factor Productivity

The concept of the TFP, as developed by Robert Solow, provides an approach to measuring the extent of "technological learning" taking place in an industry. It is estimated by subtracting from the value-added figures that portion of the contribution made jointly by labor and capital. The estimate is often made assuming the Cobb-Douglas production function.[4]

Although some researchers would call such estimates an "index of our ignorance" because the determinants of TFP are yet to be proved, it can be interpreted as a "summary index of overall learning." It provides a useful tool (i.e., an index) for studying the aggregate pace of absorbing new ways of doing things.

Table 2.4 presents the latest available estimates of average annual TFP growth rates for the 1967–93 period by 36 manufacturing subsectors.[5] Note that the subsectors belonging mainly to the heavy and chemical industries indicate higher TFP growth rates, suggesting speedier learning than in other subsectors. The ten fast-growth subsectors include tobacco (4.28 percent), office machines (3.45 percent),

Table 2.3
Annual average growth rates of labor productivity in Korean manufacturing industries, 1974–1992

Industry	Growth rate (%)
Food	10.0
Beverages	10.4
Textiles	9.9
Apparel	10.0
Leather	12.6
Footwear	8.0
Wood products	7.1
Furniture	8.5
Paper	8.4
Printing	8.3
Industrial chemicals	9.6
Other chemicals	14.2
Petroleum refining	0.0
Petroleum products	14.4
Rubber	13.7
Plastic	9.0
Earthenware	7.8
Glass	9.3
Nonmetal	9.0
Iron and steel	10.5
Nonferrous	14.0
Fabricated metal	14.3
Machinery	9.5
Electric-electronics	17.3
Transport	9.2
Precision instruments	13.3
Other	13.7
All manufacture	12.3
Manufacturing wages	9.2

Source: Computed from data provided in *Major Statistics of the Korean Economy 1994* by Korean Foreign Trade Association, Seoul, 1994.

Table 2.4
Annual growth rates of total factor productivity by 36 manufacturing sectors, 1967–1993

Sector	1967–1973	1973–1979	1979–1985	1985–1993	1967–1993
Food	1.08	0.27	1.67	0.82	0.95
Beverage	4.92	1.61	−3.45	1.78	1.22
Tobacco	8.77	7.83	−1.56	2.89	4.28
Textile yarns	3.16	1.56	0.24	0.48	1.29
Knitted products	4.78	2.71	1.41	1.90	2.63
Textile	3.52	2.46	1.17	2.30	2.35
Apparel	1.60	1.59	0.36	2.65	1.63
Leather	1.92	−0.01	1.63	0.58	0.99
Wood	3.42	1.03	0.48	0.75	1.36
Paper	2.03	1.42	1.75	0.99	1.50
Printing	1.53	1.81	1.81	2.55	1.97
Industrial chemicals	6.29	4.63	0.42	0.92	2.87
Other chemicals	5.06	4.33	0.22	1.65	2.71
Petroleum refining	2.59	1.08	−2.06	0.48	0.51
Petroleum and coal	0.52	−0.41	0.79	−0.46	0.06
Rubber	3.05	2.62	1.55	0.58	1.84
Plastic	1.84	0.26	0.99	1.35	1.13
China	2.95	2.56	1.64	3.80	2.82
Glass	3.46	2.96	1.08	2.47	2.48
Nonmetal minerals	3.28	2.15	−1.75	2.29	1.54
Iron and steel	2.71	0.33	0.34	0.64	0.97
Nonferrous metal	0.61	1.96	0.87	0.89	1.07
Fabricated metal	2.86	2.79	0.83	1.46	1.94
Engines	1.51	6.33	4.32	0.67	2.99
Industrial machines	5.06	1.83	2.40	3.03	3.07
Office machines	4.45	3.18	3.19	3.10	3.45
Electric machinery	0.50	3.73	0.53	1.90	1.67
Audio, communications	8.91	1.60	1.93	1.30	3.23
Home electronics	−1.84	7.30	0.66	0.13	1.40
Other electronics	1.45	0.99	1.13	1.78	1.37
Shipbuilding	7.17	0.82	4.39	1.30	3.23
Railway	3.18	4.83	1.63	2.02	2.84
Automobiles	3.53	3.50	2.41	2.16	2.84
Airplanes	3.44	−1.05	2.54	1.92	1.72
Medical, optical equipment	4.77	3.99	1.16	1.63	2.78
Others	2.02	2.37	1.95	0.06	1.48

Source: Sung-Duk Hong and Jung-Ho Kim, *Long-Term Changes in Total Factor Productivity of Manufacturing 1967–93* (in Korean), KDI (Seoul, Korea, June 1996), pp. 62–63.

audio and communication equipment (3.23 percent), shipbuilding (3.23 percent), industrial machines (3.07 percent), engines and turbines (2.99 percent), industrial chemicals (2.87 percent), railways (2.84 percent), automobiles (2.84 percent), and china and earthenware (2.82 percent), in that order.

Note also that the first subperiod (1967–73) saw a faster TFP growth rate in general than the following subperiods. Recall that this was the period in which labor-intensive light industries thrived as a result of rapid export expansion. Rapid TFP growth was then achieved apparently through the development of organizational and marketing skills rather than through technological learning (in the sense of engineering complexity). But with the Heavy and Chemical Industry Development Program launched in 1973, the sudden drop in TFP growth rates in the following subperiods would seem to suggest the difficulty (or costliness) of learning new technologies. These new technologies were mostly imported, but they represented state-of-the-art technologies at that time. The drop may also reflect, in part, the adverse impact of the oil crisis in 1974.

Nevertheless, it is interesting to note that there are indications of persistent learning, for example, in the case of industrial machines. The recorded TFP growth rates of that subsector were 1.83 percent annually between 1973–79, 2.40 percent between 1979–85, and 3.03 percent between 1985–93, a steadily increasing speed of learning. The iron and steel subsector, another example, recorded a slowly increasing TFP growth of 0.33 percent between 1973–79, 0.34 percent between 1979–85, and 0.64 percent between 1985–93.[6]

In the case of office machines and other related machines (subsector number 26), the TFP grew at a relatively high rate of 3.45 percent annually over the 1967–93 period. The subperiods also recorded a steady, high rate of over 3 percent throughout. This sector covers products such as computers, peripherals, facsimiles, modems, switches, and electrical control devices. This subsector will probably be quite important in transmitting growth impact to other sectors of the economy (externalities) in the future. Recall that this subsector did not exist at all in the 1950s. The speed of learning recorded in this subsector may herald it as a leading sector in the next decade, especially given the trend toward an "information society."

If these estimates are valid, the negative assessment of the Heavy and Chemical Investment Program (1973–79) should be re-examined. It has been alleged that too ambitious a push toward heavy and chemical

industries (against Korea's then comparative advantage) distorted resource allocation in a static sense and brought about a slowdown in
growth as a consequence as well as the suppression of banking-sector
development.[7]

Looking back from the vantage point of today, the program could
have proved beneficial had it started even earlier than it did. That is
because learning here is a long-term as well as a cumulative proposition, spanning a ten- to twenty-year period. The earlier the learning
begins, the better the results obtained.[8]

For the purpose of elaborating the argument further, let us take the
case of the iron and steel industries. It should not have been recommended that this sector be built according to the static comparative
advantage theory. Indeed, a corporate history of the Pohang steel complex recorded the reason why the World Bank refused a loan application submitted by the South Korean government, namely economic
nonviability and Korea's inability to repay the loan.[9] The country
lacked iron ore, coking coal, knowledge of steelmaking, and engineers
needed for steelmaking. In addition domestic market demand was insufficient to provide economies of scale. A benefit–cost ratio proved
to be less than one, a perfect economic reason for rejection. Nevertheless, Korea went ahead with this massive project and succeeded beyond anybody's wildest predictions. The only way this success can be
explained adequately is by understanding how this technology was
mastered.

The importance of having an efficient steel industry for downstream
industries such as automobile, shipbuilding, machinery, and construction cannot be overemphasized. These latter industries also emerged
as competitive export industries during the 1980s, thanks to the steady
supply of steel products for the user industries and the steady improvement in the quality of steel products. The TFP estimates presented
above seem to lend supporting evidence, demonstrating the importance of learning and mastering new technology in those industries.

At this point it seems useful to clarify the difference between the
meaning of TFP measurement in industrial countries and in developing
countries. In developing countries like Korea and other NICs, growing
TFP over a period of time can be regarded as a measurement of the
pace of the catch-up process. Normally technological knowledge is
"transferred" from industrial countries in diverse forms such as licensing, importing of machines embodying advanced technology, inviting
foreign expert engineers or consultants, foreign direct investment, and

joint ventures. These transferred technologies usually require local adaptation by going through collective testing, exercises, and drilling until they are mastered, meaning that the original machine or plant capacity and operational efficiency as defined by the designers is fully reached. Some analysts prefer to call this type of learning "imitating or copying" in order to distinguish it from a learning process in an industrial country that results in the creation of new knowledge at a technological frontier. In this sense Korea has been "learning through imitating and copying" technologies largely developed in the United States and Japan. As shown by the relatively high TFP estimates in heavy (engineering intensive) industries, the speed of learning (imitating) would seem to have been quite rapid. TFP estimates subsume effects of many dynamic elements such as increasing skill levels through education and training; injection of superior technology, imported or domestically invented; successful introduction of new products, particularly with higher-income elasticities; new ways of organizing factory floors; improved organization of workers (X-efficiency) and management hierarchy (e.g., a flatter pyramid); upgrading of output mix by an industry as well as by the manufacturing sector as a whole, in addition to the usual macro-influences. All of these phenomena can be observed in Korea. TFP estimates provide a convenient index summing up in one figure the effects of all of these diverse activities relating to skill or technology upgrading.

TFP Estimates in Other Studies: A Comparison

Hollis Chenery and associates have conducted a comparative study on productivity growth in manufacturing in Japan (1955–73), South Korea (1960–77), Turkey (1963–76), and Yugoslavia (1965–78). Their estimates of TFP growth were based on a translog production function rather than Cobb-Douglas production function (the author's approach). Table 2.5 presents their results. It is remarkable that the estimates for Korea exceed all other countries in every subsector category. It should also be noted that the electrical machinery subsector tops the ranking for Korea with a 7.25 percent annual growth rate of TFP. The corresponding figure for Japan shows a 4.42 percent annual growth of TFP, still ranking at the top among all subsectors in Japan. Then comes the fabricated metals subsector with a 6.01 percent annual growth rate of TFP in Korea, which compares with 0.84 percent for the corresponding figure for Japan. The machinery and transport equipment

Table 2.5
Annual growth rates of output and total factor productivity by manufacturing sectors in Japan, Korea, Turkey, and Yugoslavia

Manufacturing sector	Japan (1955–1973)		Korea (1960–1977)		Turkey (1963–1976)		Yugoslavia (1965–1978)	
	Output	TFP	Output	TFP	Output	TFP	Output	TFP
Food processing	9.36	2.21	16.09	5.26	8.47	1.91	7.20	−0.65
Textile	7.49	1.70	18.88	4.51	9.47	1.44	9.77	−0.17
Apparel	12.52	1.94	23.34	1.62	18.30	2.74		
Leather	11.15	0.95	25.20	2.80	6.41	−0.98	11.69	−0.14
Timber	7.94	1.12	16.32	5.62	7.35	−1.20	10.85	−0.60
Furniture	11.83	−0.09	13.49	4.88	12.37	3.23	10.77	0.07
Paper	11.25	1.62	19.41	4.52	13.53	1.41		
Chemical	12.23	2.50	21.33	4.49	15.23	1.62	12.14	0.10
Petroleum and coal	15.28	−0.43	22.81	0.68	16.60	0.45	10.09	0.18[a]
Rubber	9.79	−0.22	20.90	5.88	19.19	5.80	13.19	2.35
Stone, glass	12.43	1.73	18.93	4.53	12.80	0.26	9.90	−0.05
Basic metals	12.11	0.96	25.68	1.87	14.98	0.87	6.08	−0.63[b]
Fabricated metals	14.33	0.84	22.19	6.01	7.57	1.51	12.58	0.60
Machinery	15.90	3.14	23.01	5.73	17.61	1.33		
Electric machinery	18.26	4.42	36.00	7.25	19.34	1.83	15.55	−0.25
Transportation equipment	16.69	2.53	28.68	5.10	19.48	3.33	3.09	−0.25[c]

Source: Hollis Chenery et al., *Industrialization and Growth: A Comparative Study*, Oxford University Press for World Bank, 1986.
a. Coal only. Output: 1.32%; TFP: 1.10%.
b. Nonferrous metals only. Output: 7.54%; TFP: −0.65%.
c. Figures are only for shipbuilding.

subsectors follow with 5.73 percent and 5.10 percent annual growth of TFP, respectively, in Korea. This observation confirms in a broad way the one made earlier, namely that the capital goods sector has performed relatively better than other sectors.

A more recent estimate of TFP is provided by M. Ishaq Nadiri, which compares the manufacturing sectors of the United States, Japan, and Korea.[10] For the manufacturing sector as a whole for the 1975 to 1990 period, his estimates for the United States yielded an 0.77 percent annual growth, 1.23 percent for Japan, and 3.32 percent for Korea. But subsectoral estimates were not attempted in his study. Nevertheless, the Korean rates of TFP growth exceed those of the United States and Japan, and this would seem to support the prediction that Korea could catch up with Japan sometime early in the next century. How early might that occur? Here the idea of catching up is defined as the productivity of Korean labor approaching that of Japanese labor. Using his econometric model along with some plausible assumptions about inputs (i.e., labor, capital, and R&D expenditures), Nadiri provided a set of scenarios for catching up with Japan. The most likely scenarios are (1) 2002–03, if R&D expenditures grow at a rate of 25 percent annually, or alternatively, and (2) 2004–05, if R&D expenditures grow at a rate of 20 percent annually. These outcomes assume a "moderate" growth in labor, material inputs, and capital (meaning some plausibly slower rates than the historical averages experienced during the 1981–90 period). These scenarios, for whatever they are worth, seem to argue for the importance of accumulating R&D capital in raising labor productivity. (See note 16 of chapter 2 for the definition of R&D capital. Note also that the 1997–98 financial crisis forced the government as well as the private sector to curtail R&D expenditures drastically.)

Nadiri's analysis offers insights and advice concerning the supply of human capital, if the projections (scenarios) are realized: "Korea may have developed sufficient research facilities, but now may have to shift resources to hire more scientific and technical personnel. This may not be very easy to do in the short-term if the educational and training institutions have difficulty producing the required scientific skills. . . . If bottlenecks develop in producing the required number and types of scientists and engineers, or if the quality of the scientists and researchers is not adequately high, the likelihood of the planned increase in R&D expenditure to achieve a substantial increase in the rate of technological progress may diminish considerably." The role of human capital will be the topic for the following chapter.

Another study of TFP growth yielding a comparative perspective is provided by Alwyn Young.[11] The study reveals that the Korean manufacturing sector registered the highest TFP growth rate among the East Asian countries selected for estimation. South Korea registered a 3.0 percent annual growth (1966–90) compared with a 1.7 percent growth for Taiwan (1966–90), a −1.0 percent growth for Singapore (1970–90), and a 2.3 percent growth for Hong Kong (1966–91), though the latter is not strictly comparable because the figure is not just for the manufacturing sector but for the economy as a whole. Nonetheless, Alwyn Young argues that the premise that "productivity growth in these economies, particularly in their manufacturing sectors, has been extraordinarily high" is incorrect.[12] His argument appears supported when the entire economies (not just manufacturing) are considered. In the South Korean case, the economy as a whole registered a 1.7 percent annual growth in TFP for the 1966–90 period, which is not a particularly outstanding record compared to other countries.

There are a number of other studies employing different assumptions (e.g., Hicksian neutrality), forms of production functions (e.g., translog, Cobb-Douglas, etc.), periods covered, definitions of inputs and outputs (e.g., gross output, value added, etc.), and so on.[13] The magnitude of TFP estimates appears to be sensitive to these assumptions, definitions, and periods. Some studies even adjust for labor quality, for example, by taking the amount of education into consideration, which tends to lower the estimated figures.[14] Nevertheless, the broad pattern of TFP growth across subsectors in manufacturing would appear similar; that is, the performance of the capital goods subsectors is superior and robust. This generalization appears to hold regardless of production functions assumed, periods analyzed, and definitions adopted for inputs and outputs. This evidence lends credibility to the policy implications that can be drawn, namely that more resources should go to capital goods industries for R&D capability building, particularly to the electrical and electronic machinery subsectors.

2.3   Accumulation of R&D Capital Assets and Technological Spillover Effects

Technology has been recognized as an important determinant of industrialization since the beginning of the First Five-Year Economic Development Plan (1962–66). The formulation of the technology learning plan as reported in the document entitled: First Five-Year Plan for

Technical Development (Supplement to First Five-Year Economic Plan), Economic Planning Board, Republic of Korea, 1962, bears witness to the awareness of technology needs.[15] The Korea Institute of Science and Technology (KIST), a key player in developing technological capability in the Korean economy (see chapter 5), was established in 1966. However, wholesale investment in R&D began to surge only in the early 1980s. Major indicators of R&D activities demonstrate that 1982 was the turning point, ushering in the era of rapid upgrading in technological capability. The time shape of some major indicators is presented in figures 2.1 to 2.8 (and listed in appendix A). Note that R&D expenditures, number of researchers, technology licenses imported, capital goods imported, patents applied for and granted, all hew to a similar curve. The short time period in which technological capability was built should be kept in mind to appreciate what has been achieved. Technological learning took off, it seems, in the latter part of 1970s.

Analyses of R&D capital formation have only begun recently. So far, three studies have appeared, one published by KDI (1989), one by STEPI (1994), and the third by KERI (1995).[16] They have attempted to estimate Korean R&D capital stock for the first time. The estimate made by Jin Kyu Chang is presented in table 2.6, since it is more recent and more detailed. The manufacturing total of R&D stock reached 5,641.4 billion won in 1991, up from 407.8 billion won in 1982 (both figures in

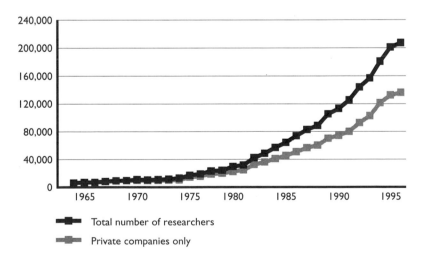

Figure 2.1
Number of researchers in South Korea, 1964–1996

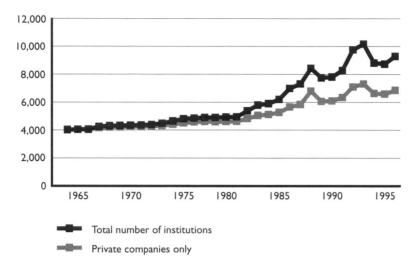

Figure 2.2
Number of R&D performing institutions in South Korea, 1964–1996

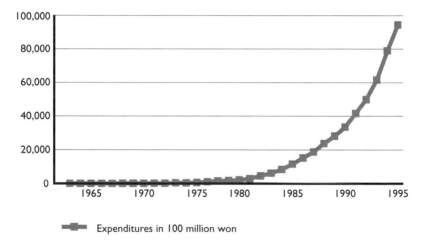

Figure 2.3
Total R&D expenditures in South Korea, 1963–1996

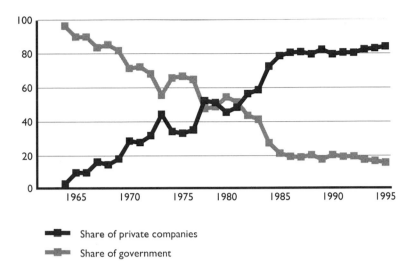

Figure 2.4
Percent of R&D expenditures by government and private companies

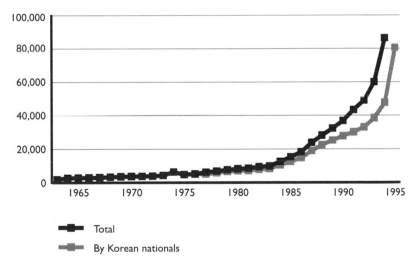

Figure 2.5
Number of patents applied for

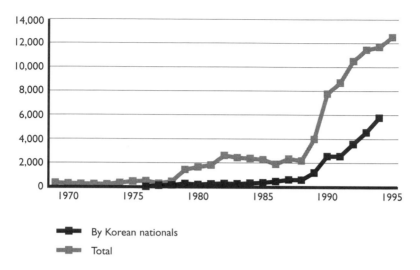

Figure 2.6
Number of patents granted

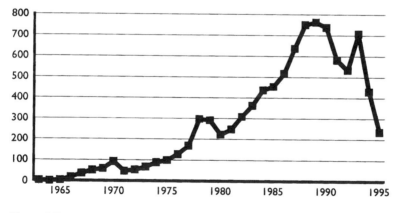

Figure 2.7
Number of technology imports

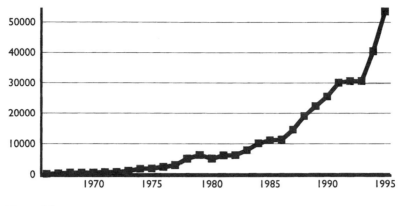

Figure 2.8
Capital goods imported (in millions of dollars)

1985 constant prices). The figures are equivalent to $0.5 billion and $7.0 billion for 1982 and 1991, respectively. The fact that General Motors alone spends approximately $7.0 billion a year for R&D puts the Korean figures into perspective.

The subsectoral distribution of R&D capital stock indicates a diverse relative magnitude and commitment to technology upgrading. Far ahead in ranking is the electrical and electronic subsector with 2,185.8 billion won (or $2.7 billion), 38.8 percent of the manufacturing total. Then comes the transport equipment subsector with 804.0 billion won ($1.0 billion), 14.3 percent of the total. Third in the ranking is the general machinery subsector with 544.2 billion won ($0.7 billion), 10 percent of the total. The dominance of the top three subsectors in R&D activities is expected to continue well into the next century. Moreover R&D investment is expected to accelerate as the leading companies in these subsectors expand their markets and R&D activities on a global scale.

For instance, Samsung, Hyundai, Lucky-Goldstar (L-G), Daewoo, and Sunkyung, the five largest *chaebol* groups, have begun competing, announcing their respective plans to build up and globalize R&D, production, and marketing networks. There is some evidence that gives the announcements credibility. Chapter 4 provides more details on R&D activities by individual *chaebol* groups. Furthermore the Korean government has committed itself to raising expenditures for science and technology to 4 percent of GNP by the year 2001 and also to assist the globalization movement by private enterprises.

Table 2.6
Estimate of R&D capital stock in Korean manufacturing industries, 1982–1991 (unit: billion won in 1985 constant prices)

Sector	1982	1983	1984	1985	1986	1987	1988	1989	1990	1991
Food and drink	69.1	77.0	96.9	114.4	142.9	197.0	221.7	277.9	319.5	356.1
Textiles and clothing	40.7	48.3	56.0	71.5	93.0	112.7	131.8	159.0	201.1	235.4
Wood	9.0	9.3	10.4	10.2	10.1	10.1	9.5	9.6	11.0	14.7
Paper	10.9	12.4	15.6	18.1	25.6	35.9	43.4	52.7	56.3	59.9
Industrial chemicals	37.6	39.3	44.3	66.0	69.0	92.4	120.6	131.8	150.4	170.6
Other chemicals	34.6	41.5	51.1	69.4	113.2	142.5	182.3	263.7	327.6	418.4
Petroleum refining	2.3	3.2	8.3	13.0	20.3	29.7	45.2	61.4	82.9	96.8
Petroleum and coal	1.5	1.8	2.8	3.3	3.5	4.1	12.3	16.7	19.0	18.8
Rubber	36.7	40.6	50.3	63.7	71.8	79.8	98.9	126.5	140.7	160.8
Plastics	2.2	2.9	17.0	24.6	23.9	29.4	30.4	31.8	34.3	34.8
Nonmetal minerals	9.4	12.3	16.7	25.2	35.4	50.0	62.9	76.3	97.8	125.6
Primary metals	26.6	32.6	39.1	49.6	65.0	81.3	113.8	130.0	174.6	206.4
Fabricated metals	9.5	11.4	17.8	30.6	37.6	49.4	59.0	72.0	94.8	122.0
General machinery	13.7	20.2	32.2	62.7	89.7	133.7	194.9	306.5	440.8	544.2
Electronics and electrical equipment	60.1	92.2	141.8	223.3	406.4	642.4	956.6	1244.4	1625.5	2185.8
Transportation equipment	34.2	45.1	59.8	109.3	160.6	252.5	342.9	490.3	626.6	804.0
Precision equipment	1.4	2.1	4.1	4.1	6.0	12.1	18.6	28.1	43.6	54.2
Other	8.3	8.5	9.0	15.6	16.9	20.0	20.6	28.0	28.1	32.9
Total	407.8	508.7	673.2	974.7	1390.9	1975.0	2655.4	3506.7	4474.6	5641.4

Source: Jin Kyu Chang et al., *Analysis of R&D Investment and Spillover Effects* (in Korean), STEPI, January 1994, p. 45.

The commitment by both leading businesses and government carry some weight in Korea, mainly as a result of the track record of industrialization during the last thirty years. Such a concentration of R&D resources in a few sectors naturally raises a simple but serious question: Is it worthwhile? Chang et al. (1994) addressed this question by estimating private as well as social rates of return on R&D investments. Following the method of estimation adopted by Jaffe (1986), Chang et al. (see note 16 of chapter 2) calculated the rate of return on R&D investment in the eight manufacturing subsectors shown in table 2.7.[17] Note first that the chemicals subsector exhibits the highest rate of return, followed by electric and electronic machinery, and finally by the transport equipment, machinery and metal fabrication subsectors combined in one. Second, the estimates for social rates of return for the electrical, electronic, and precision machines (combined) indicate a coefficient almost ten times higher than the private rate of return, followed by the subsector which combines transport equipment, general machinery and metal fabrication. These figures suggest an enormous technological spillover effect among manufacturing subsectors.[18]

A graphic summary of the spillover effect is given in figure 2.9. The electric, electronic, and precision machines (combined) subsector appears to have the largest linkage with five other subsectors. The rubber, plastic (combined) subsector has spillover linkage with four other subsectors, and so on. These represent the so-called pecuniary technological externalities. In other words, the cost reduction or

Table 2.7
Private and social rates of return to R&D investment

Industrial groups	Private rate of return	Social rate of return
Food, drinks, wood, paper	0.0223	0.0223
Textile, clothing, other manufactures	0.0477	0.0477
Nonmetal minerals, primary metals	0.0587	0.0587
Industrial and other chemicals	0.4365	0.9429
Rubber and plastic	0.0394	0.7096
Petroleum refining, coal products	0.2298	0.2399
Transport, general machines, fabricated metals	0.2939	2.0388
Electronics and precision equipment	0.2960	2.8042

Source: J. K. Chang, S. C. Chung, and K. K. Kim, *Economic Effect Analysis of R&D Investment* (in Korean), STEPI, January 1994, p. 101.

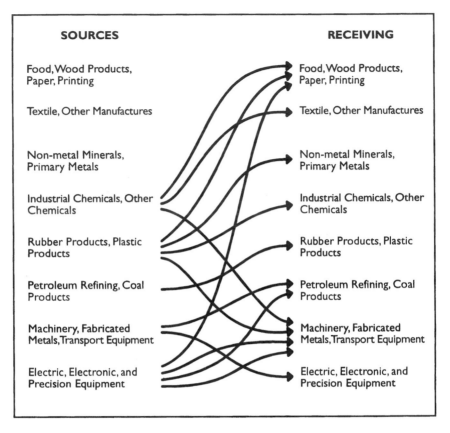

Figure 2.9
R&D spillover network (Source: Same as table 2.7)

quality improvement due to a successful commercialization of technology in one sector reduces the cost to other sectors that use the output of the source sector as their input. This benefit accrues to the user, but the source producer does not gain a benefit. The beneficial effects could multiply rapidly if all the subsectors could cooperate jointly to engage in R&D activities in order to internalize the externalities. This appears to be what is happening in the Korean manufacturing sector, although further research is needed to corroborate this trend.

Just to illustrate, technology developments in electronic devices and precision equipment are known to reduce the costs of output in many other subsectors that use those devices and equipment. The reason is that as the food-processing subsector, for example, introduces an electronic automated system to integrate output, inventory, sales, and advertising, the unit cost goes down in the long run. Likewise technological improvements in plastics production will benefit all the industries using plastics through lower prices and better quality of plastic. Such spillover effects mean that TFP growth could be influenced not only by internal efforts for innovation but also by the reception of benefits from outside of the firm or other linked industries (positive externalities).

So far, we have reviewed the private and social rates of return on R&D capital. Now we turn to the question of the extent to which R&D capital affects the productivity of labor. It would be of interest to compare the effects of raising labor productivity between physical capital and R&D capital. Byung-Ki Lee (1995) has addressed the question by estimating a revised Cobb-Douglas production function that includes R&D capital as an explanatory variable for labor productivity.[19] He used the data from 15 manufacturing subsectors for the 1988–92 period by pooling the time series with the cross-section data for regression. Table 2.8 summarizes his results.

It is to be noted that output per labor man-year is determined more by physical capital per labor man-year than by R&D capital per labor man-year. The coefficients show 0.733 and 0.045, respectively, for the former and the latter variable. This finding suggests that Korean industrialization can be characterized by resource-intensive growth rather than idea-intensive growth. And this interpretation is corroborated by other studies.[20] It is interesting also to note that the R&D capital accumulated by the government appears less significant than that accumulated by private enterprises, and further that basic research is less significant than applied research.

Does this mean that investment resources should be reallocated to favor private and applied R&D activities? To address this question more research that incorporates a time horizon will be necessary. Basic research may not have an impact on labor productivity immediately, but in the long run it may and with abundant dividends. The existing studies failed to capture this aspect of the policy issue. Furthermore R&D capital accumulation without a supporting accumulation of human capital (more highly trained engineers and technicians, more specialized managers, etc.) would appear to be inadequate to impact labor productivity in the long run. More sophisticated R&D normally requires more capable researchers, engineers, and scientists. This concern presents itself as a possible hypothesis to be tested.

Table 2.8
Influence of R&D on labor productivity: Regression analysis with 1982–1991 pooled data

CON	KL	TRL	BRL	ARL	GRL	PRL	EOS	T	R^2
Total									
1.069	0.733***	0.045**					−0.092*	0.074***	0.96
(1.30)	(10.72)	(2.06)					(−1.78)	(3.29)	
2.551***	0.602***				0.023		−0.199***	0.078***	0.96
(2.98)	(9.33)				(1.644)		(−3.64)	(3.40)	
1.085	0.733***					0.044**	−0.093*	0.074***	0.99
(1.33)	(10.87)					(2.04)	(−1.82)	(3.28)	
2.126**	0.692***		0.028*				−0.161***	0.068***	0.96
(2.42)	(10.22)		(1.74)				(−2.76)	(2.89)	
1.095	0.731***			0.044**			−0.093*	0.074***	0.96
(1.33)	(15.23)			(2.03)			(−1.82)	(3.30)	
Small and medium businesses									
1.332***	0.629***	0.049***					−0.121***	0.063***	0.96
(2.92)	(9.75)	(3.34)					(−4.18)	(4.46)	
1.503***	0.571***				0.005		−0.165***	0.085***	0.96
(4.73)	(9.50)				(0.55)		(−7.03)	(5.31)	
1.213***	0.676***					0.049***	−0.106***	0.058***	0.95
(2.67)	(11.90)					(3.72)	(−3.80)	(4.13)	
1.758**	0.656***		0.019				−0.155***	0.067***	0.95
(5.68)	(10.83)		(1.57)				(−6.64)	(4.88)	
1.316***	0.625***			0.051***			−0.119***	0.063***	0.96
(2.83)	(9.67)			(3.40)			(−4.07)	(4.63)	

Large businesses

CON	KL	TRL	BRL	ARL	PRL	GRL	EOS	T	R^2
1.352	0.749***	0.036					−0.115*	0.068**	0.94
(1.37)	(9.83)	(1.28)					(−1.91)	(2.14)	
0.731	0.471***		0.038				−0.113	0.079**	0.93
(0.55)	(3.58)		(1.87)				(−1.50)	(2.22)	
1.27	0.756***			0.037			−0.111	0.072**	0.93
(1.29)	(9.92)			(1.29)			(−1.83)	(2.26)	
1.868	0.696***				0.025		−0.149*	0.049	0.94
(1.37)	(9.15)				(1.45)		(−1.67)	(1.59)	
1.379	0.751***					0.036	−1.116	0.068**	0.94
(1.41)	(9.92)					(1.26)	(−1.94)	(2.15)	

Source: Byong Ki Lee, *Effects of Technology Development by Private Enterprise and the Government: Implications for Technology Policy* (in Korean), Seoul: Korea Economic Research Institute, 1995.

Note: (1) *t*-values are in parentheses. (2) *** indicates 1% significance level, **, 5% significance level, and *, 10% significance level. (3) CON: constant; KL: capital per labor; TRL: total R&D capital per labor; BRL: basic research per labor; ARL: applied research per labor; GRL: government research per labor; PRL: private research per labor; EOS: economics of scale; T: exogenous technical progress.

2.4   Human Capital and Returns to Investment in Education

In principle, the growth-promoting effect of education appears to be well accepted, although some contrary views exist. Basic education provides workers with opportunities to acquire and sharpen cognitive skills. Further, higher education endows students with professional tools and language for technical communication, which is necessary when an economy attempts to climb the technology ladder from a low level to a higher level with greater complexity. Thus an important factor to explain "an economy's ability to absorb information and new technology is the education of its populace."[21]

However, a contrarian view advances the notion that education is merely a method of screening talent and giving credentials rather than enhancing technological skills or risk-taking capability. If this is so, an increase in wages associated with educational level may not reflect the true productivity contribution to the society. But the latter hypothesis has yet to be supported by convincing evidence.[22] In the Korean experience the circumstantial evidence presented in the next chapter suggests that education makes a powerful contribution to learning and productivity growth.

Korea has been widely acknowledged as being a country blessed with an abundant supply of well educated labor.[23] But the analysis of how human capital has been accumulated and how it has supported the technological upgrading of Korean industry is rather scanty. This study points to the importance of human capital, particularly highly trained employees, in facilitating technology absorption by Korean industry. In this section some indicators of human capital accumulation in manufacturing are briefly reviewed as a prelude to the following chapter.

Table 2.9 shows the pace at which the educational level of workers employed in the manufacturing sector since 1962 has risen. In that year, the overwhelming proportion (74 percent) of manufacturing employees had only 0 to 6 years of education. By 1990, only 13 percent of workers remained in that category. By contrast, those who had 10 to 12 years of education increased from 9 percent in 1962 to 48 percent in 1990. Note also that those who had 16 or more years of education (college graduates) increased to 12 percent in 1990 compared with only 3 percent in 1962, and that an acceleration in the employment of college graduates is observable only since 1980. This phenomenon underscores

Table 2.9
Employees in manufacturing sector by years of education, 1962–1995

Year	Total number of workers in manufacturing	Years of education (%)				
		0–6	7–9	10–12	13–14	>16
1962	196,872	74	14	9		3
1963	252,345	64	19	12		5
1964	266,458	60	21	14		5
1965	294,261	60	21	14		5
1966	316,430	58	21	15		6
1967	349,599	56	23	15		5
1968	381,699	51	27	16		6
1969	503,571	56	24	15		5
1970	616,629	55	24	16		5
1971	742,993	55	25	16		5
1972	778,158	51	26	16	1	5
1973	918,366	52	26	16	1	5
1974	1,011,219	47	29	18	1	5
1975	959,818	35	37	22	1	6
1976	1,506,381	34	38	22	1	5
1977	1,716,009	32	40	22	1	5
1978	3,016,000	*	68	24	1	5
1979	3,126,000	*	68	26	1	5
1980	2,797,028	*	66	27	2	5
1981	2,859,000	*	65	28	2	5
1982	3,033,000	*	62	30	2	6
1983	3,266,000	*	59	32	2	6
1984	3,348,000	*	55	36	3	6
1985	3,503,000	*	53	38	3	6
1986	3,826,000	*	50	40	3	7
1987	4,416,000	*	46	44	3	7
1988	4,667,000	*	41	47	4	7
1989	4,882,000	*	40	47	4	8
1990	4,320,603	*	35	48	5	12
1991	4,994,000	*	38	45	6	11
1992	4,828,000		34	49	5	12
1993	4,652,000		37	48		14
1994	4,695,000		36	50		15
1995	4,773,000		35	50		15

Sources: For 1985–93, *Comprehensive Time Series Report on the Economically Active Population survey (1963–93),* National Statistical Office, December 1994. For 1962–77, Chong-kee Park (ed.), *Human Resources and Social Development in Korea,* Seoul: Korea Development Institute, 1979, pp. 73–93. For 1995, National Statistics Office, *Annual Report on the Economically Active Population Survey (1995).*

the emphasis given to the technology factor in the industrialization policy of the 1980s. By 1990, over two-thirds of all employees had a high school level of education or better.[24]

Returns on Investment in Education

The relationship between technological upgrading and educated manpower should go hand in hand (complementarity assumption). Highly educated workers possess a comparative advantage in learning new skills and implementing new technologies. Demand for highly educated workers therefore would tend to increase during phases of rapid technological upgrading, and hence their wages and salaries would tend to increase faster than those of less educated workers.

This hypothesis has been tested by a recent study (Kang-Shik Choi 1993).[25] It concludes that, "Using a Mincerian earnings function, we find that the marginal private return to education in Korea increases with the level of education in contrast to the case in the U. S. and some other countries." This finding seems to suggest that the normal force of decreasing returns in a static sense can be offset by learning and mastering new technologies faster, which is a result of higher education. The study concludes further that, "workers are paid more in industries where technology changes rapidly than in industries where technology changes slowly."

Other studies that estimate the rate of return on educational investment using conventional accounting methods (not regression analysis as in the above work) appear to confirm the above finding. Table 2.10 summarizes the estimates made by various researchers. It is surprising to observe, if the estimates are valid, that college education appears to yield the highest returns, followed by junior college education, high school education, and middle school education, in that order. This pattern of estimates applies to both male and female workers alike, although in general, the rate of return on education for females is higher than males (a rare phenomenon).

This pattern stands in contrast to the general conclusions reached by studies on developing countries as a group. Psacharopoulos (1994), for example, summarizes his findings as follows: "The rate of return patterns established in earlier reviews are upheld, namely, that primary education continues to be the number one investment priority in developing countries; the returns decline by the level of schooling and the country's per capita income."[26]

Table 2.10
Republic of Korea: Mincer (private) rates of return by level of schooling, gender, and year, all employed and manufacturing workers, 1974–1988

Year	MS/PS+ M	MS/PS+ F	HS/MS M	HS/MS F	JC/HS M	JC/HS F	COL/HS M	COL/HS F
All workers								
1976	2.1	1.6	9.1	11.9	13.6	19.2	16.8	19.6
1981	1.7	1.2	6.5	9.1	13.0	26.6	15.4	19.4
1986	2.8	3.4	4.6	5.6	8.3	17.3	14.4	19.3
1988	1.9	2.7	3.9	5.2	6.5	14.0	12.2	15.0
Manufacturing workers								
1974	8.0	7.5	14.8	14.8	12.5	20.2	16.5	15.1
1976	3.2	1.6	8.7	9.3	14.7	15.8	17.5	16.7
1979	6.1	3.1	11.7	12.4	15.0	17.4	17.8	18.8
1981	2.9	1.0	6.0	6.5	12.8	19.3	16.1	18.7
1986	4.2	2.2	10.0	9.0	12.2	15.4	17.8	20.3
1987	3.4	2.3	4.6	4.0	9.0	8.5	13.4	20.0
1988	2.7	1.8	4.4	4.4	6.3	6.2	11.0	11.8

Source: Jai-kyung Ryoo, Young-sook Nam, and Martin Carnoy, "Changing Rates of Return to Education over Time: A Korean Case Study," *Economics of Education Review* 12 (1993): 71–80.
Note: MS: middle school; PS: primary school; HS: high school; JC: junior college; COL: college.

One can conjecture that the rate of return on university education can be maintained at a high level if college graduates command skills that are in highly demand by expanding industries. The fast pace of learning new skills could help maintain higher return on university education. Indeed, since the 1960s demand for skills obtained in colleges and universities have been increasing. For instance, English language proficiency coupled with an area of specialization such as law, economics, accounting, and engineering have been in great demand because the rapidly expanding export volume required these skills. Such demand was not so great in manufacturing per se since that sector used a more unskilled labor force. Skills were needed more in social overhead sectors (transportation, communication, electricity, water supply, etc.) and also in professional services sectors (banking, legal services, engineering services, etc.). These sectors had to provide services to the export-driven manufacturing sectors in addition to import-competing industries; otherwise, the galloping growth of exports could not have been sustained.[27]

One can further conjecture that as digital technology spreads to all industries, the earnings and productivity of university graduates (particularly in science and engineering) will probably increase even more. New industries will be created requiring workers with high-tech skills, as exemplified by HDTV (coupled with telecommunication technology) and clusters of related industries. Furthermore it must be borne in mind that digital technology, applied in an industry, is capable of saving all types of resources at once (i.e., labor, capital, energy, raw materials, space, and time), but only if educated people are available to harness it. In an era in which a new technological paradigm is developing, the race for competitiveness may amount to a race for human capital accumulation. As Thurow (1996) has aptly said, "With everything else dropping out of the competitive equation, knowledge has become the only source of long-run sustainable competitive advantage, but knowledge can only be employed through the skills of individuals."[28]

2.5   Concluding Remarks

This review of productivity-growth performance as well as studies on R&D activities and human capital formation allows us to draw some (preliminary) conclusions. Some of these are to be tested with more details in the following chapters.

First, productivity growth in Korean manufacturing, however measured, has exceeded other countries (even compared to Japan), although different researchers produced varying estimates, owing to different periods covered, basic data sources, and forms of production function. The findings imply that a significant amount of "learning of new technologies" has been achieved. So long as wages and salaries do not grow faster than the pace of learning in the long run, the competitiveness of Korean products should remain strong. If the past long-term record suggests anything, the future competitiveness of Korean industries looks promising.

Second, human capital (i.e., educated human resources) has grown more rapidly in Korea than in other developing countries as well as industrial countries. Human capital provided a basis for harnessing imported, state-of-the-art technologies, and mastering them fast. Productivity growth and industrial competitiveness in Korean manufacturing owe a great deal to the abundance of human capital.

Third, the electric and electronics subsector has demonstrated outstanding performance in raising productivity, increasing shares in output, employment, and export coupled with burgeoning R&D activities. Substantial spillover effects were detected from this subsector to other subsectors. Such a record argues for allocating greater resources to the subsector in the future for expansion and development. The fast-expanding global market for electronics and related products offers a challenging field for the Korean electronics industry.

Fourth, the machinery and transport equipment subsectors are set to become the second most successful Korean industry in the global market, after electronics. Automobiles have also emerged as a leading export item since the mid–1980s, when Hyundai began exporting Ponys to the North American market. Along with semiconductors, automobiles promise to lead in raising labor productivity and competitiveness of Korean manufactures for the coming decades.[29]

The following chapters aim to explain these records of outstanding performance in terms of historical and institutional perspectives. Chapter 3 delves into what roles the colleges and universities have played in producing human capital, particularly scientists and engineers. Chapter 4 examines what *chaebols* and small and medium industries have done to learn and master new (imported) technologies. And chapter 5 looks at what the government sector has done to enhance the technological capabilities of Korean industries. These three chapters address, in the Korean context, the "appreciative theory" which Richard Nelson (1996) thought important for understanding the logic of innovation.[30]

3

Human Capital Accumulation and the Role of Universities

In the previous chapter we reviewed indicators of Korean productivity growth that are comparable (or even superior) to the best performers (e.g., Japan). This chapter explores the sources and process of human capital accumulation that provided a fundamental building block needed to upgrade Korean industry's technological capabilities. Due to a paucity of information, only educated workers will be considered. The inquiry addresses the following set of questions: Where did scientists, engineers, and university professors come from? What role have they played in building the R&D infrastructure vital to Korean industry's technology capabilities? What role have Korean universities played in supplying (highly) educated manpower, particularly scientists and engineers? What do the long-term human capital requirements look like? In exploring these issues, I emphasize the structure of the incentive system as an explanation for observable behavior, such as de facto tenure given to assistant professors at the time of employment, resulting in poor research output.

3.1 Human Capital Accumulation: A Building Block for Industrialization

In 1945, Korean industry inherited some physical capital, called "enemy assets," that the Japanese left behind after their defeat in World War II. In technological terms, however, these "assets" proved inadequate to the needs of Korean industry. Human capital and organizational skills, which determine capability, were absent because Japanese policy makers did not want Koreans to learn essential skills. Just before the end of the World War II, the Japanese owned and operated more than 80 percent of the capital assets in manufacturing, and industrial engineering was virtually monopolized by the Japanese. The Japanese occupation government saw to it that Koreans did not get an education beyond the primary school level. According to Noel F. McGinn (1980), "In 1939, for example, there were 143 Japanese students enrolled in primary schools for every 1,000 Japanese living in Korea, while there were only 55 Korean primary students for every 1,000 Koreans. . . . There were only 1.3 Korean students in high schools for every 1,000 Koreans, compared to 32.7 Japanese students for every 1,000 Japanese. The Korean fraction in colleges and universities were even smaller."[1]

The existing colleges and universities primarily served the interests of Japanese residents in Korea with only a nominal Korean quota; in 1944, "only 800 Koreans had graduated of which 300 were from the Medical School and about 40 from the School of Science and Engineering."[2] Among 873 professors in higher educational institutions, only 215 were Korean, mostly in the medical field.[3] The number was totally inadequate to the nation's needs. This systemic discrimination against Koreans was part of Japan's colonial economic policy.[4]

Without experienced top-level managers and engineers when the Japanese left, the "enemy assets" sufficed to produce only about 40 to 50 percent of factory capacity. The business environment was not helpful either. After the war the Korean economy struggled through similar adverse conditions to those faced by the present-day Confederation of Independent States (CIS). For example, the economic structure was dismembered (e.g., bisection of the country into North and South Koreas); international and interregional trade relations were disrupted (e.g., disconnection from markets such as Manchuria, northern China, and Japan). This resulted in a loss of trade partners; factories were dismantled and plundered; interindustry linkages were broken up; industrial infrastructure and supporting facilities were in disarray, including the banking system, transportation, and communication networks, for example, all of which had been owned and operated mostly by the Japanese.

Thus rebuilding the institutional-organizational edifice to make the system workable remained the most challenging task for policy makers. The Japanese colonial government was not interested in cultivating Korean values, norms, routines, and social consensus, which could lay the foundation for indigenous industrial growth. On the contrary, the Japanese colonial government had tried to force the "Japanization" of Korean culture and people, a policy that Koreans resisted overtly and covertly.[5] Nevertheless, it is fair to say that the "enemy assets factories" provided a physical means by which a trial-and-error learning could be attempted. It should be understood, however, that the benefits accruing to Korea from the Japanese legacy has often been overstated in the literature. Creating human capital and institutional devices to organize the productive system presented a far more pressing challenge than merely acquiring physical capital assets because it required creative adaptation.[6]

Under very pressing circumstances, the policy makers saw that the long-term challenge came from the need to eliminate pervasive illiteracy; three-quarters of the populace had no formal education whatsoever. Given such illiteracy, nation-building efforts would be inefficient if not futile. Fortunately, from 1945 onward, the social consensus was that a system of compulsory education, at least at the primary level, deserved top priority in the agenda of nation building. The Education Law, enacted in 1949, made primary education compulsory and tuition free. By 1959, 96 percent of school age children were enrolled in primary schools, up from 70 percent in 1950. About 75 percent of the national education budget up to the early 1960s was spent on primary education.[7] Subsequently, especially after the Korean War (1950–53), an extraordinary amount of educational investment took place compared with other countries at a similar economic level. Table 3.1 gives some selected indicators of development in higher education since 1945. Annual data are given in the table in order to emphasize the time shape of changes that the average (e.g., ten-year) conceals.

The elimination of illiteracy through compulsory primary education was a necessary precondition for effective nation building. But equally important was the development of higher education. The record shows that the number of college and university graduates has grown rapidly throughout the postwar period. The factors explaining the rapid growth of higher education can be summarized as follows: (1) The pent-up demand released after the Japanese occupation ended. (2) The proliferation of private colleges and universities established to meet the ever-increasing demand for higher education. (3) The willingness of Korean households to spend an increasing portion of their income on their sons' and daughters' higher education, despite their low income level, especially during the 1950s and 1960s.

The pressure of pent-up demand can be seen by the pace at which the number of students enrolled in colleges and universities grew during 1945–49 period, a 3.5-fold increase (from 7,819 to 28,000). Back then, the lack of qualified professors with proper training, a result of the departure of the Japanese professors, was often dealt with by recruiting

Table 3.1
Selected indicators of higher education in Korea, 1945–1996

Year	Total college students (includes junior colleges)	Students in 4-year colleges	Faculty in 4-year colleges	Faculty with PhDs (includes junior colleges)	Students in science and engineering in 4-year colleges	College students per 10,000 persons
1945	7,818	n.a.	1,390	n.a.	n.a.	4.1
1946	10,315	n.a.	1,170	n.a.	n.a.	5.3
1947	25,813	n.a.	2,775	n.a.	n.a.	13.4
1948	24,000	n.a.	1,265	n.a.	n.a.	12.0
1949	28,000	n.a.	1,800	n.a.	n.a.	13.8
1950	11,358	n.a.	1,100	n.a.	n.a.	5.7
1951	20,000	n.a.	1,300	n.a.	n.a.	9.7
1952	34,089	n.a.	1,823	n.a.	n.a.	16.3
1953	48,554	n.a.	1,912	n.a.	n.a.	23.0
1954	66,415	n.a.	4,511	n.a.	n.a.	31.2
1955	84,996	n.a.	2,626	n.a.	n.a.	39.5
1956	96,754	n.a.	3,161	n.a.	n.a.	46.7
1957	91,153	n.a.	3,257	n.a.	n.a.	42.8
1958	79,449	n.a.	4,315	n.a.	n.a.	41.6
1959	81,519	n.a.	4,027	n.a.	n.a.	35.5
1960	101,041	n.a.	3,803	n.a.	n.a.	40.4
1961	142,232	n.a.	4,002	n.a.	n.a.	55.2
1962	134,470	n.a.	4,058	n.a.	n.a.	50.7
1963	131,777	n.a.	4,496	n.a.	n.a.	48.3
1964	142,629	n.a.	5,351	n.a.	n.a.	51.0
1965	141,626	105,643	5,305	727	27,269	49.3
1966	175,349	131,354	5,808	896	31,901	59.6
1967	168,460	124,029	5,985	991	31,342	55.8
1968	172,410	123,659	6,572	1,109	34,473	55.9

Year						
1969	178,965	132,930	7,160	1,283	38,574	56.7
1970	193,591	146,414	7,779	1,440	36,671	61.5
1971	202,077	155,369	8,071	1,692	50,685	61.4
1972	222,224	163,932	8,949	1,820	53,599	66.3
1973	246,663	178,050	9,253	2,208	57,156	72.3
1974	269,899	192,308	9,492	2,403	57,677	77.8
1975	278,381	208,986	10,080	2,807	59,760	84.2
1976	325,234	229,811	10,080	3,609	73,231	90.7
1977	365,107	251,329	10,902	3,564	79,475	103.6
1978	418,875	277,783	11,475	3,833	92,584	113.3
1979	509,308	330,345	13,059	4,309	114,706	135.7
1980	616,462	403,989	14,458	4,835	139,261	161.7
1981	797,152	535,876	17,481	5,450	179,911	205.9
1982	984,062	661,125	20,137	6,092	231,635	242.6
1983	1,075,953	772,907	22,473	7,024	255,324	269.6
1984	1,193,007	870,170	24,406	7,976	267,222	295.3
1985	1,277,828	931,884	26,047	9,090	336,624	313.3
1986	1,332,455	971,127	27,580	10,219	350,105	321.1
1987	1,361,949	989,503	28,642	11,278	362,437	327.6
1988	1,387,170	1,003,648	29,885	12,753	382,172	330.5
1989	1,434,259	1,020,771	31,675	14,468	401,227	340.0
1990	1,490,809	1,040,166	33,340	16,155	419,891	343.6
1991	1,540,961	1,052,140	35,175	18,143	433,847	351.0
1992	1,982,510	1,070,169	37,287	20,132	448,899	363.0
1993	2,099,755	1,092,464	39,511	22,510	467,291	378.0
1994	2,196,930	1,132,437	41,576	27,650	493,046	396.0
1995	2,343,894	1,187,735	45,087	30,806	523,002	419.0
1996	2,541,659	1,266,876	48,581	33,718	562,593	452.0

Source: Ministry of Education.

high school teachers with university degrees. For instance, a number of Kyunggi High School mathematics, biology, physics, and philosophy teachers were hired by Seoul National University as part-time lecturers. This makeshift arrangement was thought better than nothing, to be used until the new doctoral degree holders would return from abroad to assume professorships. Nevertheless, graduates of these colleges and universities with makeshift programs were hired as managers by government agencies, business enterprises, and the service sector. Standards were compromised in order to alleviate the urgent problems of the period. The quality of instructors was poor. Also the work provided by college and university graduates at that time was sub-par by today's standards. Just to illustrate, modern double-entry accounting was rarely practiced in firms well into the 1960s. The effort to improve the quality of higher education continues today, but some of the habits and mind-sets acquired in those early years remain a challenge (e.g., rote memorization rather than creativity in teaching and learning).

The pressure for higher education also spawned an increasing number of private colleges and universities. In a way the government felt relieved by their birth because of budget constraints and soaring demand. The government then adopted an open-door policy, meaning anyone could found a college provided that some initial capital could be raised for financing the institution. The open-door policy has been revised several times subsequently in order to control the number of graduates, but in the main it failed to reduce graduates' unemployment. Today the private part of higher education produces over 75 percent of the total graduates, quite a contrast to other developing countries. With a few exceptions, however, many of these latecomer (and regional) institutions of higher education are considered to be inferior to already established institutions that have made a name for themselves. For instance, regional universities tend to have more crowded classrooms, fewer "bright" students, less equipment for experiments, fewer PhD holders on the faculty, higher teaching loads, and so on. Thus the ranking of colleges and universities was initiated. Usually Seoul National University is considered to be the top-ranked school, followed by Yonsei University and Korea University (about equal in ranking), with Sogang and others down the ranking order. (KAIST is discussed later.)

Apparently such an ordering system is of some usefulness to employers of graduates. The national system of competition for entrance to higher-educational institutions ranks the exam-takers according to their test performance, and the more famous universities end up picking the "brighter" examinees. In other words, the higher educational institutions function as a sifter of ability or intelligence. Such a function may reduce the transaction costs on the part of private or public employers in identifying talented recruits. One could of course argue whether an examination system really tests innate ability or intelligence. Some even hypothesize that affluent families have an advantage in being able to transfer parental social status and income to their children. In this view, higher-educational institutions provide a mechanism for carrying out the transfer process by conferring diplomas (credentials).

A counterargument maintains that the higher-education system in Korea inherited the tradition of selecting intellectual elites from any social status group so long as one passes the examination. The Yi Dynasty used the "Kwa Ko" system to select government officers, although the examination was mainly on one's ability to comprehend and compose poems and prose in Chinese. The present-day university system serves as part of a mechanism to select potential achievers in society. The higher-education facilities cull students with the potential for learning skills and conceptual tools (professional languages) that they can use in earning a living.[8]

The debate may provide an interesting area of research for years to come. But casual observation as well as the research results that are coming in would seem to suggest that the reality is mixed. The university system functions as both a sifter of ability and at the same time an enhancer of useful skills. And both functions can be useful, in certain cultural contexts, for upgrading technological capability.

One study on Korea (McGinn 1980) concludes: "The evidence is not consistent with a conclusion that education generated growth, through some transformation of individuals from traditional to modern men or through the formation of human capital. . . . Education in Korea does not appear to have expanded as a response to technological improvements in the economy requiring higher levels of ability among workers. Nor is there evidence that increase in the number of educated people anticipated (in some causal way) the economic boom of the 1960s."[9]

This investigator was obviously looking for a "single-variable causal relationship" in Korea. It seems to make more sense to regard educated, trained manpower as only one of several "inputs" enabling firms, industries, and the economy as a whole to learn new or imported technologies. In turn, mastering them leads to productivity growth and ultimately to international competitiveness. An explanation for this aspect of structural upgrading needs at least three factors and their interactions, namely technological knowledge, human capital able to master the knowledge, and an institutional setup, organizing them into a firm, industry or a "national system of innovation." An abundance of human capital, if unorganized or inefficiently organized, may mean little. The cases of the Philippines and the CIS (the former USSR) provide apt examples.[10]

With regard to the question of educational expansion in Korea unrelated to "technological improvements in the economy requiring higher levels of ability among workers," a brief explanation can be offered.

First, the Todaro (1969) model of rural–urban migration could be adapted to the case of education.[11] His model is intended to explain why people move, even anticipating possible unemployment in the city. The basic idea is that the mover calculates the "expected future income" in the city, multiplying the probability of getting employed by urban wages. If this sum exceeds by far the rural wages (plus probable costs of moving), then it is rational for the person to move. Similar reasoning applies to education. One would decide to get an education and training, even if one anticipated possible unemployment immediately after graduation, provided that the "expected lifetime income" reflecting the received education exceeds the probable costs of education.

Second, education may be regarded as not just an asset creating income but as an asset generating respect, social prestige, and the ability to appreciate the artifacts of intellectual life such as art, music, literature, history, philosophy, science, and technology. Moreover the Confucian tradition values learning in general, and the desire for learning was released from Japanese suppression. As a result education is highly valued by Koreans and governs their consumption behavior. This explains the exceptionally high level of educational expenditures (over 10 percent of income) appearing in the survey data of household income-expenditure, even in the lower-income brackets.

Third, besides the investment-plus-consumption values of education, the demand for education would seem to reflect the consensus that "national independence (liberation from Japanese domination) and survival depend on uplifting the level of enlightenment of Koreans through education." This thought permeates virtually all writings and speeches concerned with education and the future of the nation. It is difficult to demonstrate the quantitative strength of the enlightenment campaign on the psyches of the Koreans and the demand for education it fostered. But neglect of this factor seems unjustified, despite the measurement problem.

Fourth, recently a study on social capital advanced the hypothesis (supported by evidence from Korea) that university education confers on graduates a diploma as well as a social network within and outside the firm in which they find employment. This network provides an effective tool for solving problems connected with company operations and hence ultimately the company profits. To a certain extent, this aspect of the university alumni network also operates in the United States. But the study reveals culture-specific human skills and patterns of reciprocity governing the exchange of valuable information. This exchange is often accompanied by favors. The social network capital is shown to be highly valuable when dealing with a government-business relationship. The employers consider this problem-solving capability of an employee very important (i.e., profitable for the company), hence the graduates of prestigious universities command higher salaries. This represents a phenomenon cutting across the opposing camps of debates concerning the productivity role versus credentialism.[12]

The exceptional zeal for education serves the goal of industrialization well, particularly if education externalities are real and strong. Theodore Schultz (1990) advances the idea that human capital has external effects. "These effects spill over from one person to another. People at each skill level are more productive in high than in low human capital environment. Human capital enhances the productivity of both labor and physical capital. . . ."[13] Rapid urbanization and the geographical concentration of the highly educated in Korea seem to support this view. The Yongsan electronic enclave seems to emulate Silicon Valley in California and Route 128 in Massachusetts. The education-externality hypothesis remains to be tested in the Korean experience. However, the evidence that exists, though scanty, suggests rather significant externalities.

3.2 Education-Productivity Nexus: Issues and Evidence

In recent years a debate has erupted as to whether the so-called East Asian miracle is so miraculous at all. Paul Krugman (1994), for instance, asserted that the performance of Japan and the four "dragons" (Korea, Taiwan, Hong Kong, and Singapore) in raising total factor productivity has not been, according to his new calculation, particularly impressive compared to other industrialized countries.[14] His argument considers

human capital formation just as resource-using as physical capital formation. And if the productivity effects of these two forms of capital is
removed, there is little left in the estimates of total factor productivity
(or residual) associated with "pure and true innovation" based on new,
frontier knowledge.

This section examines Korean data available on productivity in the
light of the above argument. By doing so, the meaning of technological
learning in the Korean context can be clarified or even redefined.

It was noted earlier that human capital accumulation has been recognized as an important contributor in raising output per laborer in Korea, but precious little study has been available to provide supporting
evidence. Apparently, a statistical correlation between productivity
and human capital (e.g., educated human resource) has been difficult
to establish. However, a recent study by Hak K. Pyo provides some
long-sought evidence. One of his regression results follows:

$$\log \frac{GDP}{L} = -0.346 + 0.370 \log \left(\frac{K}{L} \right) + 0.406 \log \left(\frac{H}{L} \right),$$

$$\phantom{\log \frac{GDP}{L} = }(0.142) \quad (0.098) \qquad\qquad (0.039)$$

$$R^2 = 0.99,$$

$$DW = 1.51,$$

where GDP/L is labor productivity, K/L is physical capital per labor,
and H/L is human capital per labor. Standard errors are in parentheses. He used a set of aggregate time series data covering the 1955–90
period. A condition of constant returns to scale was imposed in regression exercises. Ninety-nine percent of variations in GDP/L are explained by two forms of capital (physical and human) per labor, a
remarkable statistical fit.[15]

It is noted that the contribution by human capital appears to be
greater than the contribution by physical capital in raising labor productivity. This piece of evidence suggests that human capital helped
employees and firms to speed up the pace of learning and mastering
imported technologies. Also it is interesting that a similar regression
conducted on a set of the U.S. data (1940–69) indicates the opposite,
namely that the contribution made by physical capital far outweighs
that made by human capital. The coefficient of $\log(K/L)$ turns out to
be 0.858 (standard error: 0.231) while that of $\log(H/L)$ is 0.028 (standard error: 0.258). This result prompts us to wonder how to interpret

it. (Why was human capital relatively less important in the U.S. case than in Korea? One could hypothesize that the United States was saturated with an abundance of human capital and its economic worth therefore was less.) At any rate Pyo's (1995) regression result (with a 99 percent of R-square) is consistent with Paul Krugman's thesis that the East Asian growth is characterized by resource-intensive growth, which he compares with the resource-intensive growth of the former USSR.

One could argue, however, that Paul Krugman's likening the Korean experience to that of the former USSR is misplaced. An estimate of total-factor-productivity growth rates for the latter follows (in percent per annum)[16]

1928–40	1940–50	1950–60	1960–70	1970–75	1975–80	1980–85
1.7	1.6	1.6	1.5	0.0	−0.4	−0.5

In a fundamental sense, the decline in efficiency as shown by these figures provides one of the reasons for the USSR's collapse. The rigid economic system could not reverse the long-run trend of cumulative, structural inefficiency. Furthermore the incentive (performance-reward) system in the USSR failed to motivate workers to learn new ways of doing things or to become efficiency conscious. However, the South Korean performance of TFP growth in manufacturing compares favorably with any other countries including the United States, Japan (as shown in the previous chapter), and Germany.[17] The argument to be developed in this study is that the learning process in South Korea involved rapid absorption of imported knowledge, helped by an abundant supply of educated workers and by the organizational flexibility to ensure the right kind of incentive structure.

Returning now to the question of the education-productivity nexus, some preliminary regression exercises are reported as follows. Instead of labor productivity, total factor productivity is chosen as the dependent variable to be explained by education and R&D. This approach could prove useful in reinterpreting the meaning of TFP growth as a learning index. According to a recent finding reported by Vikram Nehru and Ashok Dhareshwar (1994), "The cross-country profile of TFP growth and the role of initial conditions point toward the dual role played by human capital in the development process: as a standard factor of production to be accumulated and *as a source of learning and entrepreneurship* [emphasis added] and hence of interesting growth dynamics. It may be necessary to rethink the concept of 'TFP as the residual' in models with human capital."[18]

Since reliable R&D data are only available from early 1980s onward, an approach of pooling cross-sectional data with time series is used in this regression exercise. The data covers 36 manufacturing subsectors for the period 1982 to 1992. The regression on pooled data yields the following coefficients:

$$LTL = C + 0.020\ RDR(1) + 0.033\ RDR(2) + 0.047\ RDR(3) + 0.029\ ED,$$

$$(1.958)\qquad\qquad (3.090)\qquad\qquad (4.762)\qquad\qquad (5.878)$$

$$R^2 = 0.786,$$

$$DW = 0.486,$$

Number of observations = 340,

where LTL is the natural log of total factor productivity estimates, C is a constant of fixed effects model with 36 subsectors, RDR(1) is the R&D expenditure over sales (ratio) with a one-year lag, RDR(2) is the same with a two-year lag, RDR(3) is the same with a three-year lag, and ED is the average education year of the workforce. The figures in parentheses are t-values of the coefficient. See appendix B for other details on the regression results.

It is interesting to note that the effect of R&D on total factor productivity is most significant when there is a three-year lag, and also that the effect is least significant with a one-year lag. The result seems to suggest that it takes three years to exploit fully the knowledge obtained by R&D activities. The average education year of the workforce has the expected plus sign and is statistically significant. Unfortunately, the effect of organizational, institutional variables could not be measured.

Education as a Determinant of Wages and Salaries

Wages and salaries of educated labor are higher than those of the less educated. Numerous studies in other countries bear this out.[19] This section adds to the existing evidence to confirm the positive correlation between education and remuneration in Korea. The regression exercises enable us to evaluate the relative importance of education in comparison with other determinants such as work experience, age, and sex. This information, along with others, will provide a useful basis for policy discussion on education and industrial technology upgrading.

Fortunately the basic statistics that the Ministry of Labor (Korean government) collects every year was made available for this study for the 1980 to 1994 period. The annual sample has more than 30,000 observations of working individuals. With these data the following (semilog) form of wage and salary income function has been estimated:

ln Wage = C + $b1$ EDUYEAR + $b2$ DSE

$$+ b3 \text{ AGE} + b4 (\text{AGE})^2 + b5 \text{ DSEX},$$

where C is a constant, EDUYEAR is the number of years for schooling (6, 9, 12, 16 years), DSE is the dummy variable for scientists and engineers, AGE is the age of workers, DSEX is the dummy variable for sex (male = 1). Table 3.2 summarizes the regression results for every two years during the period. More details on the regressions appear in appendix C.

Notice that an additional year of schooling increases one's income by over 6 percent. In other words, a college graduate would earn over 24 percent more compared to a high school graduate, assuming that college takes four years to finish. Notice also that scientists and engineers enjoyed a wage premium of 18.4 percent over other college graduates in 1980. But the premium dropped to an insignificant 0.46 percent by 1994. This can be explained by several factors operating in the labor market for scientists and engineers (presumably, university graduates or higher). To begin with, there seems to be a gross mismatch between skills demanded and those supplied, due to failures of forecast and labor supply rigidities (more on this later). For instance, skills relating to software, semiconductor, electronics, or information technology (e.g., telecommunication) are in great demand compared to other skills. Furthermore there has been an inundation of college and university graduates and many have been unemployed since the early 1980s. Many recent graduates had to take lower paying, less-skilled jobs after an extended period of job hunting. The labor market for scientists and engineers seems to have borne severely the brunt of these skill mismatch problems.

The coefficient for age variable indicates that every additional year (in cross-sectional data, not longitudinal) increases income by 6.8 to 9.1 percent. Much of the income increase may reflect the time-honored seniority system, although some portion may represent a genuine increase in productivity based on increased experience (a sort of learning by doing). Thus well-educated, senior workers have an advantage over

Table 3.2
Regression results for a wage function, estimated every two years, 1980–1994

Year	C	b1	b2	b3	b4	b5	R^2
1980	9.465222 (398.7085)	0.067925 (90.77804)	0.183732 (15.29666)	0.078451 (49.15531)	−0.0008 (−34.3741)	0.320444 (55.45386)	0.614333
1982	9.651034 (394.2437)	0.069787 (88.57183)	0.191618 (17.80752)	0.083071 (51.79928)	−0.00084 (−36.5031)	0.317562 (53.69177)	0.610143
1984	9.77609 (396.9347)	0.071369 (90.73118)	0.176852 (20.19489)	0.083789 (52.82497)	−0.00082 (−36.0709)	0.315621 (55.26985)	0.633869
1986	9.920412 (418.9959)	0.06931 (91.54721)	0.13868 (14.70618)	0.090523 (61.31232)	−0.0009 (−43.7931)	0.252798 (38.22108)	0.581521
1988	10.48892 (432.2613)	0.070483 (85.6308)	0.103415 (11.79942)	0.067666 (45.8538)	−0.00065 (−31.087)	0.310154 (57.80176)	0.560205
1990	10.60717 (465.8176)	0.070545 (97.27495)	−0.04758 (−5.42416)	0.07856 (63.13708)	−0.00082 (−50.2032)	0.315899 (64.13048)	0.425846
1992	10.92503 (540.5867)	0.66476 (96.91107)	0.035444 (6.101939)	0.080198 (72.09236)	−0.00084 (−56.4978)	0.30635 (71.82204)	0.532184
1994	11.09231 (424.1115)	0.0556 (64.74918)	0.004582 (0.71208)	0.090191 (63.22736)	−0.00093 (−49.6908)	0.356196 (63.40474)	0.426731

Data source: KLI (Korea Labor Institute), occupational wage survey samples.
Sample size:

1980	1982	1984	1986	1988	1990	1992	1994
30,551	30,743	31,147	31,003	30,872	47,005	40,982	42,328

Note: Figures in parentheses are t-values.
Regression equation:

$$\ln \text{Wage} = C + b1\,\text{EDUYEAR} + b2\,\text{DSE} + b3\,\text{AGE} + b4\,(\text{AGE})^2 + b5\,\text{DSEX},$$

where EDUYEAR: educational year attained (6, 9, 12, 14, 16 years), DSE: dummy variable for scientists and engineers, AGE: real age, and DSEX: variable for sex dummy (male = 1).

less-educated, young workers in any workplace. However, the deluge of well-educated young workers who graduated from colleges and universities has tended to lower their own wages relative to less educated workers in general as suggested by table 3.3. As a by-product, the educational system produces an income equalization effect.[20] One could argue that in the Korean case the declining college wage premium could have made technological upgrading in factories less expensive than otherwise.[21]

The coefficient for sex dummy indicates that male workers earn approximately 25 to 35 percent more income than female workers. Such inequality seems to have worsened after 1986. It has been increasingly recognized that the sex bias should be eliminated soon, not only for the sake of justice but also for increasing efficiency in the labor market. A large pool of female talent, especially college and university graduates, seems to be waiting to be tapped in such areas as software and information technology. Only about 50 percent of female college and university graduates is reported to gain employment on leaving school. The inequality, if corrected, could provide an avenue to alleviate shortages of one of the most sought after skills in the future.

3.3   Universities and Human Capital Accumulation

From the viewpoint of technological upgrading, the higher education system in a developing country has three functions to perform. The first is to train scientists and engineers who are to supply the industrial sectors and other supporting agencies. The second is to create technical knowledge through research, particularly knowledge that is useful for the absorption of imported (or invented) technologies. The third is to provide services, based on professional expertise, to industries that aspire to innovate with new technology. These propositions represent a special application of the time-honored general function of a university, namely teaching, research, and service. In this section these functions are examined within the context of the Korean experience.

If one regards the function of colleges and universities as a supplier of scientists and engineers to industries, the record shows mixed results. There is abundant supply, but the average quality (competence) of graduates seems to have fallen. Problems abound such as high unemployment among graduates and skill mismatches, which will be discussed below. Figure 3.1 reveals that the number of engineering students in colleges and universities began to soar in about 1975. The

Table 3.3
Wage levels by educational attainment (in won), 1975–1992

Year	Middle school graduates	High school graduates	Junior college graduates	College and university graduates
1975	32,019	55,982	76,248	120,021
1976	43,226	73,144	106,256	167,982
1977	53,889	88,939	131,122	204,955
1978	72,947	116,898	174,469	269,998
1979	104,034	157,790	232,884	364,010
1980	124,435	180,919	254,762	413,318
1981	150,775	218,502	313,087	491,546
1982	174,191	249,169	325,678	552,191
1983	193,855	267,442	372,638	604,662
1984	213,985	287,004	378,099	650,739
1985	226,272	303,049	393,450	686,490
1986	250,958	323,542	417,361	718,266
1987	279,342	347,876	442,487	779,332
1988	339,947	414,084	501,402	839,441
1989	404,910	487,013	580,133	930,396
1990	476,949	569,394	668,200	1,055,950
1991	567,630	671,103	787,938	1,202,953
1992	686,481	744,491	895,158	1,326,795

High school graduates = 100

Year	Middle school graduates	High school graduates	Junior college graduates	College and university graduates
1975	57.2	100.0	136.2	214.4
1976	59.1	100.0	145.3	229.7
1977	60.6	100.0	147.4	230.4
1978	62.4	100.0	149.2	231.0
1979	65.9	100.0	147.6	230.7
1980	68.8	100.0	146.3	228.5
1981	69.0	100.0	143.3	225.0
1982	69.9	100.0	130.7	221.6
1983	72.5	100.0	139.3	226.1
1984	74.6	100.0	131.7	226.7
1985	74.7	100.0	129.8	226.5
1986	77.6	100.0	129.0	222.0
1987	80.3	100.0	127.2	224.0
1988	82.1	100.0	121.1	202.7
1989	83.1	100.0	113.0	191.0
1990	83.8	100.0	119.1	185.5
1991	84.6	100.0	117.4	179.3
1992	92.2	100.0	120.2	178.2

Source: Korea Education Research Institute, *Korea Educational Indicators,* Seoul, 1993, p. 343.

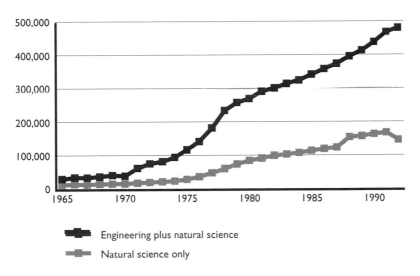

 Engineering plus natural science
Natural science only

Figure 3.1
Number of engineering and natural science students in colleges and universities, 1965–1993

number of students in natural sciences also rose, although at a slower pace than engineering students. This surge in supply seems to coincide with the drive for the Heavy and Chemical Industry (HCI) Program (1972–79), which provided the major impetus for a rising demand for science and engineering graduates. The Ministry of Education permitted colleges and universities to take in an increasing number (and also share) of students in those fields. (See figure 3.1.)

However, the unemployment rates among university graduates posed a serious problem. Table 3.4 presents the rate of university graduates unable to find employment upon graduation during the 1965–89 period. In 1989, for example, 166,845 students graduated from four-year colleges and universities. Of those, 145,106 attempted to enter the job market; however, only 76,594 could find immediate employment. Graduates without immediate employment tended to find a job after one or two years of searching, but often below the skill level they had acquired at college or university. A study reported that during the 1960–70 period, 22.4 percent of college and university graduates were thus employed in an occupation "inferior" to their training.[22] In other words, there has been a great deal of mismatching between skills demanded and those supplied. The problem is further exacerbated by an excess supply across all the disciplines.

Table 3.4
Employment conditions for four-year college and university graduates, 1965–1989

Year	Graduates	Annual growth rate	Graduates seeking jobs	Annual growth rate	Persons employed	Annual growth rate
1965	36,180		29,375		12,564	
1970	23,515	−7.5	19,463	−4.5	13,743	3.4
1975	33,610		27,352		19,635	
1980	49,736	7.9	38,851	7.3	28,348	8.3
1981	55,846	12.3	41,402	6.5	28,524	0.6
1982	62,688	12.3	47,037	13.6	33,988	19.2
1983	77,272	23.3	57,547	22.3	38,489	13.2
1984	90,888	17.3	69,142	20.1	43,907	14.1
1985	118,534	30.5	93,143	34.7	48,552	10.6
1986	137,848	16.1	113,140	21.5	51,667	6.4
1987	149,582	8.5	125,752	11.1	60,718	17.5
1988	161,983	8.3	139,785	11.2	70,732	16.5
1989	166,845	3.0	145,106	8.3	76,594	8.3
1981–1985		19.2		19.5		11.5
1986–1989		9.0		13.3		12.9
1981–1989		14.7		16.6		11.1

Source: *Educational Statistics Yearbook, 1965–1989*

The inefficiencies in the labor market can be corrected by restructuring the educational institutions, for example, by reducing the quotas for colleges and universities and increasing quotas for technical junior colleges and vocational schools. If this is not done, the anticipated structural change of Korean industries toward high-tech fields during the coming decade could exacerbate the skill mismatch problems even further.[23] Preferably the incentive system could be restructured so that technicians with skills in great demand could command monetary and nonmonetary remuneration equal to (or even in excess of) those of college and university graduates. Such a task represents a major overhaul of the existing higher education system. (More discussion will come below on this issue.)

The poor quality of university graduates in science and engineering poses an even more distressing problem (evidence follows), creating a disadvantage for industrial-sector employers who must compete in the fast-moving global market. The employers complain that university graduates have to be retrained in order to make them fit the needs of the enterprise. The graduates may have textbook knowledge but little training with experiment and factory-floor problems. Retraining takes one or two years according to company executives. Nonetheless, it is not difficult to find causes for the deteriorating quality of university graduates, particularly in science and engineering. Research is expensive, and recruiting qualified professors is not easy. Most of the private colleges and universities cannot afford to keep up with public universities financed by the government. Consequently the conventional indicators all exhibit a deteriorating trend, such as a rising student/faculty ratio, a falling school-space/student ratio, library books/student ratio, and so on (see table 3.5). Investment in educational infrastructure has not caught up with the soaring pace of student enrollment in colleges and universities.[24]

Quality deterioration can be traced back to the structure of incentives for faculty members.[25] To begin with, faculty promotion has not been linked to performance in teaching, research and service, as is the case in the Western university system. A faculty member obtains virtual tenure at the point of employment, normally at the level of an instructor or assistant professor. This system is coupled with a tendency toward inbreeding, meaning that universities have been hiring their own graduates as faculty at the recommendation of senior professors who taught them. Quite often more than three-quarters of the faculty were trained within their department. The social hierarchy in a department is marked by Confucian philosophy, so the authority of elders is given

Table 3.5
Deterioration of school facilities per student in colleges and universities, 1965–1993

Year	Students per faculty	Students per clerical staff	School (m²) per student	Library books per student
1965	19.9	21.2	135.6	
1970	18.8	17.7	177.1	26.3
1975	20.7	18.4	101	21.4
1980	17.9	26	91.1	17.3
1985	35.8	46.9	58.1	13.9
1990	31.1	37.7	60.1	18.5
1991	29.9	37.1	65.4	19.3
1992	28.7	42.7	65.2	16.4
1993	27.6	44.5	62.4	16.9

Source: Korean Educational Development Institute, *Educational Indicators in Korea*, 1993, p. 248.

automatic respect in departmental decision making. There is neither effective peer-group evaluation nor competition for promotion, as is the case in the Western university system (especially in the American system).[26]

In addition, faculty members have been struggling under heavy teaching loads, 5 to 6 three-hour courses a week being not unusual in many universities. The salaries are also meager. Small wonder that research output is poor; for example, 0.092 is the figure for papers published per faculty member in the field of science and engineering in 1994.[27] What this means is that the university system can hardly be regarded as productive in creating basic knowledge, let alone knowledge that is useful to industry. (See table 3.6 for a comparison, by country, of publication records in science and engineering.) The case of KAIST, an exception, is discussed below.

Teaching quality seems to have suffered as well from the heavy teaching load. Students have little opportunity to receive personal attention from the faculty, owing to the large enrollments. In the engineering field, for example, the student/faculty ratio soared to 55.4 students per faculty in 1985 from 30.3 in 1968. In 1993 the ratio stood at 35 students per faculty in the engineering college of Seoul National

Table 3.6
Ranking of nations by the number of science and engineering papers published, 1991–1994

Country	1994	1993	1992	1991
United States	267,125(1)	258,776(1)	254,373(1)	224,955(1)
United Kingdom	65,159(2)	61,853(2)	62,027(2)	53,644(2)
Japan	55,142(3)	51,199(3)	51,772(3)	44,521(3)
Germany	49,552(4)	45,941(4)	47,380(4)	40,412(4)
France	38,623(5)	36,195(5)	36,418(5)	30,102(5)
Canada	32,219(6)	31,252(6)	31,435(6)	27,181(6)
Italy	23,527(7)	21,668(7)	21,392(7)	32,838(7)
Russia	17,919(8)	19,952(8)	17,803(8)	17,803(8)
Australia	16,052(9)	15,172(9)	14,700(9)	12,592(9)
Netherlands	15,944(10)	14,984(10)	14,663(10)	12,699(10)
Spain	14,498(11)	13,282(11)	13,078(11)	6,369(11)
Korea	3,910(24)	2,997(27)	2,461(30)	1,818(32)

Source: Korea Industrial Technology Association, *Industrial Technology White Paper 1995*, p. 74.
Note: Figures in parentheses indicate ranking order.

Table 3.7
Number of students enrolled per academic staff in higher education, selected countries

Country	1975	1980	1984	1985	1986
Korea	20.9	28.8	37.0	37.7	37.5
Japan	19.8	18.5	17.4	17.1	17.2
United States	16.7	n.a.	15.5	15.6	n.a.
West Germany	8.1	8.1	9.8	n.a.	n.a.
France	20.0	n.a.	21.7	21.6	n.a.
United Kingdom	7.5	7.4	11.1	n.a.	13.9
Canada	17.8	19.0	21.0	21.3	n.a.
Hong Kong	14.6	12.5	13.0	n.a.	n.a.
Argentina	13.2	10.6	10.5	12.0	n.a.
USSR	15.3	14.3	14.0	13.6	n.a.
Taiwan	21.3	20.8	20.6	20.6	20.3

Source: Min Won Suh, *Statistical Indicators of Korean Higher Education,* 1989.1.
Korean Council for University Education; Directorate-General of Budget, Accounting and Statistics, *Statistical Yearbook of the Republic of China, 1988,* Executive Yuan, Republic of China.
Note: (1) In Japan, students in university and college + academic staff in university and college; (2) in United Kingdom, students in university (4 years) + academic staff in university (4 years).

Table 3.8
Student–faculty ratio in the engineering colleges in Korea

	1978	1979	1980	1982	1983
Engineering schools	40	39	39	42	42
National, public	40	32	27	31	31
Private	40	43	43	47	47

Source: Same as for table 3.7.
Note: Graduate schools are included.

University as compared to 13 in the University of Tokyo Engineering College. This figure compares with less than 10 students per faculty at MIT, or 15.6 students per faculty for the U.S. average in engineering undergraduate education. KAIST in 1990 had 13.4 students per faculty. (See tables 3.7 and 3.8 for further comparisons.) The teaching overload in Korea has led to inferior teaching methods, namely a rote memorization of textbook and lecture notes, rather than experimentation with technological innovations. Naturally this is because of the expense of equipment and also of additional faculty required to supervise its use.[28]

Furthermore student evaluations of faculty have not been an accepted practice in the Korean university system.

An increasing awareness of the quality problem among policy makers in recent years has ushered in serious discussions of educational reform. A novel idea advocated by some is to institute a market mechanism for competition in higher education. A noteworthy aspect of the discussion is the idea of opening the education market to foreign universities (particularly American universities), which may be interested in opening branch campuses in Korea, staffed mainly with American professors. In principle, the new competition would help to weed out inefficient universities. Thus the problems of substandard quality of graduates and mismatch of skills could be solved through the "survival of the fittest." In what form and how fast such a mechanism should be put in place remains an open question. But the frequency of debates on television programs and newspaper editorials suggests that serious soul-searching has begun among university presidents, policy makers in educational fields, as well as journalists and other critics.

While the higher education system as a whole is currently undergoing a critical self-evaluation, the Korea Advanced Institute of Science and Technology (KAIST) seems to provide a fitting model. It was established in 1971 with a set of innovative features designed to produce mainly masters degrees and doctorates as well as research of a world-class standard. The U.S. Accreditation Board for Engineering and Technology (ABET) conducted an evaluation of KAIST in 1992, applying U.S. evaluation criteria. The conclusion stated: "KAIST is a first quality institute. Its engineering and science programs are of high caliber, are offered by a highly enthusiastic faculty and, with few exceptions, are supported with adequate facilities. The students are well qualified, aggressive and anxious to learn; they are loyal to the institutions, highly motivated, articulate and career oriented."[29]

It seems worthwhile therefore to scrutinize how (through what strategies) KAIST succeeded in achieving a quality standard comparable to the top 10 percent of colleges and universities offering science and engineering degrees in the United States. This will help us to ascertain what lessons it might hold for other institutions of higher learning in Korea. The example of KAIST illustrates the value of a well-crafted institutional apparatus in producing high-quality scientists and engineers.[30]

Essentially top-quality professors and intelligent students with high aspirations constitute the basic ingredients for building a successful higher-learning institution. KAIST started out by crafting incentive devices that would motivate Korean scientists and engineers working in the United States to return to teach and do research at KAIST. The incentive package included a salary two or three times higher than the going rate in Korean universities, the provision of a modern apartment built near the campus, paid moving expenses, and the provision for research equipment as requested by the recruited professors. This package enabled KAIST to mobilize the best Korean scientists and engineers (54 of them in the first five-year plan period) who had already been teaching and doing research with distinction at leading U.S. universities. As of 1993, KAIST has employed 336 faculty members, over three-quarters of whom hold PhDs from leading U.S. universities, while the remainder obtained their doctorates from European, Japanese, and Korean universities.

KAIST faculty members have proved their ability as researchers by leading the country in the publication of research results. On average, a faculty member published 1.52 papers a year in refereed journals (foreign plus domestic), which turns out to be 28 times higher than the national average in Korea (according to the 1988 statistics).[31] This superior performance is largely due to the KAIST regulation that bases faculty promotion on publication, particularly in internationally established journals.[32] It should also be noted that faculty as well as students show great pride in having been selected to lead the nation in learning and research. Social expectations seem to work as a stimulant for excellence in research. Faculty are also provided with the best research equipment that the nation can afford; the operational budget of the institute is 100 percent financed by the government, even though KAIST was established with a $6 million aid fund initially provided by the U.S. Agency for International Development.

The quality of KAIST graduates also turns out to be very high. PhD candidates for the KAIST are required to publish at least one article in an established international journal. This requirement represents an innovative feature yet to be emulated by other universities in Korea. Furthermore every student admitted to the Institute receives a full scholarship, including tuition, room and board, and some spending money for textbooks and supplies. Moreover the graduates are exempt from compulsory military duty. This provision is something that cannot be found in other countries and is something that Korean youth seem to covet. This incentive package has proved to be powerful enough to attract the most qualified students in the country. Only those high school graduates in the top 3 percent of their classes are eligible for admission.

As of August 1996, 3,108 bachelor degrees, 9,566 master degrees, and 2,647 doctorates have been conferred. The graduates have found employment predominantly in industries (42.2 percent of graduates, 1993 data), research institutes (18.8 percent of graduates, 1993 data), universities (8.2 percent of graduates, 1993 data), and government agencies (1.8 percent of graduates, 1993 data). The remainder (29 percent) have pursued higher degrees. Yet, the demand for KAIST graduates has exceeded the supply to such an extent that private enterprises were willing to pay a part of the education costs for the students whom they were able to hire. This is in marked contrast to the excess supply of other university graduates noted earlier. An encouraging aspect is that some graduates opened their own companies based on the technology that they themselves developed as a part of research they conducted together with professors. Most of them were in cutting-edge, high-tech areas (25 venture companies so far), and some even started businesses by first exporting before turning to domestic markets. The "ultrasonic medical imaging system" developed at KAIST provides an excellent example. A graduate was able to form a thriving company in 1985 (Medison Co. Ltd.) based on the newly developed technology.

As a result of its research capabilities, KAIST began to attract outside research projects and contracted with private enterprises and with government R&D agencies. The cumulative sum amounted to 5,841 project cases for a total of 92,621 million won as of 1993, and the trend has been accelerating in value and volume.

These observations lead us to conclude that KAIST has succeeded as a provider of trained scientists and engineers as well as technological ideas that Korean industries need. Institutional arrangements at KAIST (particularly the incentive-motivation devices) have been effective in enticing professors and students alike to produce high-quality research. And the KAIST experience carries some lessons, at least in principle, applicable to other higher-learning institutions in Korea and in other developing countries.

For drawing lessons, it should be borne in mind that KAIST has been given autonomy in its governance, except its broad mandate under the jurisdiction of MOST. By contrast, colleges and universities have normally been placed under controls of MOE (the Ministry of Education). The Ministry of Education micromanages universities with myriad rules and regulations regarding such issues as annual admission quotas, tuition fees to be charged, number and contents of courses to be offered, graduation requirements, hiring and firing professors, and expansion of classroom areas and sports facilities. Originally the rules and regulations were intended to prevent corruption. But they have proved to be stifling to the progress of quality education. Fortunately a national consensus has emerged for the need of educational reform. But the issue of what, how, and when for such a reform is still being debated. Evidently KAIST offers a model to be emulated.

The evaluation of KAIST's successes, however, has to be tempered by some criticism of weaknesses. The ABET report has pointed out that the design training program is deficient in virtually all departments of engineering. The list includes aerospace, chemical, civil, and industrial engineering, material science, mechanical engineering, and the precision and mecha-tronics engineering departments. For example, the report said of the mechanical engineering department that "the program would be much improved if the engineering design experience was strengthened including the addition of a capstone design course (major senior design experience integrating and drawing upon previous course work in the discipline)."[33]

This deficiency seems to represent the next hurdle that Korean universities and industries must overcome. However, the effort to meet the challenge must begin at the university level. Apparently the importance of designing skills has not yet been fully appreciated by university faculty, industry executives, or policy makers. Considering that KAIST is the best engineering school that Korea has ever had, and yet still has a deficient program in engineering design, says something important. Designing is where creativity comes in, and future industrial competitiveness depends on it. Advanced design means not just producing a set of blueprints but creating a conceptual map encompassing the flow of ideas from the initial product concept through the selection of the technology mix—scanning the global knowledge shelf, manufacture, cost efficiency, marketability, meeting environmental requirements—right down to consumer satisfaction in global-local markets. The university is the place to imbue student scientists and engineers with the proper attitude toward design. To do that effectively, it is necessary to make the factory-floor experience an important part of the curriculum.

Box 3.1

Kwangju Institute of Science and Technology

Another higher-learning institution is being established in Kwangju, modeled after KAIST, namely the Kwangju Institute of Science and Technology (K-JIST, located in southwest Korea). It began admitting graduate students in 1995 in MS and PhD programs. It has five departments, including (1) the information and communication engineering with a research focus on opto-electronics communication, (2) new materials engineering (high-tech advanced materials development), (3) electro-mechanical engineering (helicopter system and core technology), (4) environmental engineering (pollution control technology), and bioscience engineering (cell function control and signal media). These departments are designed not to reproduce what KAIST has but to complement it in areas of teaching and research. Furthermore, from the beginning, K-JIST assumed a global outlook. For example, all the courses are to be taught in English. Foreign students will comprise about 15 percent of the student body. Seven faculty members have been recruited from foreign countries already, and 23 visiting professors have given two- to four-week of special seminars and advised students. The institute has invited foreign research outposts (or branch companies) to settle on the campus, including a United Nations environmental management research institute, which is now at the feasibility study stage.

Summing up, the university system in Korea has "succeeded" in supplying graduates with science and engineering degrees quantitatively (though in excess of demand). But the success must be qualified by a "diploma mill" effect, that is, an excess supply of degree-holders, often with substandard competency. Even so, university education is valuable in the sense that graduates have acquired at least the professional language needed for communication in science and engineering, albeit through a rote-memory method that hampers creativity. Furthermore, from the employers' viewpoint, the abundance of graduates has created a buyer's market wherein companies pick and choose qualified graduates at reasonable wages. Looking into the future, those who may have been placed in a job slot below their university level of skills and intelligence may prove to be a useful asset when the waves of computerization upgrade their jobs.

The problem of educational quality requires a fundamental overhaul of the incentive structure for faculty members (the tenure system, less teaching load, peer group evaluation, etc.). This institutional reform has to be supported by large investments to improve the educational infrastructure (experimental equipment, more faculty to reduce class size, etc.) and by research funding to allow faculty members to develop their teaching knowledge and publish their research results. University-industry cooperation could alleviate imbalances in R&D resource allocation and at the same time exploit the complementarity between university and industry sectors. The next section considers this issue.

3.4   University-Industry Complementarity and Cooperation Programs

Traditionally there has been little cooperation between universities and industries beyond the supplying of graduates with BS degrees. The law prohibited joint appointment of a professor by a university and by an industry. As in Japan, professors were supposed to conduct research within the context of an organized program within the university, and not elsewhere, even in other universities. Professors preferred theoretical research to developing ideas for practical, factory-floor applications. Their job security had been guaranteed by the practice of de facto lifetime employment. Their dignity had been assured by the Confucian tradition of high esteem for scholars.

Small wonder that the university system in Korea has been attracting so many PhDs, especially in science and engineering. According to 1994 statistics (the latest available), the total R&D personnel with PhD degrees in the country numbered 33,998, of which 26,475 (or 78 percent) were employed by colleges and universities. By comparison, the industrial sector has only 2,798, or 8.2 percent of PhD degree-holders. (See table 3.9

Table 3.9
Distribution of R&D personnel by academic degrees and by employers in 1994

	Total	Government	Universities	Enterprises
Total	117,446 (100)	15,465 (13.1)	42,700 (36.4)	59,281 (50.5)
PhD	33,998 (100)	4,725 (13.9)	26,475 (77.9)	2,798 (8.2)
MS	38,725 (100)	7,083 (18.3)	15,050 (38.9)	16,592 (42.8)
BS	40,893 (100)	3,409 (8.3)	1,105 (2.7)	36,379 (89)
Other	3,830 (100)	248 (6.5)	70 (1.8)	3,512 (91.7)

Source: MOST, *Science and Technology Yearbook 1995*, p. 298.

Table 3.10
R&D investment per researcher by government, universities, and enterprises, 1990–1994
(unit: thousand won, %)

	1990	1991	1992	1993	1994
Total average	47,514	54,536	56,206	62,300	67,220
Growth rate	11.7	14.8	3.1	10.8	7.9
Government	70,063	85,875	73,462	81,564	99,619
Growth rate	22.7	22.6	−14.5	11	22.1
Universities	11,453	13,959	13,023	15,539	14,259
Growth rate	4.2	21.9	−6.7	19.3	−8.2
Enterprises	61,298	65,839	70,991	81,322	96,916
Growth rate	7.9	7.4	7.8	14.6	19.2

Source: MOST, *Science and Technology Yearbook 1995,* p 296.

for more details.) And yet, university R&D programs have suffered from meager R&D expenditures and inadequate experimental facilities. For instance, in 1994, universities were allocated only 7.7 percent of the total R&D expenditures of the country, while the industrial sector enjoyed 72.8 percent.[34]

In terms of per-researcher expenditures, the university researchers spent only 14,259,000 won (about $18,000) compared with 96,916,000 won (about $121,000) for industry researchers and 99,619,000 won (about $122,000) for government researchers. (See table 3.10.) The underutilization of the brain power available in university settings is rather conspicuous.

Yet the industrial sector has been searching eagerly for PhD recipients, aiming to raise their in-house R&D capabilities in advanced technology (in electronics, information science, mechatronics, software design engineering, robotics, etc.). Obviously the current situation presents a human-made complementarity between the university sector and the industrial sector. On the one hand, the university sector needs research funds and R&D equipment that can be used for research as well as for teaching. On the other hand, the industrial sector needs research ideas in applied as well as in basic research, while its technological requirements are being upgraded constantly to meet the global competition. Furthermore the industrial sector needs a continuous flow of well-trained graduates with both theory and factory-floor experience. Some ingenious institutional arrangements mediating those needs between the two sectors could bring about handsome payoffs beneficial to both sectors.[35]

Fortunately increased recognition of these needs has motivated major actors in the R&D community as well as policy makers to act or to search for workable forms of cooperation. Some examples are briefly examined below.

Several leading universities have recently established Cooperative R&D Complexes on their campuses. These consist of physical facilities (land, building, equipment, etc.) and logistic support for recruiting professors and graduate students in order to serve the industry demand for a particular technology development. Industry is encouraged to open R&D branches to send researchers for a certain period of time for a joint project or for the purpose of participating in seminars and conferences, to contract out certain mission-oriented research projects. Industries can also give gifts of money or equipment to the university in exchange for receiving good graduates at a later date.[36] Examples include the Korea University Techno-Complex, Kwang-Un University Science Park, Seoul National University Research Park, Sung-Kyun-Kwan University S&T Research Complex, Yonsei University Research Complex, and Postech Techno-Park. Notably these universities have taken initiatives to suggest, plan, implement, and negotiate with potential participants. These actions are encouraging because the past pattern of seeking special government support and leadership is apparently changing.

Each complex or park has its own strategies and approaches to building on its resources and visions. Kwang-Un University's Euro-Asia Science Park deserves special attention. It plans not only to do joint research but also to manufacture capital goods and parts for assembling semiconductors and related products. The Park will sell these for profit. This means that the Park will be experimenting with a vertically integrated approach covering all phases of R&D and value-chains from product concept, research, design, production, marketing to distribution.

It remains to be seen whether the incentive (performance-reward) system will become firmly institutionalized through experiments or trial and error. For example, sooner or later the problem of how research results (successes and failures) should be shared among participants will have to be answered. The issue of differences in attitude toward disclosure must be addressed, in particular, the conflict between professors' desire to publish and companies' need to keep company secrets. Trust must be developed between universities and industries regarding each other's competencies, norms, values, and credibility, all of which have been major hindrances to cooperation. This also means breaking the traditional idea deeply rooted in the Korean psyche that scholarly activities are holier than commercial ones.[37]

Box 3.2

The MIT Model

The Massachusetts Institute of Technology (MIT) has demonstrated that industry-university cooperation can yield synergy effects with multiplying benefits to both actors. It is worthwhile for Korean universities with engineering schools to pay attention to the MIT model and try to emulate it. An important lesson to learn is how MIT has managed to construct the incentive structure for industry-university cooperation programs for all the parties without compromising the fundamental goals of a higher educational institution.

According to a study recently published, the economic impact of MIT in the United States includes (1) over 4,000 companies founded by its graduates and faculty members, plus firms spun off from major MIT labs as well as those launched with licensed MIT technology; (2) global sales totaling U.S.$232 billion (equivalent to a national economy ranking the 24th largest in the world economy); (3) an employment size of 733,000 in 1994; and (4) many companies keeping close, long-term technological ties with MIT because their knowledge base is heavily weighted toward software, high-tech manufacturing, and consulting.*

MIT conducts day-to-day administration of industry-university cooperation business through a MIT Technology Licensing Office (TLO). This office has two principal goals: "The first is to facilitate the transfer to public use and benefit of technology developed at MIT. The second, where consistent with the first, is to provide an additional source of unrestricted income to support research and education at MIT." Over 40 percent of MIT's annual budget comes from outside research funding. The TLO functions as the mediator between the MIT researchers (students, faculty, joint researchers, etc.) and industry. The TLO activities are guided by a well-defined set of rules and regulations, which have undergone time-honored tests and calibrations. To be noted, for instance, is the rule of giving one-third of the license fee income to the inventor annually, a powerful monetary incentive. The following reference document is recommended: "Guide to the Ownership, Distribution and Commercial Development of M.I.T. Technology," an unpublished report prepared by the MIT Technology Licensing Office (May 24, 1989).

* See "M.I.T.: The Impact of Innovation," a special report prepared by Wayne M. Ayers, chief economist of BankBoston, March 1997, pp. 36.

3.5   Centers of Excellence Program to Uplift University Performance

The low evaluations given R&D performance at Korean universities have been a major concern of policy makers. The previous sections of this chapter noted some of the important reasons for poor performance, to recapitulate, the inadequate incentive structure for motivating professors and researchers. Heavy teaching loads, insufficient funds and equipment for research, tenure and promotion unrelated to performance in teaching and research, lack of a peer-group evaluation system, inbreeding tendencies in hiring, and the like, constituted a formidable set of barriers confronting policy makers. Resistance to any reform came from vested interests rooted in the existing institutions. It took several years of debate among policy makers, professors, journalists, business executives, and others, before the need for reform was accepted. The idea of creating centers of excellence with government financial support was adopted in 1989. The major focus of reform was the distorted incentive structure, which was addressed by introducing a system of competitive application and selection.

From 1990 to 1995, Korea Science and Engineering Foundation (KOSEF) selected 38 centers to receive a long-term grant (normally for nine years with a midterm evaluation every three years). Seventeen of 384 applications were selected for the Science Research Center (SRC) and 21 for the Engineering Research Center (ERC). See table 3.11 listing the recipient centers. (Note incidentally that Seoul National University and KAIST dominate.) The grant funds could be used for scaling up research activities by purchasing equipment, holding or attending conferences, exchanging research personnel, inviting foreign researchers, and so on. The selection criteria included the quality of the proposed program in terms of potential technological advances and innovation, the quality of the research team with crossdisciplinary approaches, and the quality of faculty. An important requirement was to conduct research cooperatively not only with researchers from other disciplines but also with industry and government R&D institutes as well as international research institutions.[38]

The goal of the SRC/ERC program is to strengthen the research capabilities of the universities by having them specialize in an area in which they have a comparative advantage and thereby to enhance the competitiveness of Korean industries through university-industry cooperation. The goal can be achieved through the dissemination of basic

Table 3.11
List of Centers of Excellence established

Name of center		Location	Director
Science Research Centers			
TGRC	Topology and Geometry Research Center	Kyungbuk National University	U-Hang Ki
CTP	Center for Theoretical Physics	Seoul National University	Hi-Sung Song
SPRC	Semiconductor Physics Research Center	Jeonbuk National University	Hyung-Jae Lee
OCRC	Organic Chemistry Research Center	Sogang University	Nung-Min Yoon
RCMM	Research Center for Molecular Microbiology	Seoul National University	Yung-Chil Hah
PMBBRC	Plant Molecular Biology and Biotechnology Research Center	Gyeongsang National University	Moo-Je Cho
GARC	Global Analysis Research Center	Seoul National University	Sang-Moon Kim
RCDAMP	Research Center for Dielectric and Advanced Matter Physics	Pusan National University	Min-Su Jang
CBM	Center for Biofunctional Molecules	Pohang University of Science and Technology	Dong-Han Kim
CMS	Center for Molecular Science	Korea Advanced Institute of Science and Technology	Mu-shik Jhon
RCCD	Research Center for Cell Differentiation	Seoul National University	Man-Sik Kang
CRC	Cancer Research Center	Seoul National University	Jae-Gahb Park
CMR	Center for Mineral Resources Research	Korea University	Chil-Sup So
RCNBMA	Research Center for New Bio-materials in Agriculture	Seoul National University	Kwan-Hwa Park
ASSRC	Atomic Scale Surface Science Research Center	Yonsei University	Chung-Nam Whang
HRC	Hormone Research Center	Chonnam National University	Hyuk-Gang Kwon
CMC	Research Center for Molecular Catalysis	Seoul National University	Jung-Hun Suh

Table 3.11 (continued)

Name of center		Location	Director
Engineering Research Centers			
AFFRC	Advanced Fluids Engineering Research Center	Pohang University of Science and Technology	Chung-Mook Lee
CAIR	Center for Artificial Intelligence Research	Korea Advanced Institute of Science and Technology	Jung-Wan Cho
STRC	Sensor Technology Research Center	Kyungbuk National University	Byung-Ki Sohn
SaTReC	Satellite Technology Research Center	Korea Advanced Institute of Science and Technology	Soon-Dal Choi
RETCAM	Research Center for Thin Film Fabrication and Crystal Growing of Advanced Materials	Seoul National University	Dong-Nyung Lee
BPERC	Bioprocess Engineering Research Center	Korea Advanced Institute of Science and Technology	Ho-Nam Chang
ARRC	Animal Resources Research Center	Kon-Kuk University	Chang-Won Kim
RCNDD	Research Center for New Drug Development	Seoul National University	Won-Keun Chung
RASOM	Rapidly Solidified Materials Research Center	Chungnam National University	Byoung-Sun Chun
CISEM	Center for Interface Science and Engineering of Materials	Korea Advanced Institute of Science and Technology	Cuk-Yong Yoon
ERC-ACI	Engineering Research Center for Advanced Control and Instrumentation	Seoul National University	Wook-Hyun Kwon
TPMRC	Turbo and Power Machinery Research Center	Seoul National University	Sung-Tack Ro
CARR	Center for Advanced Reactor Research	Korea Advanced Institute of Science and Technology	Byong-Whi Lee
RCCT	Research Center for Catalytic Technology	Pohang University of Science and Technology	Young-Gul Kim

Table 3.11 (continued)

Name of center		Location	Director
ARC	Automation Research Center	Pohang University of Science and Technology	Kyu-Dae Cho
RCOID	Research Center for Ocean Industrial Development	National Fisheries University of Pusan	Ryu-Ryang Pyun
BRC	Bioproducts Research Center	Yonsei University	Young-Se Kwon
OERC	Opto-Electronics Research Center	Korea Advanced Institute of Science and Technology	Li-Hyung Lee
STRESS	Advanced Structure Research Station	Hanyang University	Nack-Joon Kim
CAAM	Center for Advanced Aerospace Materials	Pohang University of Science and Technology	Jae-Chan Choi
NSDM	Engineering Research Center for Net-Shape and Die Manufacturing	Pusan University	
Regional Research Centers			
CACP	Research Center for Advanced Mineral Aggregate Composite Products	Kangwon National University	Je-Seon Park
MRRC	Medicinal Resources Research Center	Wonkwang University	Jae-Baek Kim
FACPV	Factory Automation Center for Parts of Vehicles	Chosun University	In-Young Yang

Source: Korea Science and Engineering Foundation.

knowledge, improved coordination of research between universities and industries, preparing scientists and engineers to catch up with advanced practices, and international cooperation in education and research.[39] The designated center of excellence functions as a focal point for diverse activities such as conducting joint research on a crossdisciplinary project involving professors, graduate students, and industrial researchers from member companies; organizing seminars, workshops, intensive training, and publication; retraining engineers from industries and other R&D institutions; and sending professors and graduate (as well as undergraduate) students to the factory-floor of member companies for hands-on experience.

For instance, the Engineering Research Center for Net-Shape and Die Manufacturing at Pusan National University, consists of 30 faculty members coming from 14 universities and research institutes in the country. The Center brings together various research activities such as precision forging and semisolid forming, computer-aided preform design in metal forming, precision machining for die manufacturing, mechatronics in the metal forming industry, intelligent process planning, and robot systems for polishing. Also, on average, the Center gives financial support to 40 MA students and 20 PhD students a year. Corporate participants include Samsung Heavy Industry, Samsung Aerospace, Lucky-Goldstar (L-G), Mando Machinery, and others. These industrial participants contribute to the Center financially by offering contracts and grants for projects of their choice.

The significance of the SRC/ERC program lies in the fact that both the grant giver (KOSEF) and the receivers (university science and engineering communities) have committed themselves to the evaluation mechanism in a meaningful way, that is, linking rewards to performance. The initial award depends on competitive application and selection. Subsequently, upon receipt of a midterm (third-year) report, KOSEF undertakes a review process involving peer reviews, site visits, and a final evaluation, which will affect the level of financial support. The initial contract can also be terminated if performance is judged as a failure. Renewal of the KOSEF grants also depends on a performance evaluation, just as in the case of the initial application. This evaluation process provides an incentive-motivation mechanism for the centers to compete and excel.

It is too early to make a comprehensive evaluation of the program, especially because the time lag between academic research and first commercial introduction is long (according to the U.S. experience, 5 to 9 years). But the first (three-year) interim reports submitted by the 13 Centers of Excellence selected in the 1990 competition appear encouraging. (For a summary, see table 3.12.) Note that a total of 1,667 papers were published in domestic academic journals and 1,157 in international journals (i.e., 218 papers per center). In the realm of international cooperation, 35 international conferences were held, 398 foreign scholars were invited, and 201 joint research projects were carried out with foreign institutes and universities. A total of 862 students graduated from MS degree programs and 203 students in PhD degree programs. And, a total of 75 patent applications have been submitted. An overall evaluation of the 13 centers gave six centers an A

Table 3.12
Selected performance indicators for the first 13 Centers of Excellence evaluated for the 1990–1992 period

Category	Major achievements
Budget acquired	41 billion won; 3.2 billion won per center
	18.4 billion from KOSEF
	14.5 billion from extramural sources
	8.0 billion from intramural sources
Number of R&D Projects	1,224 projects or 94 projects per center; 742 for KOSEF
	421 for extramural
	61 for intramural
Research papers	1,667 for domestic journals
	1,157 for foreign journals; 218 papers per center
International cooperation	35 international conferences
	398 foreign scientists invited
	201 international joint research projects
R&D human resources	862 MSs (66 per center)
	203 PhDs (16 per center)
	72 post docs
Industry-university cooperation	2,970 persons trained in 44 sessions
	46 technology transfers for 56 companies
	75 patent applications submitted

Source: Korea Industrial Technology Association, *Industrial Technology Whitepaper* (in Korean), 1994, p. 79.

grade, while the remaining seven centers earned a B grade. (No C grade.) This experience could signal a paradigm shift from the past practice of dividing up research funds from the government "equally" among recipients without any performance evaluation or feedback mechanism.

The six-year interim reports submitted more recently by the same 13 centers seem to indicate that the new incentive device is working as desired. The total number of papers published reached 3,287, a 16 percent increase since the three-year interim reports. The number of papers published in foreign journals climbed to 1,367, an 18 percent increase. In addition the number of university-industry cooperative research projects soared to 298, a 48 percent increase. The figure for technology transfer and commercialization recorded 134 items, a 91 percent increase. Patent applications increased to 307 items compared with 75 in 1993. Consequently, KOSEF decided to award additional research funds to the outstanding performers, which included the Research Center for Molecular Microbiology (Seoul National University), the Center for Theoretical Physics Seoul National University), and the Center for Artificial Intelligence Research (KAIST).[40]

3.6   Korea–U.S. Linkages and R&D Human Resources

The university system in the United States has been the major source of educated and trained Korean scientists and engineers. After graduation many PhDs have stayed in the United States for postdoc training or practical experience in teaching or even employment in leading R&D centers and enterprises such as AT&T, GE, GM, IBM, Motorola, NASA, and SRI. Their return to Korea, either permanent or temporary, has provided an invaluable avenue for technology transfer from the United States to Korea, especially in high-tech areas. This human bridge between the two countries is expected to play an even more significant role in the future. As Korea climbs further up the technology ladder, highly sophisticated technology will become needed. Thus scientists and engineers with training and experience in strategic technology, unavailable in Korea, will more likely come from the United States than from other countries.

An apt example of this situation is Samsung's recruitment of Korean-American scientists and engineers in the development of semiconductor chips. In 1985, Chin D. J. (Stanford PhD) was recruited from IBM to lead Samsung's fledgling semiconductor research unit. Kwon O. H. and Hwang C. K. (both Stanford PhDs) joined soon afterward. They were given a "blank check" to equip their laboratories as well as to reward themselves. In return, they have provided technological expertise which led to the invention of 4 mega DRAM (1988), 16 mega DRAM (1990), 64 mega DRAM (1993), 256 mega DRAM (1994), and 1 giga DRAM (1996). The "economic value of these experts" to Samsung would appear priceless, as was well symbolized by the blank check tendered during the negotiation process. They were seen as having the ability to trigger "human-capital externalities" in the remaining members of Samsung's R&D establishment.[41]

This "Stanford connection" also led to the importation of American know-how (e.g., as compared to Japanese know-how) when additional knowledge was required to advance to the next stage of the chip-development cycle. (Table 4.9, in the next chapter, lists the sources and contents of Samsung's imports of foreign electronics technologies between 1983 and 1991. As is evident in the table, the U.S. sources provided 35 items compared to only 8 items from Japan.) Aside from the human bond created by the connections to Stanford, Japanese reluctance to provide technologies to Korean firms has also played a role. The competitive relationship with the Japanese electronics industry is expected to increase as Korean firms catch up. It is also possible that Japanese firms may change their minds and find reasons to cooperate strategically with Korean firms.

Korean universities have also benefited from the Korea–U.S. human-resource bridge. The contribution made by U.S. trained engineers in upgrading the KAIST faculty has already been noted. Those Koreans who returned from the United States to join faculties of Korean universities are in the vanguard of the transfer of T&S knowledge to lecture rooms and textbooks. They have kept up with new developments by subscribing to journals and have updated their lecture notes. On sabbatical, they went back to the universities from which they graduated. They have thus contributed to breaking cultural and language barriers between the two countries. All this may seem trivial at first glance, but in the long run, they will build an information network with a leader in science and technology in the United States.

An important element of the human bridge is the pool of Korean-American scientists and engineers employed by U.S. universities and R&D centers, estimated at over 10,000. They have been active in learning and creating knowledge in diverse, specialized areas of science and technology. Table 3.13 presents the numbers of R&D personnel in the United States in specialized areas of electronics and information technology (as an illustration of a potential nodule for a future Korean-American S&T information network).

3.7   Challenges to Science and Technology Education in the Twenty-first Century

The emergence of digital technology has brought with it an era of "technology fusion." The combination of mechanics with electronics gave birth to a new breed of technology, mechatronics. This prompts us to anticipate various possible combinations, such as biotronics and optotronics. Fumio Kodama explains the meaning of fusion in the following terms:

Table 3.13
List of Korean-American scientists and engineers in electronics and information-computer technology, 1994

Classification code	Field	Number
EL020	Communication	160
EL030	Computer/microprocessor	109
EL040	Control electronics	54
EL050	Design/electronics	10
EL070	Electronic/electric machines	36
EL080	Electro-physics	52
EL090	Electro-optics	6
EL120	Mechatronics	1
EL130	Microwave	8
EL160	Research, electronic	5
EL170	Test, electronic	1
EL180	Other electronics	76
Subtotal		508
C0000	Computer science	112
C0010	Artificial intelligence	69
C0020	Computer algorithm	38
C0030	Computer application	9
C0040	Computer systems	85
C0050	Database management	57
C0060	Fault tolerance/reliability	25
C0070	Image processing	73
C0080	Information science	3
C0090	Pattern recognition	44
C0100	Software engineering	94
C0110	System analysis	6
C0900	Other computer science areas	53
Subtotal		668
Grand total		1,176

Note: Only those scientists and engineers registered in the *Directory of Korean-American Scientists and Engineers,* published by the Korean-American Scientists and Engineers Association Inc., Vienna, VA, 1994.

As the names mechatronics and optoelectronics imply, "fusion" means more than the summation and combination of different technologies, and it implements an arithmetic in which one plus one makes three. . . . Fusion is more than complementarities, because it creates a new market and new growth opportunities for each participant in the innovation. Fusion goes beyond the accumulation of small improvements, because it blends incremental improvements from several (often previously separate) fields to create a product endowed with some extra ingredient not found elsewhere in the market. It also goes beyond interindustry relationships, because different innovations in different industries progressed in parallel with each other, taking the form of joint research.[42]

These new areas of technology are being harnessed to create unprecedented new business opportunities in the global trade of information-based services, and along with it follows the spurt of demand for high-tech engineers.

Mechatronics has created demand for a new breed of scientists and engineers capable of thinking in terms of systems building, incorporating technologies from diverse disciplines. Furthermore, these will integrate not only diverse technologies but also the whole chain of value-adding processes into the system structure from product vision, design, prototype, manufacturing, marketing, through to distribution and final disposal. Great optimization can be brought about in this framework with the help of ever more powerful computors that the digital revolution permits. It poses a formidable task for the higher education system to devise a new curriculum with which to train this new breed of scientists and engineers to meet the challenges of next century.

In terms of quantity the future looks quite daunting. Table 3.14 shows the shortage of S&T personnel expected during the 1992 to 2010 period. The researchers calculated the shortage figures by subtracting the estimated increase in demand from the estimated increase in supply. The demand estimate depends on the assumption that the past trends will obtain in the future, and the resulting figure of extrapolation is adjusted by the Japanese pattern of changing skill-input coefficients as the output composition changes. The supply estimate depends on the assumption that the university entrance quotas, controlled by the Ministry of Education, remain unchanged. The total shortage of engineering PhDs, for example, amounts to 35,735. Of that total, electric and electronic engineering graduates top the shortage list with 10,146, machinery and shipbuilding engineering comes next with 5,478, metal and materials engineering follows with 3,914, and so on.

These shortages imply a need for large-scale investment in education and in infrastructure for education and training. But it must also be

Table 3.14
Demand, supply, and shortage of PhD-holding science and technology personnel, 1992–2010

Field		1992–1996	1997–2001	2002–2010	1992–2010
Science	Demand (A)	2,964	5,527	10,307	18,798
	Supply (B)	1,777	2,135	3,912	7,824
	B − A	−1,187	−3,392	−6,395	−10,974
Engineering	Demand (A)	6,992	16,323	28,304	51,619
	Supply (B)	3,568	4,374	7,942	15,884
	B − A	−3,424	−11,949	−20,362	−35,735
Machinery and ship-building	Demand (A)	1,216	1,893	4,839	7,948
	Supply (B)	566	679	1,235	2,470
	B − A	−650	−1,214	−3,604	−5,478
Metal and materials	Demand (A)	663	1,893	3,113	5,669
	Supply (B)	400	478	878	1,756
	B − A	−264	−1,415	−2,235	−3,914
Electrical and electronic engineering	Demand (A)	2,349	4,635	8,462	15,446
	Supply (B)	1,158	1,492	2,650	5,300
	B − A	−1,191	−3,143	−5,812	−10,146
Chemical engineering	Demand (A)	818	1,175	2,434	4,427
	Supply (B)	310	394	704	1,408
	B − A	−508	−781	−1,730	−3,019
Food and genetic engineering	Demand (A)	426	1,599	2,462	4,487
	Supply (B)	164	181	345	690
	B − A	−262	−1,418	−2,117	−3,797
Medical and pharmaceutical	Demand (A)	3,784	4,951	10,574	19,309
	Supply (B)	3,941	4,458	8,399	16,798
	B − A	157	−493	−2,175	−2,511
Agricultural and marine	Demand (A)	1,474	2,015	4,218	7,707
	Supply (B)	896	1,006	1,902	3,804
	B − A	−578	−1,009	−2,316	−3,903

Source: STEPI, *Long Term Plan for Science and Technology Development toward 2010* (Human Resources Section), Research report 95-09 (in Korean), Seoul, 1995.

kept in mind that in the estimation procedure, nothing has been mentioned about the potential impact of the information-based society and economy on the demand for high-tech engineers and researchers. That aspect has been ignored for a good reason. Past experience is not helpful for an extrapolation due to the technological paradigm shift. But, considering the potential development of a vast global market for knowledge-based service industries and trade opportunities that the digital revolution permits, the potential impact seems to be too important to ignore. Korea should pay serious attention to the growth of information-based industries, particularly telecommunications, multimedia, and information processing, which are not classified as manufacturing. Demand for high-powered engineers by the latter industries could easily exceed the demand for engineers by the Korean manufacturing industries, since the global information and telecommunication market seems virtually unlimited.

In terms of quality, engineering education demands a departure from the traditional reductionist approach that led to minute specialization and compartmentalization of disciplines. The walls between disciplines and departments must be dismantled. Students must be allowed to become creative and to formulate their own curriculum by mixing different disciplines and setting goals for themselves. One would of course be allowed to follow the traditional disciplinary approach if one chooses. Professors can be ready to guide and teach flexibly within the new paradigm of technology fusion and cross-disciplinary integration. A set of courses could be created to increase students' ability to solve factory-floor problems that may arise with the application of the technology fusion approach. A new standard for grading students' performance could be devised, especially for giving credit to factory-floor experiences and multiple skills as opposed to a single skill.

One possible way to manage all of these issues effectively would be to design *a pilot school* with an industry-specific curriculum content. For example, a graduate school of automotive technology (Automobile Polytechnic Institute, hypothetically) could be envisaged, where diverse engineering courses are taught in an integrated manner. A course could bring together concept-car development, technology scanning, designing, manufacturing, component production, electronic devices, emission control, special auto-marketing techniques, and automobile-specific accounting procedures. One could think of a Multimedia Polytechnic Institute or a Software Design Polytechnic Institute, a Biotronics Polytechnic Institute, a Textile Polytechnic Institute, and so on, all designed to confer graduate as well as undergraduate degrees. These institutes would emphasize practical experience by inviting retired company engineers to give lectures, and this "experimental content" of the syllabus would be adequately balanced with theory.

4   Corporate Organization as
       a Learning Institution

This chapter reviews the process of technological upgrading in *chaebols* as well as in small- to medium-scale enterprises. *Chaebols* have led the way in the absorption and implementation of imported technologies, and their competitive advantages have been strengthened as a result. Recently they have been providing the major thrust for continuing export-oriented growth in the Korean economy. Success stories include the production and export of semiconductors by Samsung and automo bile manufacture by Hyundai. This review addresses the following questions: Will the strategies for technological upgrading which worked in the past, also work in the future? What new strategy options will be available? How should cooperative schemes be designed so as to create a positive-sum-game result between *chaebols* and small to medium enterprises (SMEs)?

4.1   *Chaebols* as Learning Organizations

Chaebol groups, or industrial conglomerates, as in the case of Japanese *zaibatsu* groups, have been the leading actors in the transformation of an agrarian Korea into a capital-cum-technology intensive industrial economy.[1] The dynamism of this institutional form is manifested in various performance indicators such as rapid growth of sales, exports, employment figures, asset values, and consequently in business concentration indexes. However, *chaebols* have often been the target of criticism regarding their greed; exploitation of consumers; government-business symbiosis at the expense of the public in general, in particular the poor, small scale industries; unfair practice of "octopus-like preying" on weak enterprises, etc. Regardless of the variety (and verity) of the criticisms, their contributions to technological learning and rapid industrial growth are certain.

The record of applications for intellectual property rights and the number of patents, utilities, designs, and trademarks applied for are shown in table 4.1. These figures represent the top 29 companies ranked by the number of applications. It is to be noted that almost all the companies listed belong to the most successful *chaebol* groups, namely Samsung, Lucky-Gold Star (L-G), Daewoo, Hyundai, and Kia. Furthermore applications are concentrated in the fields of electronics, telecommunications, automobiles, and machinery. These fields represent battle grounds of fierce competition in learning new technology that began in the 1980s.

The reasons for *chaebol* leadership in technological risk-taking activities are several. Since the early 1960s, when industrialization began, *chaebols* have been following a diversification strategy as a means of quickly building empires. Part of this strategy was to employ college graduates from top universities by the thousands every year, to indoctrinate them in the company culture, and enhance their company-specific skills and technologies. (See table 4.2 for expenditures by leading *chaebols* for training.) Competition for well-educated college graduates has raised salaries well above the national average. *Chaebols* had deep pockets and easy access to subsidized loans, which enabled them to pay. Furthermore, under the *chaebol* system, the failure of a new project in a member company could be covered by successes of projects in other member companies—a convenient form of risk-sharing in an economy where fundamental uncertainties prevail.

Byong Ho Gong (1995) studied the history of *chaebols* and concluded that the high-growth strategy through diversification results in what he calls an "economy of growth."[2] High growth tends to increase the efficiency of line workers because of the rapid accumulation of production-related experience (often called "learning by doing," "learning by imitating," and "learning by using"). It also tends to create greater opportunities for promotion, an added incentive that lowers the average age of employees and reduces risks and uncertainties. Thus bankers are more willing to lend money to *chaebols*, which diversify and grow faster than smaller companies. Diversification normally necessitates learning new technologies for product and process development.

Gong concluded that the *chaebols*, with an aggressive diversification strategy into new products and markets, had a greater survival potential as a result of their rapid learning-productivity linkages. The linkage led either to improved product quality or to unit cost reduction, or

Table 4.1
Number of applications for intellectual property rights by 29 leading companies in 1992

Company	Patent	Utility	Design	Trademark	Total
Samsung Electronics	3,410	1,933	355	299	5,997
GoldStar Semiconductor	2,318	3,234	174	159	5,885
Daewoo Electronics	435	1,397	384	33	2,249
Hyundai Automobile	348	1,062	606	17	2,033
Hyundai Electronic Industry	930	490	367	13	1,800
Samsung Electricity	198	551	24	2	775
GoldStar Communication	344	324	30	5	703
GoldStar Electron	318	351	2	0	671
Samsung Display Devices	300	266	11	1	578
Orion Electricity	73	452	50	0	575
Kia Automobile	74	306	174	2	556
GoldStar Telecom	235	207	21	0	463
POSCO	197	253	3	0	453
GoldStar Industrial System	76	321	8	4	409
Korea Electronics	349	1	0	1	351
Daewoo Motor Co.	35	193	85	5	317
Mando Machinery	52	182	49	1	284
GoldStar Cable	127	121	20	9	277
Daewoo Telecom	67	145	48	16	276
Samsung Aerospace	87	149	8	2	246
Samsung Heavy Industry	59	147	4	30	240
Asia Automobile	27	94	99	9	229
Daewoo Electronic Component	52	160	13	0	225
GoldStar Electric Machinery	50	151	3	5	209
GoldStar Alps Electronics	39	101	1	0	141
GoldStar Instruments and Electric	36	92	1	0	129
Daewoo Heavy Industry	11	67	1	2	81
Samsung Corning	38	34	0	0	72
Daewoo Ship Industry	15	35	1	18	69
Daewoo subsidiaries (7 total)	687	2,449	582	74	3,792
Samsung subsidiaries (6 total)	4,092	3,080	402	334	7,908
GoldStar subsidiaries (9 total)	3,543	4,902	260	182	8,887
Hyundai subsidiaries (2 total)	1,278	1,552	973	30	3,833

Source: Republic of Korea Government Patent Office.

Table 4.2
Investment expenditures for education and training of employees by major *chaebol* groups in 1992 and 1993 (unit: million won)

Company	1992	1993
Samsung	31,348	40,837
Hyundai	11,498	13,935
Daewoo	15,530	19,218
L-G	18,333	23,319
Hanjin	9,290	10,016
Kia	6,761	8,211
Sunkyung	6,637	7,223
Ssangyong	5,991	7,334
Daelim	1,732	2,019
Byupsan	1,977	2,147
Hanil	230	190
Hanhwa	2,482	3,185
Kumho	3,328	3,711
Dusan	3,058	3,302
Dongkuk Steel	577	575
Hyosung	1,277	1,460
Lotte	4,097	4,208
Sammi	168	110
Kohap	201	158
Kolon	3,095	3,649
Dongyang	2,482	3,617
Halla	1,449	2,583
Haitai	2,293	2,254
Dongah	1,939	2,639
Woosung Construction	604	1,130
Dongbu	1,167	1,872
Kumkang Shoes	710	477
Kukdong Construction	1,878	1,573
Hanbo	270	176
Miwon	1,507	1,877

Source: Hankook Kyungje Shinmun (Korea Economic Daily), July 6, 1994.

even both at once. One must also add that those with superior export-performance records, benefited more from government incentive schemes, such as tax breaks, subsidized-interest loans, and access to foreign-exchange uses.[3] Thus the *chaebols*, which could diversify into foreign markets and into new products for export, further increased their advantages.

High rates of technological learning and diffusion among *chaebols* have been supported by high-growth policies. Yang Taek Lim (1988), has estimated the rate of new technology diffusion for numerical control (NC) equipment and compared the diffusion speed between Canadian and Korean industries. In the case of the general machinery sector, Korean large-scale enterprises have achieved a speed index 0.3929, a threefold rate over their Canadian counterparts at 0.1303. Korean small and medium enterprises have achieved a rate 0.2070 or 1.6 times that of their Canadian counterparts. Similar results have been recorded in other sectors, including electronic equipment and transportation equipment.[4]

To conclude this section, it can be stated that the *chaebol* has served Korea well and has been a prime mover in building technological capability. It has helped to reduce the risk and uncertainty of new projects, to diversify product portfolio and overseas markets, to exploit dynamic scale economies, to internalize externalities (positive side), and to benefit from the cumulative knowledge within their member companies. But it should be stressed that Taiwan, a reputable rival to South Korea, did not rely on anything like conglomerates. For historical reasons the Chang Kai Shek government shunned conglomeration, and instead nurtured medium- and small-scale enterprises. The *chaebol*, as an institutional form, was neither a necessary nor a sufficient condition for industrialization based on technological learning but only a convenient "institutional tool" adopted to organize and manage market imperfections (and even market failure) in Korea.

Finally it must be pointed out that *chaebols* were used during the initial phases of Korean industrialization as an instrument to compensate for the absence of a venture capital market. In industrialized countries, venture capital helps entrepreneurs to initiate risky projects by spreading risks and uncertainties over the whole set of venture businesses. The fundamental uncertainties in developing countries preclude such venture capital.[5] Under the circumstances the government provided subsidized loans (e.g., the "policy loans") to *chaebols*, de facto creating a risk-sharing partnership. If the project was successful, the profit so earned would belong to the *chaebols,* and if the project failed, the government and ultimately the tax payers would bear the cost.[6]

Having fattened the *chaebols* for some time, the government encouraged family-owned companies to list their stocks in the slowly developing equity market. In the absence of an efficient capital market in Korea, this approach of "enticing capital formation and its stock market" may be considered far better than doing nothing. The basic reasons for the absence of a capital market were fundamental uncertainty, poverty, and lack of technical knowledge and experience. The policy loans functioned as surrogate venture capital. This makeshift arrangement provided an opportunity for private enterprises to engage in learning by doing, imitating, and using. But the usefulness of this makeshift arrangement has disappeared, even for helping technological learning by a firm, and a new institutional device seems necessary for future technological learning. (More on this at the end of this chapter.) Witness that the system has permitted an excessive leverage (e.g., debt–equity ratio of over 400 percent) of *chaebols,* and this *"addictive"* borrowing habit in the domestic market as well as abroad has contributed, at least in part, to bringing about the financial calamities of the 1997–98 period.

4.2   Diversification as a Strategy for Technological Learning

Looking at the performance indicators, the current ranking of *chaebol* groups appears to be clearly defined. For instance, in terms of sales, employment, export, and capital assets, Samsung ranks at the top followed by Hyundai, L-G (formerly, Lucky-Goldstar), Daewoo, Sunkyung, and so on down the line. But these giants today began as humble small- to medium-sized enterprises when they entered into the market. Samsung started out in 1953 with a single product, refined sugar. Hyundai entered the market as a construction company in 1946. Lucky Chemical Co. came into being in 1947 as a toothpaste maker. And Daewoo was born much later, that is, in 1967 as a textile merchant (mainly as an exporter). Byung Ho Gong's study concludes that three factors can explain their growth and capability building in technology and organization. The first is the ability to adjust continuously to the changing business environment. The second is a good relationship with the government, since the latter provided opportunities and means (e.g., subsidized loans) for enterprises to participate in the learning process. The third is the aggressive diversification strategies that the successful companies adopted.[7]

Diversification strategies coupled with inter-*chaebol* competition for market share has, indeed, provided an effective paradigm for these firms to import new technologies and master them in the shortest possible time. The major thrust of company-level diversification initially originated with the Heavy-Chemical Industry Development Program of the 1970s. Table 4.3 indicates the wholesale participation of *chaebol* group companies in the program. To be noted is that the allocation of individual projects to the participating companies at that time seems to have defined today's pattern of market competition. For instance, Samsung, L-G, and Daewoo, which at the time were selected to participate in electronics projects, constitute the market leaders today. Likewise, in shipbuilding, Hyundai, Daewoo, and Samsung dominate the current industry. In the automobile industry, Hyundai and Daewoo remain the major competitors today. Kia and Ssangyong became bankrupt in 1998. As will be shown below, all these companies have been investing an ever-increasing amount of capital in building technological capabilities in their respective fields of assignment since the 1970s.

When these companies negotiated the allocation of projects with the government, they had little experience in making the products involved, whether automobiles, ships, television sets, cranes, gasoline, or steel. They had to import technologies from abroad and learn. Instead of following a given comparative advantage for specialization in industry, they decided to build competitive assets from a virtual zero level to state-of-the-art technological capability. The aim was to learn and master the relevant technology as fast as possible, an aim shared by both private enterprises and government planners. The practical target for each new factory built with foreign technology was to exceed, in the shortest possible time, the stipulated maximum output capacity as defined by the machine builders. Furthermore, to become competitive in international markets, the companies wanted from the beginning to import state-of-the-art technology, not a second-rate or labor-intensive technology that would be obsolete soon. When negotiating with foreign companies for technology importation, the ignorance of technology market conditions (often called the problem of information asymmetry) on the part of Korean companies, was often alleviated with government assistance. During that early period the government agencies seemed to have a better set of information sources and bargaining power vis-à-vis foreign technology sellers.[8]

Table 4.3

Pattern of *chaebol* groups participating in Heavy and Chemical Industry Development Program, 1973–1979

Industry	Plan	Outcome (actual)
Iron and Steel	POSCO expansion	Increased to 8.5 million ton capacity
	Second complex construction	Kwangyang Bay Branch
	Facilities for specialty steel	Daehan Heavy Equipment Co. (currently Kia Specialty Steel, '86), Sammi Specialty Steel
Nonferrous metal machines	Onsan base to be adapted	Koryo Metal (currently L-G Metal, '82)
		Hyundai undertaking Daehan Aluminium
	Changwon base to be adapted	Hyundai, Hyundai Heavy Industry
		Daewoo (Hankook Machine), Daewoo Heavy Industry
		Hyosung (Hanyung Co.), Hyosung Heavy Industry
		Samsung (Daewung Heavy Industry), Samsung Heavy Industry
		Ssangyong (Jinil Co.), Ssangyong Heavy Industry
	Promoting auto export	Kia undertaking Asia Motor Co.
		Daewoo (GM Korea), Daewoo Motor Co.
Shipbuilding	Goje Island base to be adapted	Hyundai, Hyundai Shipbuilding and Heavy Industry (currently Hyundai Heavy Industry), Hyundai Mipo shipbuilding
		Daewoo, Daewoo Shipbuilding (currently Daewoo Heavy Industry)
		Samsung, Samsung Shipbuilding (currently Samsung Heavy Industry)
Electricity	Promoting export	Samsung, Samsung Electricity, Samsung Corning (Hankook Semiconductor, Hankook Electricity and Communication), Samsung Electronics
	Expanding Gumi complex	L-G, GoldStar Electric Machinery, GoldStar Instruments and Electric (Daehan Semiconductor), L-G Telecom
		Daewoo, Daewoo Electronics undertaking Daehan Cable '83
Chemical	Yeochon base construction	Honam Ethylene (Privatization currently Daelim Industry)
		Honam Oil and Chemical (Privatization currently Lotte Group)
		Kumho, Kumho Chemical (currently Kumho Shell Chemical)
		L-G, L-G Oil and Chemical
		Samsung, Samsung Oil and Chemical (Ulsan)
		KOLON, KOLON Oil and Chemical (Ulsan)
		Namhae Chemical (state owned)
	Refinery construction	Ssangyong, Ssangyong Refinery

Source: KERI, *The Korean Business Group 1995*, p. 244.

During the 1970s and 1980s *chaebol* diversification continued despite temporary setbacks in the 1979–80 recession.[9] Mergers and acquisitions (M&A) added impetus for *chaebols* to expand into new industries. For instance, Daewoo's major industries today (e.g., automobiles, electronics, and shipbuilding) came into Daewoo's possession when the government offered it failing firms at a bargain price, namely with subsidized loans for re-engineering or re-organization. When a new venture was undertaken, a team of engineers experienced in re-organization along with production-line technicians was formed as a task force. Often the team was sent abroad to be trained in a "best-practice" firm in Japan, the United States, or Europe. New technologies were imported to upgrade the firm's capability. (See table 4.4, indicating a trend of accelerating imports of foreign technologies by five leading *chaebols*.) These accumulated experiences provided a fundamental corporate resource (or know-how) for innovation that was combined with an aggressive diversification strategy. Table 4.5 provides information on the current status of four *chaebols'* diversified structure.

In the 1980s the leading *chaebols* began to compete in building in-house R&D capabilities. Table 4.6 presents Samsung's R&D facilities as an example. Note that all of the 27 research institutes have been launched since 1980. An interesting game to watch is which *chaebol* gets ahead in recruiting more PhDs in science and engineering. As of 1995, Samsung is leading with 482 PhDs, followed by L-G with 311, Hyundai with 225, and Daewoo with 203. (Korea Industrial Technology Association compiles biennially a compendium of research institutions for all manufacturers with in-house R&D labs, i.e., Research Institution Yearbook. The publication has rich data useful for monitoring R&D competition among manufacturing enterprises. Table 4.6 illustrates the sort of data available in the yearbook.)

The establishment of an R&D institute in an industrial branch, such as in semiconductors, signified that the company was committed to investing in new ideas in-house in order to accelerate technological upgrading. In-house R&D activities can provide a powerful tool for creating ideas, for improving productivity, for enhancing bargaining power in technology transactions, and even for figuring out competitive and cooperative strategies in technology markets. Building R&D institutes even has an advertising effect that can be helpful in establishing brand name. It can be seen from the table that Samsung, the leader of R&D in Korea, has been competing in building R&D capabilities since the early 1980s. In particular, collecting the largest number of

Table 4.4
Number of technology imports by five major *chaebol* groups, 1964–1988

Year	Samsung	Hyundai	Daewoo	L-G	Sunkyung	Total
1964				1		1
1965						
1966			2	2		4
1967				3		3
1968		2	1	3	1	7
1969	3		3	2		8
1970		3		6		9
1971	2	1	6	2		11
1972	2	1	1		1	5
1973	3	6	1		1	11
1974	2	6	3	4		15
1975	4	4	5	4		17
1976	3	8	5	7		23
1977	3	12	8	2		25
1978	9	43	12	5		69
1979	12	23	7	10	2	54
1980	13	15	10	12	1	51
1981	10	24	14	12		60
1982	20	13	12	23		68
1983	34	18	15	28	6	101
1984	24	42	25	32	1	124
1985	35	32	36	37	1	141
1986	44	31	13	30	1	122
1987	38	40	23	42	4	147
1988	70	32	25	55	3	185
Total	331	356	230	322	22	1,261

Source: Korea Industrial Technology Association, *Current Status of Technology Imports Contracted*, Seoul, 1989.

PhDs has been a symbolic game, a competition for building up the enterprise's visibility.

Several factors can be identified that help explain the rush toward building R&D institutions. The diversified corporate structure of the *chaebols* necessitated more specialized engineering services as new firms were added. Furthermore, as these companies climbed up the technology ladder in each industry, they found it increasingly difficult to buy and transfer foreign technology. The foreign companies were naturally concerned about creating potential competitors. In addition

Table 4.5
Indicators of diversification by four large *chaebol* groups, 1992

Industry	Hyundai Percentage of sales	Hyundai Number of companies	Samsung Percentage of sales	Samsung Number of companies	Daewoo Percentage of sales	Daewoo Number of companies	L-G Percentage of sales	L-G Number of companies
Fishing and mining	0	2	0	0	0	0	0.04	1
Food	0	0	3.41	2	0	0	0	0
Textiles	0	0	2.85	3	0	0	0	0
Other light industry	0.99	2	1.67	2	0	0	0	0
Chemical and petroleum	3.29	2	1.73	6	0	1	24.8	10
Nonferrous metal	1.16	2	0	0	0	0	0	0
Metal (primary)	3.85	3	0	0	0.15	1	3.86	3
Electrical and electronic	3.76	4	23.48	10	17.49	7	35.16	20
Heavy industry	31.8	11	4.83	2	28.25	9	0	0
Power	0	0	0	0	0	0	0	0
Construction	10.74	2	3.58	1	1.98	1	4.95	2
Trade	31.09	1	31.92	2	49.91	1	18.26	1
Distribution	2.31	3	1.56	5	0	0	7.82	7
Hotel	0	0	0.44	2	0.32	1	0.27	1
Transportation	2.50	3	0	1	0	0	0.50	2
Finance	2.39	4	22.9	4	1.74	1	0	5
Other services	9.12	9	1.64	14	0.13	4	1.37	11
Total	100	48	100	54	100	26	100	63

Source: Korea Economic Research Institute.

Table 4.6
Samsung's technology capability indicators, 1995

Names of R&D establishments under Samsung *chaebol* group	Number of			R&D expenditures in 1994 (million won)	R&D/ sale (%)	Date of establishment
	PhDs	MAs	BAs			
Construction Institute of Technology	27	40	30	28,800	1.5	85.7
Construction Machines	1	1	8	413	0.03	93.5
Data System Information Technology	34	166	622	3,145	0.81	85.7
Corporation Apparel Technology			6	7,676	0.13	92.2
Petrochemical Co. R&D Lab	1	3	6	1,450	0.43	88.3
Engineering R&D Center	6	25	10	7,943	1.7	87.3
Engineering R&D Center Branch		2	11	2,968	0.64	94.9
Display Devices Center	26	68	74	47,500	3.45	83.6
Electronic Device Production Engineering	5	21	53	18,288	1.30	90.7
Electromechanics R&D Center	16	64	126	25,726	3.14	82.4
Electromechanics MLB		1	9			95.1
Electronic Co. Technical Lab	108	538	1,861	773,550	1.50	80.4
E.C. Semiconductor R&D Center	100	400	1,100	161,600	6.00	81.10
Electronics LSI Design	6	18	287	22,400	6.00	88.11
Electronics Information Computer System	7	103	446	26,480	4.60	87.9
Biomedical Research Institute	28	15	5	1,849	0.02	94.9
Fine Chemicals R&D Center	7	6	2	1,135	0.49	86.3
Knitting Needle Engineering Research Lab		1	4	69	0.69	92.8
Chemical Technology Center	44	42	49	11,893	2.40	89.11
Gereral Chemicals Technical		7	27	4,429	0.87	90.3

Heavy Industries Daeduck	29	63	49	15,305	0.83	92.3
Heavy Industries Maritime Research	11	29	96	20,100	2.70	84.3
Heavy Industries Machinery and Electronics	9	40	41	7,826	1.80	82.3
Heavy Industries Manufacturing Engineering		2	28	4,153	1.00	91.11
Heavy Industries Technical Construction Division	3	4	13	14,438	2.30	91.1
GE Medical System			16	2,000	4.00	95.1
Corning R&D	14	35	23	8,436	1.80	84.4
Total	482	1,695	5,000	1,219,572	1.64	

Source: Korea Industrial Technology Association, *Research Institution Yearbook*, 1995–1996.

Korea's advantage in cheap labor has been eroded as China and Southeast Asian countries have emerged as major traders in the world market. This was so even before Korean wage rates soared in 1987 owing to the entry of democracy.

The configuration of these structural changes prompted the Korean government to announce a major policy shift in the early 1980s: "Technology-led national development." Under that slogan the government enacted a set of laws in order to assist technology upgrading of industries by providing tax benefits, technology information, low-cost financing, and infrastructural services of various kinds. (See table 4.7 for beneficial tax laws enacted in succession and also table 4.8 for a record of low-cost loans provided to investors to take risks in technology related activities.)

In short, the 1980s saw the incentive structure redesigned to entice private enterprises into technological risk-taking. As a consequence private enterprises, particularly the *chaebols,* responded quickly to take advantage of the new laws, while the international market environment was forcing them to act anyway. Thus one could argue that the market forces were "catalyzed" by new institutional devices, bearing on risk-taking decisions by private enterprises.

Effective competition among producers was neither reduced nor compromised by the new system. Doing new things was the way to compete. This mode of government activism has been utilized over and over again in many other areas of policy making throughout the last three decades. This mode of government involvement is fundamentally different from the one that prevailed in Latin America and South Asia during the 1980s. There, government protective policies often obstructed market forces and created rent-seeking opportunities, to put it bluntly. These institutional differences between regions appear to offer a lesson worth paying special attention to.

4.3 Samsung's Semiconductor Development: A Model

Samsung announced in November 1996 that its engineers succeeded in constructing a prototype for a 1-Giga DRAM for the first time in the industry. This event signaled Samsung's lead in DRAM technology among all the memory-chip producers in the world market. The speed with which Samsung has overtaken the world-class DRAM producers deserves an explanation. In September 1982 Samsung began an intensive study to formulate investment schedules and strategies to enable

Table 4.7
Development of tax benefit system for R&D by the year of new tax laws enacted, 1960–1986

Years	1960s	'73	'74	'75	'76	'77	'78	'79	'80	'81	'82	'83	'84	'85	'86
Promotion of R&D			*Reserve Fund for R&D (since 1988 the upper limit of tax benefit was abolished)		*Tax exemption or special depreciation rate on purchases of R&D equipment					*Tax exemption on R&D and training expenses (since 1988, the upper limit of tax benefits was abolished)	*Exemption of local real estate tax on buildings plus land of R&D institutes	*Reduction of custom duties on R&D equipment	*Special consumption tax exempted on R&D sample		*Tax credit on spending for human resource development
Promotion of technology transfer	*Tax exemption or reduction on payments for technology imports			*Tax exemption or reduction on income from R&D activities			*Income tax exemption on foreign engineers and researchers								
Promotion of R&D commercialization					*Tax exemption and social depreciation rate for assets of newly commercialized technology	*Income tax exemption on engineering consulting services							*Special tax benefits for R&D based SMEs		
Promotion of demand									*Special consumption tax rates for products of pioneering technology						
Promotion of venture capital formation										*Reserve fund system for investment losses of venture capital firms	*Exclusion of capital gains from taxable income for venture capital firms			*Tax benefits for dividends paid by venture capital firms	*Tax exemption on capital gains from venture stock trading

Source: Kyun Kim, *A Study of Technological Capability Development in Korea during the 1980s* (in Korean), PhD dissertation, Seoul National University, February 1994, p. 98.

Table 4.8
Record of low-cost loans to encourage R&D activities and technology upgrading, 1981–1990 (unit: 100 million won)

	1981	1982	1983	1984	1985	1986	1987	1988	1989	1990
Financial supports		134	221	221	301	518	632	842	1,112	1,693
Special R&D project		133	220	220	300	517	550	650	870	1,200
Basic industrial technology development			1	1	1	1	81	190	240	491
Prototype development of inventions		1			1	1	1	2	2	2
Special funds	56	95	83	124	143	595	1,517	1,859	1,869	3,059
Industrial development funds	56	95	74	91	139	195	314	603	805	630
National investment funds			9	33	4	194	314	375	499	340
Industrial technology promotion funds						206	889	881	444	250
SME structural adjustment funds									121	840
Special plant equipment funds										999
Loans from banks	136	528	883	920	864	1,332	1,459	1,985	1,911	1,975
Industrial bank	35	408	579	520	364	810	915	1,051	863	1,175
SME bank	101	120	304	400	500	522	544	934	1,048	800
New technology project loan company	62	223	521	632	871	983	1,049	1,117	1,237	1,947
Investment	1	5	33	63	97	146	162	195	211	376
Loan	61	218	489	569	774	837	887	922	1,026	1,571
Total	254	980	1,708	1,897	2,179	3,428	4,657	5,803	6,129	8,674

Source: Kyun Kim, op. cit., p. 108.

it to catch up. Subsequently Samsung announced a series of R&D achievements (prototypes) as follows: 64K (November 1983), 256K (February 1986), 1M (July 1986), 4M (February 1988), 16M (August 1990), 64M (January 1993), 256M (August 1994), and 1G (November 1996).

This experience offers an interesting case study of how a latecomer can overcome technological barriers of various kinds, including formidably high risks and uncertainties in R&D and marketing, the "techno-nationalism" of advanced producers, and shortening product life cycles. More fundamentally, one may ask where the three necessary factors came from, namely knowledge, engineers, and organizational skills and strategies. These elements represent basic constraints on firms in developing countries and challenge entrepreneurs in developed ones. The firm-level experience in accumulating these assets provides the very basic (micro-micro) materials for understanding the broader picture of industry-level and economy-level upgrading processes.[10] Samsung demonstrates what is possible in industry and in the economy as a whole if Samsung's practices could be diffused to other firms.

Knowledge

The crucial first step Samsung took for knowledge acquisition was to build a multipurpose R&D institute in Santa Clara, California, the heart of the electronics industry in the United States. This "outpost" institute assumed the roles of (1) information scanner to identify knowledge holders (e.g., license sellers) for potential agreements, (2) R&D center equipped with a pilot plant for the purpose of designing and testing, (3) recruitment center for talented and experienced scientists and engineers not only for the outpost itself but also for R&D institutes in Korea, (4) training center for production-line operatives of chip-making plants in Korea, and (5) office of marketing research and sales outlet. For a fledgling enterprise with little experience in high-tech business or international management, the idea of establishing an R&D institute in the United States was audacious, a firm commitment to learning (even if by costly trial and error). The idea itself was born out of an extensive (12-month) feasibility study by a team of experts, including Samsung executives, Korean-American engineers, and other American consultants. The goal was to make Samsung a global player in chip making within the shortest possible time.

The first success by the Santa Clara institute was to mediate an agreement between Samsung and Micron Technology Inc. The latter signed a contract to transfer a chip design technology for 64K DRAM in June 1983. The first 3,000 units of chips were handed over to the Bucheon plant, which were used mainly for training researchers as well as production-line operatives to learn and raise the "yield." The latter term means the proportion of output passing a quality test. Normally, the first batch of output is expected to yield only about 10 percent. The record shows that a 92 percent yield was reached within 40 days from the starting date.[11] By November 1983, only 6 months after the launching of the project, the development team succeeded in ironing out the problems in the last 8 core process technologies out of the total 309 processes involved. These last problems were actually solved by hiring engineers who received training from Micron Technology Inc. and had experience in developing 64K DRAM prior to their employment at Samsung.[12]

Intricacy and extreme precision characterize the technologies involved. For example, a clean room is required where less than 10 pieces of dust less than 0.3 micron in size can be allowed per cubic meter of room space. Purity in gas and water is a must. No interruption in electricity supply is permitted. No vibration. The reason for these exacting requirements is that a circuit board with dimensions of 2.5 mm $\times$ 5.7 mm (14.25 mm^2) must contain 8 million lines, each 2.5 micron wide, all connected and imprinted with precision.[13] As the new generation of chips were added to the agenda of technology upgrading, these intricacies multiplied at an exponential rate. In meeting these new challenges, the R&D outpost proved to be an essential institutional device for Samsung, providing a transoceanic bridge. The speedy information-scanning service, servicing new agreements with technology suppliers in the United States, recruiting new talent, particularly Korean-American scientists and engineers with research experience at IBM, AT&T, GE, and the like, were all readily provided by the outpost.

Table 4.9 lists the technology agreements reached between Samsung and foreign companies during the 1983 to 1997 period. Note that foreign technologies came predominantly from the United States and that agreements included information, service, and patent licensing most of the time. Note also that the frequency of agreements has been accelerating. This out-sourcing policy reflects the sophistication of Samsung's technology management as the experience of exploiting world technology resources accumulates. As Samsung's technological capa-

Table 4.9
Samsung's technology imports and semiconductor strategic alliances, 1983–1995

Date	Partner	Subject Agreement	Subject
1983	Micron Tech. (U.S.)	ABC	CMOS process and IC
1983	Sharp (Japan)	ABE	Optical fiber and related IC
1983	ISE (U.S.)	ABC	Bipolar IC
1984	DITTI (Germany)	ABE	16K EEPROM, 256K DRAM, 64K SRAM
1984	SSI	ABE	CMOS logic IC
1985	Zytrex (U.S.)	ABC	8bit micom
1985	SGS-ATES (Italy)	ABE	MPU
1985	Intel (U.S.)	ABC	1M DRAM
1985	SSI	AB	Semiconductors
1986	IXYS (U.S.)	ABC	VTR servo controller
1986	Intel (U.S.)	ABCE	Semiconductors
1986	AMTA (U.S.)	AB	Submicron IC
1986	SSI	AB	DRAM and SRAM patents
1987	AMTA (U.S.)	ABE	LCD-CTV IC
1987	Unisys (U.S.)	AC	Semiconductors
1987	SSI	ABCE	Submicron IC
1987	Intel (U.S.)	C	DRAM and SRAM patents
1987	AMTA (U.S.)	ABE	LCD-CTV IC
1987	TI (U.S.)	CE	Semiconductors patents
1988	Norpak (Canada)	ABC	Voice multi-broadcast IC
1988	IXYS (U.S.)	ABC	Smart power IC
1988	SSI	ABC	Semiconductors
1988	Hitachi (Japan)	C	64K and 256K DRAM

Table 4.9 (continued)

Date	Partner	Subject	
		Agreement	64K and 256K DRAM
1989	Intel (U.S.)	ABCE	Video controller
1989	Philips (Netherlands)	C	Locos IC
1989	NCR (U.S.)	ABC	64K, 128K, 256K, 512K ROM
1989	NCR (U.S.)	ABC	ASIC
1989	Zigog (U.S.)	ABC	8bit MCU
1989	AMTA (U.S.)	ABC	LCD driver MCU
1989	Zilog (U.S.)	AC	85C 30SCE
1989	NS (U.S.)	ABC	Laser printer controller
1989	SSI	AC	Process automation technology
1989	SMC (U.S.)	C	Semiconductor patents
1989	Motorola (U.S.)	CE	Semiconductors
1989	SGS-Thompson (Netherlands)	C	Semiconductor patents
1989	Functional Logic (Japan)	ABC	Neutral ASIC
1989	IBM (U.S.)	C	Semiconductor patents
1989	USC, D.J. Shem (U.S.)	AC	IC simulator and device model
1989	UCLA, K.L. Wang (U.S.)	AC	Thin oxide technology
1989	SSI	ABCE	Semiconductor
1990	Integraph (U.S.)	ABCD	32bit RISC MCU
1990	AMTA (U.S.)	ABC	Camcorder servo controller
1990	ACC Microclec. (U.S.)	ABC	PC ship set
1990	UC Davis (U.S.)	ABC	Cache controller
1990	NS (U.S.)	ABC	Fax modem ASIC
1990	Samsung Japan	ABCE	8bit MCU
1990	Daniel Yun (U.S.)	ABCE	ICs
1990	AMTA (U.S.)	ABC	CCD image sensor controller

Date	Company (Country)	Content	Type
1990	SCT PTE (Singapore)	PC chip set	ABC
1990	NEC (Japan)	DRAM products	C
1990	Clarksper Design (U.S.)	DSP core	ABC
1990	TDK&S.Y. (Japan)	Semiconductor patents	C
1990	Link Research (Japan)	CCD area sensor	ABC
1990	Samsung Japan	LCD driver IC and controller	ABCE
1990	HP (U.S.)	CMOS process technology	ABC
1990	SSI	Semiconductors	ABCE
1990	ARRY Mcrosys (U.S.)	Digital signal processor	ABCE
1991	Mitsubishi (Japan)	DRAM patents	C
1991	Norpak Co. (Canada)	AVTD IC	ABC
1991	NS (Germany)	Semiconductor patents	C
1991	Hitachi (Japan)	DRAM, SRAM, EEPROM, etc.	C
Dec. 1992	Toshiba (Japan)	Development of flash memory chips	
Jan. 1993	General Instrument (U.S.)	Broad-band agreement of HDTV chips	
Apr. 1993	Array (U.S.)	Development of digital signal programming chips	
Jul. 1993	Mitsubishi (Japan)	Standard setting for cashed DRAM	
Nov. 1993	Micron Technology (U.S.)	Development of synchronous DRAM, Windows RAM, triple-port RAM	
Dec. 1993	Toshiba (Japan)	Development of LCD-motivation integrated circuit	
May 1994	ARM (U.S.)	Development of microprocessing unit	
Sept. 1994	ISD (U.S.)	Development of voice signal process chips	
Jan. 1995	Toshiba (Japan)	Technical exchange for memory and nonmemory chips	
Feb. 1995	NEC (Japan)	Production of memory chips in Europe	
Apr. 1995	Fujitsu (Japan)	Technical exchange for TFT-LCD	
Apr. 1995	Toshiba (Japan)	Development of 64M flash memory	

Source: Young Rak Choi, *Dynamic Techno-Management Capability—The Case of Samsung Semiconductor Sector in Korea*, PhD dissertation, Roskilde University (Denmark), 1994, pp. 66–67 and *Korea Economic Weekly*, May 1, 1995.

Note: (A) Technological information, (B) technology service, (C) patent licensing, (D) trademark use and (E) other agreements.

bilities grew, those foreign firms that earlier refused to sell technologies to Samsung reversed their attitude and wanted to establish a cross-licensing agreement. Furthermore Samsung is planning to exploit its current strength in DRAM technology, to branch out into other areas such as TFT-LCD (Thin-Film-Transistor Liquid-Crystal Display), and multimedia complex (HDTV, mobile communication, video-on-demand, music, etc.).[14] Another wave of diversification can be expected with a consequent upgrading of Samsung's technology base.[15]

It should not be forgotten, however, that Samsung's internal R&D investment has gone hand in hand with foreign technology sourcing. Adaptation and imported technologies have required more investment in R&D assets, both physical and human. Likewise, more specialized R&D institutes are needed along with more scientists and engineers to staff them if the diversification plans are to be fulfilled.

Human Capital

Available evidence suggests that Samsung Electronics Company has experimented boldly with implementing an innovative policy for human capital accumulation. The policy package contains three components: (1) recruit the best minds, (2) design job contents that induce creativity with opportunities for self-improvement as well as career development, and (3) reward employees with pay, promotion, and pride (personal feeling of self-worth) according to performance. This sounds like common sense. But in fact these measures proved to be *iconoclastic* in that they broke the sanctity of company traditions. A few representative events of this sort are explained below.

Samsung has been the number-one choice among college and university students from 1988 to 1996, according to *Recruit Magazine's* annual polls. This probably reflects Samsung's policy of regarding human capital as the most important asset that a company has. The company has adopted a series of measures that allow the staff to develop their careers while they are employed with the company. Bright employees are annually selected and sent abroad to earn PhD degrees at the company's expense, a good way to establish company loyalty among employees and researchers. Some 200 young, unmarried employees are sent abroad every year for six months to one year to help them become more comfortable in international settings. Their assignment is to learn about a foreign culture and language. The latest policy change (1994) is the introduction of an 8-hour work day coupled with the construction of facilities where employees can take career development or cultural courses after work. Korea has been known worldwide for its long working hours (typically 12 hours per day for staff members of a company). With its new policy Samsung signaled a break in this work regime. In return Samsung demanded intensive, concentrated work from the staff members. These developments enhanced the reputation of the company, which in turn enabled Samsung Electronics to pick and choose the best college and university graduates available in the market (between one and two thousand a year).[16]

Similar audacity may be observed in recruiting U.S. trained PhD-level scientists and engineers. It was noted earlier that Samsung Electronics offered a "blank check" to the candidate who would lead the 65K DRAM and 4M DRAM development projects. This meant that the company was willing to pay any amount of remuneration asked and at the same time to purchase any R&D equipment, however expensive, that the candidate specified. This sort of behavior was unheard of in the history of Korean enterprise. In short, if Samsung wanted someone, it got him. This has become an ongoing policy. (See table 4.10 for the recruitment record of U.S. trained scientists and engineers during the 1980s.) The number of PhDs recruited from the United States reached 417 by 1992, compared with 482, the total number of PhDs in all of Samsung's R&D establishments in 1995 (see table 4.6). In other words, U.S. trained PhDs have come to dominate. More than half have been assigned to help realize the company's R&D agenda.

Top-notch human capital resources, so recruited, are trained and "indoctrinated" into the company culture. Samsung has developed an elaborate program of in-house education for all levels of employees. The program includes a specially designed curriculum for first-time

Table 4.10
Record of recruited scientists and engineers from abroad by Samsung

Year	PhDs	MAs	Total
1987	84	76	160
1988	33	54	87
1989	61	57	118
1990	82	57	139
1991	77	60	137
1992	80	54	134
Total	417	358	775

Source: Yong Wook Jun and Jung Hwa Han, *Road to Super Enterprise; Growth and Transformation of Samsung* (in Korean), Seoul, Kimyongsa, 1994, p. 245.

employees, for middle managers promoted to a higher level, and for the highest-level executives. Group training can stretch for weeks or months in dormitory-style living arrangements. Three elements are emphasized in the curriculum, namely (1) unqualified loyalty and dedication to the company and assimilation into the Samsung-specific culture, (2) professional knowledge and expertise, and (3) creation of a network among Samsung group employees. It has been said that the discipline demanded in a training program resembles that at a military academy and that the Samsung program has been acclaimed as being superb and is therefore often emulated by other companies.[17] The following episode illustrates the "resourcefulness" of Samsung's training program. Some 200 employees, who were selected to staff the first fabricating plant, had to hike 64 kilometers as a group, symbolizing the 64K DRAM. Not one person dropped out. This symbolic act was combined with a series of lectures about how chip making, if successful, could make Korea economically strong due to the semiconductor's strategic value. Therefore it was an act of patriotism and a mission to learn the new business as fast as possible at all levels of the organization. The first training period took three months. Those who participated testify that the event aroused a feeling of oneness with other members, a sense of mission and pride in being selected, and a willingness to do one's utmost, even to obey orders from above unconditionally. In addition to courses in technical skills, Samsung's training program devises culture-based schemes (ceremonies, events, rituals, etc.) if they help evoke *boram*, that is, a feeling of self-worth in achieving something new or contributing to the company and to the country.[18] (To a Westerner, such rituals may seem stultifying.)

Samsung employees have also been motivated by the new incentive measures regarding take-home pay and other remuneration based on performance, particularly inventiveness. If an employee obtains an A grade (on a scale from A to E) in an annual performance evaluation, he is rewarded with a two-month salary bonus. If the team to which he belongs obtains an A, another two-month salary is added. And, if his company gets an A among all the group's member companies, an additional one-half month salary is added. Thus the maximum performance premium could run up to 4.5 months salary, not a small sum. Furthermore employees at Samsung collectively own about 20 percent of the company stock. This has a profound effect on the employees' motivation. In addition, if an employee wants to pursue an idea with other employees, an experimental group may be formed that might lead to a further profitable project or business. These reward schemes represent a departure from the conventional seniority system in which the length of service largely determines rewards rather than performance.

Organization and Strategies

Samsung's venture into the semiconductor business represents an excellent case of how the organizational structure of *chaebols* may be exploited for rapid learning. These structures include a highly regimented hierarchy with a dedicated and intelligent workforce. Absolute power resides at the top, resulting in speed and flexibility in redeployment of managerial resources (money and human beings) and deep pockets (financial power). In the case of Samsung Electronics Co., the founder-owner of Samsung Group (Byung Chul Lee) was fascinated with semiconductors already in the early 1970s. This provides a rare case of farsighted entrepreneurship in Korean business history.

It took one full year of feasibility studies carried out by a 26-specialist task force to come up with the strategy of technology learning. The best engineers and researchers were recruited from the member companies at the order of the group chairman. The task force produced an in-depth study and a carefully designed "road map" to reach the target (vision): (1) a total investment in plant and equipment of 440 billion won (approximately U.S.$580 million) plus R&D spending of 100 billion won (about U.S.$133 million) between 1983 and 1988, (2) an output target for memory chips and microprocessors of U.S.$200 million per annum to reach a global market share of 2 percent and 4.5 percent, respectively; and (3) as noted earlier, the establishment of a U.S. R&D center to assist and complement R&D activities in Korea, manpower training, recruitment of top-class engineers, and collection of market information and technology trends. It is significant that a contingent from the feasibility study group was dispatched to the United States for a month to check their provisional "road map" with the Korean-American scientists and engineers. Significant revisions followed regarding the timetable for reaching 1 Mega level (submicron) technology, a technology that was little understood by the Korean engineers at the time.

The years from 1983 to 1988 turned out to be difficult ones for Samsung because of the recession in the chip market and their commitment to huge, unprecedented investment. The price of memory chips plummeted to 20 cents in 1985 from $2.50 per unit. Many feared the downfall of the company. But persistent support came from top management, thanks to the built-in arrangement for a group-level sharing of risks inherent in the *chaebol* form of organization. The *chaebol* also had easy access to bank loans because of their sheer size and collateral power in addition to the government policy favoring big exporters. It is worth recalling that a number of U.S. chip-making firms went out of business during the chip-market recession due to their limited financial ability to ride out the cycle. Japanese chip-makers belonging to conglomerates (*zaibatsu*), in contrast, were able to maintain their business thanks to their financial position.

The concentrated power at the top of the Samsung Group and its highly regimented hierarchy is often credited for its ability to reach quick decisions and implement policies quickly. Thus, for example, it decided to speed up plant construction, and a plant was completed within a six-month period by the Samsung construction company. This is in marked contrast to the normal construction period of 18 months. The method used was to build continuously 24 hours a day without weekends or holidays off. The obsession with catching up with industrial countries in chip making within the shortest possible time led to a number of organizational experiments.

A notable example is the method of chronologically overlapping R&D activities for the next generation of chips: "The basic structure of this approach is as follows: one team is at the stage of defining concepts of technology and architecture, another team is at the stage of developing process technology, and the remaining one (the third team) is at the stage of improving production know-how."[19] (See table 4.11 presenting examples of "concurrent R&D" in Samsung's chip-making company in concert with its R&D outpost company in the United States.) The research outpost usually developed more advanced (high-value-adding) technologies for the purpose of transferring them to the parent company in Korea. Occasionally, as it happened, two different promising technological paths were undertaken simultaneously at two sites if it was not clear which would be chosen ultimately. Also, though only once, the two places competed on a same project.

Another example is the skillful deployment of a high-powered task force team (TFT). For each generation of chips, a TFT was formed with a set of top-notch engineers as leaders who had been educated at leading U.S. universities and also had prior experience in semiconductor R&D in leading U.S. companies. The latter qualification proved to be the decisive factor determining success and speed. The team was given the target and complete autonomy on spending, even to transport all the equipment by air to speed up R&D. However, the equipment

Table 4.11
Examples of concurrent R&D and plant construction in Samsung

Type of chip	R&D site or plant construction	Launching of		Working good die		Mass production
		R&D	Construction	R&D	Construction	
64K	Korea parent company	1983.5		1983.11		1984.9
	U.S. branch outpost					
	Plant construction		1983.9 (S)		1984.5 (F)	
256K	Korea parent company	1984.3		1984.1		1986.4
	U.S. branch outpost	1983.9		1985.7		
	Plant construction		1984.8 (S)		1985.5 (F)	
1M	Korea parent company	1985.9		1986.7		1987.11
	U.S. branch outpost	1985.5		1986.11		1989.11
	Plant construction		1987.8 (S)		1989.2 (F)	
4M	Korea parent company	1986.1		1988.2		
	U.S. branch outpost	1987.4		1988.6		
	Plant construction		1988.1 (S)		1989.11 (F)	

Source: Young Rak Choi (1994, p. 136).
Note: S: start of construction preparing for mass production; F: finish of construction.
Working good die: the stage of the semiconductor design process at which the "yield" ratio can be improved through a series of experiments in die designing.

purchased had to meet the criterion that the machines should embody the most advanced cutting-edge technology available in the market. The rationale was to learn the top technology in order to reach the top of the technology ladder in chip making in the shortest possible time.

A truly notable organizational change can be observed in the integration of R&D teams on the factory floor. Traditionally an R&D team was regarded as a group of researchers with PhDs and MS degrees, which are higher qualifications than production-line workers. Thus they were housed in separate offices and laboratories.[20] But having seen the necessity of close communication and constant information sharing between R&D personnel and line-workers, Samsung put the R&D teams under the production manager and on the same factory floor. This represented a reversal of the traditional hierarchical mentality which went completely counter to the principle of *chaebol* organization.

Still another example of organizational innovation was the creation of a technology-management team. The team collects information on technology trends, possible cooperative ventures, and alliance partners. Also, by constructing patent maps, the team attempts to forecast the future technology market in which Samsung is expected to compete as well as to figure out Samsung's priorities more systematically. Available evidence suggests that Samsung has been amassing the largest number of intellectual properties of all the *chaebol* groups in Korea. (See

Table 4.12
Industrial property rights by *chaebol* groups in 1995 (unit: thousand won)

Company	Patent right	Design right	Trademark right	Utility model patent	Total
Samsung Group					
Cheil Wool			861,867		891,867
Samsung Micro Chemical			2,089		2,089
Samsung Electronics	29,333,927	388,838	473,907	1,471,425	31,668,097
Samsung Aerospace	629			233	862
Samsung Display Devices	1,458,236				1,458,236
Samsung Electricity	218,942	309,023		416,441	944,406
Samsung Heavy Industry	63,701	4,216	87,374	27,266	182,567
Samsung Co.	88,596	4,175	798,108	5,909	896,788
Hotel Shilla		130	27,603		27,733
Hyundai Group					
Hyundai Motor Co.			1,144,635		1,144,635
Hyundai Micro Industry	3,698	1,047	10,988		16,109
Hyundai Motor Service		107,654		376	107,654
Kumkang Development		76,485			76,485
Daewoo Group					
Daewoo Heavy Industry	168,196	23,551	78,670	175,512	445,929
Daewoo Electronics	49,198	269,409	71,180	163,878	553,665
Orion Electricity			9,438		9,438
Daewoo Communication			301,261	31,527	332,788
Daewoo Co.					258,266
L-G Group					
L-G Chemical	40,493		105,006		145,499
L-G Industrial Electricity	45,971	15,974	4,755	74,756	141,456
L-G Electronics	44,173	1,563	169,399		215,135
L-G Machinery Electricity	19,300	9,313	6,475	38,642	73,730
L-G Instruments & Electric	35,813	2,304	3,662	35,074	76,853
L-G Co.	3,806	1,857	177,197	489	183,349
Kia Group					
Kia Motor Co.	294,779		291,381		586,160
Asia Motor Co.	127,029				127,029
Kia Motor Service		105,929			105,929
Ssangyong Group					
Ssangyong Paper		40,196		522	40,715
Ssangyong Heavy Industry	841	220	5,356	287	6,704
Ssangyong Motor Co.	9,734	59,176	210,134	21,071	300,115
Ssangyong Cement	3,644		98,991		102,605
Ssangyong Co.			59,762		59,762
Sunkyung Group					
Sunkyung Industry			655,540		655,540
Sunkyung Co.	691	569	302,343		303,603
Hanhwa Group					
Hanhwa Chemical	96,060	174,967	347,461		608,488
Hanhwa Co.	30,933	828	247,351	6,047	285,519
Hanhwa Machine	56	12	3,042	562	3,672
Lotte Group					
Lotte Samkang			118,249		118,249
Lotte Confectionery			421,127		421,127
Lotte Chilsung	292		138,383		141,771
Honam Oil and Chemical	19,335		5,602	2,641	24,937

Source: Korea Industrial Technology Association, *White Paper on Industrial Technology 1995* (in Korean), p. 184.

table 4.12 showing the "book values" of intellectual properties owned by the ten *chaebol* groups in the order of intellectual property ownership size.) The team is in charge of managing this asset portfolio, the first organizational device of its kind in the country. To wit, the team has the power to develop strategies for the technological advancement of Samsung, including decisions to make or buy technology from others.

To summarize, Samsung has become an innovative, growing organization. Ingenious institutional (organizational) devices have been continually designed and redesigned in order to facilitate rapid absorption of imported technologies. Concurrent engineering, time-oriented management, team-based management, and the like, which appear in the management literature in recent years, all seem to have parallels at Samsung.[21] Samsung's ability to organize and re-organize itself flexibly has given it immeasurable strength. A look at the history of the company gives some sense of its ability to furnish "institutional assets." The intellectual caliber of human resources that Samsung has been recruiting seems to have much to do with this.[22]

However, Samsung's quick success also demonstrates a structural weakness, the other side of the coin. The single-target approach aiming at DRAM chips enabled Samsung to focus limited resources effectively to win the game. But the DRAM market is well known for its volatility and high risk, owing to a short product life cycle, huge investment requirements for equipment, and fierce competition. Samsung now faces the need to diversify its chip-making business into ASIC and other software which require much higher design (as well as production and marketing) capabilities than the company now has. Mass-production technology, which gave Samsung an advantage in the past, may be of little help in mastering ASIC technology and other software requiring flexible manufacturing technology for small-lot production. This represents yet another challenge for Samsung to overcome. How their top-down decision making will affect their ability to shift paradigms is an open question.[23]

4.4   Strategic Cooperation among *Chaebols* and SMEs

The phenomenal rise of the *chaebols* since the 1960s has overshadowed the performance of SMEs. Despite the relative neglect of the latter sector by Korean economic policy makers during the past three decades, SMEs have achieved a respectable record of output expansion, employment creation, exports, and labor productivity growth.[24] This is particularly striking when Korean SMEs are compared with their counterparts in other developing countries (except perhaps in Taiwan). See table 4.13 for job creation and labor productivity of SMEs. Note that the number of workers employed by large enterprises (with 300 workers or more) grew from 618,376 in 1973 to 956,756 in 1992, an increase of 55 percent. Employment in smaller firms jumped higher by several folds during the same period, for example, 5.4 times for firms with 20 to 49 workers. This employment growth is associated with the creation of new firms, which has mostly been in the SME sector rather than in large enterprises. Furthermore growth in labor productivity was on average about 10 percent per year for the SMEs and approximately 12.3 percent for the large firms (for the 1973–1984 period for which an SME-specific wholesale price index is available).

A steady 10 percent annual growth in labor productivity (in constant price) over a period of a decade represents outstanding performance, particularly when it is compared to growth rates of SMEs' productivity in other countries. The record has only been overshadowed by an even better performance by the *chaebols*. Nevertheless, over time, this growth-rate differential between the SMEs and *chaebols* could result

Table 4.13
Labor productivity in manufacturing by firm size in 1973 and 1992 (unit: in constant 1985 won)

Firm size	Employment	Value added per employment	Labor productivity comparison
1973			
5–19	140,535	1,316,143	0.375
20–49	96,043	1,560,557	0.444
50–99	97,442	2,282,736	0.650
100–199	122,838	2,745,334	0.781
200–299	82,595	2,730,637	0.777
300+	618,376	3,514,477	1.000
1992			
5–19	470,391	14,972,053	0.322
20–49	521,764	18,594,310	0.400
50–99	361,498	22,980,641	0.486
100–199	311,794	29,423,948	0.633
200–299	179,186	32,525,743	0.716
300+	956,756	46,444,581	1.000

Source: Economic Planning Board, *Report on Mining and Manufacturing Survey*, 1973 and 1992.

in an increasing productivity gap between the two sectors because of technology-learning-productivity factors.

It is well known that SMEs have been suffering from difficulties in accumulating finance, human, and knowledge capital. The main reason for this lies in government policies favoring large enterprises over small.[25] Even though "policy loans" favoring large enterprises practically disappeared by February 1988, the SMEs still find themselves at a disadvantage in seeking access to loans. Banks would prefer to lend money to the possessors of substantial collateral, such as land, something that large enterprises are more apt to have. The primitive capital market has not been of much help. For operational cash, SMEs often had to borrow at high-interest rates (often 30 to 40 percent) in the curb (informal) market. Thus SMEs normally could ill afford to have expensive R&D equipment and risky long-range projects. Moreover they could scarcely compete with large enterprises in hiring expensive, high-caliber engineers and researchers.

Furthermore it has frequently been reported that large firms lure away well-trained workers, researchers, and engineers by offering attractive salary packages and positions. Evidence indeed shows that the turnover rate of employees tends to be higher for SMEs than for large enterprises. (See table 4.14.) This discourages SMEs from training their

Table 4.14
Monthly turnover rate of employees by size of enterprise, 1977–1990

Year	10–19	20–99	100 299	300–499	Over 500
1977	6.9	7.5	6.5	6.5	4.2
1978	7.8	8.1	6.8	6.8	5.3
1979	6.6	8.3	7.3	7.3	6.0
1980	7.2	7.9	7.2	6.3	4.9
1981	6.9	7.7	7.3	6.0	4.9
1982	6.3	7.0	7.2	5.7	4.5
1983	6.0	6.9	7.0	6.3	4.7
1984	7.5	7.3	7.6	6.2	4.6
1985	6.6	6.5	6.3	4.9	3.8
1986	6.0	6.1	5.6	4.6	3.6
1987	7.2	6.0	5.6	4.5	3.7
1988	7.6	7.6	6.5	4.4	3.0
1989	6.5	6.5	5.0	3.7	2.7
1990	6.8	6.3	5.1	3.8	2.7

Source: STEPI, Sun Koon Kim et al. *R&D and Technical Manpower of Technology Intensive SMEs* (in Korean), Seoul, STEPI (Policy Research Series 94–22), 1994, p. 106.

own employees, in contrast to the case of large enterprises or *chaebols* where long-term employment is more the rule. A weak human-capital base probably also leads to a limited ability to manage technological information and transactions. Thus SMEs are slower to learn new technology and in a weaker position to compete in the product market with large-scale enterprises.

These technological disadvantages notwithstanding, SMEs competed fiercely for survival with little assistance from the government until very recently. Only those that could adapt to these disadvantages and find a niche survived; without a government safety net (in contrast to India)[26] the others disappeared from the market. (See table 4.15 for figures on the founding and closing of SMEs during the 1991–94 period.) In 1994, for instance, 16,723 new SMEs entered the market, while 11,255 were declared insolvent. On average, 1,394 new firms were created monthly and 938 firms went out of business, leaving a net gain of 456 firms per month.

Market competition among SMEs in this harsh business environment tends to favor only the strong performers. Available evidence suggests also that the SMEs that survive are mostly suppliers of parts or intermediate inputs to large-scale assembly firms. The rapid increase in out-sourcing by the *chaebols* (buying parts from external sources for automobiles, television sets, computers, printers, etc.) appears to have created ever-increasing opportunities for new entrants, particularly since the early 1980s. (See table 4.16 which presents statistics on the

Table 4.15
Growth indicators of SMEs, 1991–1994

Indicator	1991	1992	1993	1994
Growth rate of production	7.4	5.7	2.6	12.2
Growth rate of export	4.8	6.9	14.6	15.7
Growth rate of investment	24.1	5.4	9.6	20.1
Number of new establishments[a]	12,249	13,792	11,938	16,723
Per month	1,021	1,141	995	1,394
Number of bankruptcies	6,159	10,769	9,502	11,255
Corporate	2,013	3,714	3,402	4,503
Noncorporate	4,146	7,055	6,100	6,752
Per month	513	897	792	938
Bankruptcy rate	0.06	0.12	0.13	0.17

Source: MOTIE.
a. In the largest seven cities.

Table 4.16
Number of SMEs and their distribution by proportion of long-term contract sales to assembly firms

Year	Number of firms	Total SMEs[a]	<5%	5%–10%	10%–15%	15%–20%	20%–40%	40%–60%	60%–80%	>80%
1980	9,224	30,668 (30.1)	2	1.8	1.2	1.1	6.7	9.3	7.2	70.7
1981	11,234	32,379 (34.7)	3.5	1.6	1.3	0.9	8.5	9	8.2	67
1982	12,149	35,798 (33.9)	1.1	0.6	1.1	1.3	6.9	9	6.5	73.5
1983	13,57_	35,798 (37.9)	1.6	0.6	1.3	0.7	5.3	4.8	8.1	77.6
1984	15,840	38,084 (41.6)	1.4	0.9	0.7	1.3	4.8	5.4	7.2	78.3
1985	17,020	40,480 (42.0)	1.3	1.1	1	1	4.1	5.1	4.9	81.5
1986	18,183	42,941 (42.8)	1.3	0.8	1.2	0.7	5.4	5.4	6.1	79.1
1987	23,512	48,876 (48.1)	1.2	0.3		0.9	4.5	4	5.1	83
1988	29,220	53,089 (55.0)	1.2	0.6	1.1		3.5	50.7	2.8	40.9
1989	38,929	58,496 (66.5)	0.8	0.4	0.5	0.5	1.5	3.6	4.5	88.2
1990	45,120	64,365 (70.1)	0.4	0.2	0.6	0.5	2.4	3.5	4.8	87.6
1991	49,806	67,649 (73.6)	0.9	0.1	0.4	0.2	1.6	3	5.4	88.4

Source: National SME Cooperative Federation, *Report on the Activities of SMEs* (in Korean), 1992.
a. Numbers in parentheses give the proportion of small-medium enterprises dependent on supplying parts to large assembler companies.

dramatic increase in SME subcontracting to assembly firms.) The number of subcontracting firms increased more than fivefold from 9,224 in 1980 to 49,806 in 1991 (or from 30.1 to 73.6 percent of the total number of SMEs for the respective years). Moreover SMEs selling 80 percent or more of their output to "mother companies" on a long-term contract (dependency) basis increased from 70.7 percent in 1980 to 88.4 percent in 1991.

The SME-large assembler relationship is increasingly organized along the *keyol-hwa* model, analogous to the Japanese *keiretsu* system. Under this system, a semipermanent relationship is established between the part suppliers (SMEs) and the assemblers (large enterprises) in order to share in the fruits of cooperation. The "design-in" approach is an example of such cooperation. Engineers from SMEs and assemblers cooperate in R&D to produce more efficient parts or to cut costs (or both). The resulting rents are then shared between them so as to create a synergy effect.[27]

The government "localization program" also seems to have helped spawn new SMEs in the subcontract businesses. (The next chapter gives more details on the incentive content of the localization program and how it works to accelerate the process of upgrading technological capabilities.) Here it suffices to note that the ability to learn new technologies quickly proved to be key to survival. This sort of entry into the market by new SMEs has provided a dynamic element of growth. The proliferation of SMEs seems likely to continue well into the next century, especially because of the networking that digital information-communication technology makes possible.

Two more recent developments promise to help improve SMEs' technological capabilities, one on the part of the government and the other by the *chaebols*. The government passed a law in 1996 that established an SME Agency to consolidate services for SMEs, which had been scattered among a multitude of ministries. The agency is charged with reducing restrictive regulations, information costs, risks, and uncertainties facing SMEs and, in particular, to assist SMEs in undertaking technological innovation. For example, if an SME wishes to introduce automation into a factory, consultation services (at a nominal fee) are available. These include information on how system-development engineering could be approached; what sorts of machines are available, where, and at what price; and what low-interest financial assistance might be available, and so on. Such consultation can lead to the agency certifying an SME, which in turn may be used as a form of "surrogate collateral" for borrowing development funds from the banking system. The technology-based loan guarantee could also be extended to viable SMEs that suffer from temporary cash flow problems.

A young aspirant entering a fledgling industry (e.g., computer peripherals) could also receive assistance from the agency. Agency experts may provide him with free (or nominal cost) services for marketing surveys, available technologies, production engineering, management training, access to low-cost financing (e.g., subsidized loans for a promising venture with externalities), and so on. In short, the aim is to reduce or even to eliminate constraints (or market imperfections and failures) of various kinds facing the young entrepreneur. This approach is intended to help SMEs to learn new technology and thereby to increase their competitiveness. Normally in an industrial country, a well-developed banking system or venture-capital company shares risks and uncertainties in return for a share in potential profits. But in Korea, technology-based innovation is something new, and bankers know little about it. Therefore, until experience accumulates, the SME Agency can be expected to continue to play a mediating role between new industrialists taking risks and the "rudimentary" financial system. The SME Agency could serve as a *"learning device"* until an efficient venture-capital market emerges in some later period after sufficient experience.

In the private-enterprise sector there has also emerged in recent years a corresponding movement to help SMEs. This movement reflects the realization that the technological capabilities of SMEs are important in determining the international competitiveness of large-scale enterprises because the latter buy input materials from SMEs. Furthermore, when SMEs improve the quality of their output to meet international standards, the needs of large-scale assemblers to import their inputs (parts and machines) from Japan declines. This helps to reduce the chronic deficit in Korea's balance of trade with Japan.

This increasing awareness led to a number of meetings in early 1996 between the Korean Federation of Industries (representing *chaebols*) and the Central Association of Small and Medium Industries. The meeting produced a set of agreements regarding cooperation measures between the two groups which aimed to improve SMEs' technological and managerial capabilities. The financial crisis of 1997–98 may force *chaebols* to shelve the agreements temporarily. Nevertheless, it is useful to summarize them because the agreements lay precedents for future approaches. In other words, they bear historical significance, and in the long run, the same issues are likely to re-emerge. Some of the main points were as follows:

1. Joint R&D teams should be formed to improve the quality of SME output.

2. The free lease of R&D equipment offered to SMEs by *chaebols* should be regarded as a "profit loss" for tax purposes.

3. The current limit of not more than 10 percent ownership of a SME company stocks by a *chaebol* (a Korean Antitrust provision) should be raised up to 25 percent as an exception when *chaebols* help SMEs.

4. A tax-deferred reserve fund should be allowed when *chaebols* help SMEs to "localize" capital goods (i.e., replace imports).

5. *Chaebols* should pay cash to SMEs rather than issuing IOUs for transactions of part supplies in order to solve the cash flow problems of SMEs.

Subsequently the government has accepted all of these provisions as recommended in the meetings.

Furthermore each *chaebol* individually has taken initiative to formulate its own program to help SMEs in a special way. Just to illustrate, take Samsung's program for the next few years. Samsung will dispatch 500 seasoned technicians to SMEs (which do business with Samsung) for training. Ten percent of Samsung's total R&D budget will be devoted to assist SMEs' R&D projects. Samsung will provide free services for training 10,000 managers from SMEs and also for consulting. Samsung will assist the establishment of SME mutual funds with a contribution of 10 billion won, and so on.

Hyundai provides another example of such initiative. The group will invite SMEs workers to be trained for quality control. Hyundai will transfer some of its business lines to SMEs especially (automobile) parts production. Hyundai will assist SMEs for "localization" of parts production (read import substitution) through joint development of brand-name and preferential purchase arrangements. Hyundai will provide free services for training managers in security and environmental control. Hyundai will share information with SMEs on overseas marketing as well as on CALS (computer-aided acquisition and logistics system) operation. Hyundai will participate in establishing venture-capital funds, and the like.

It is amusing to note that the 30 largest *chaebol* groups announced their individual plans as though they were in a pledging competition. In doing so, the *chaebols* participated in formulating a national consensus. The problem of raising technological capabilities of SMEs has become a national issue, since it concerns the survival of Korean industries in the face of global competition. But the pledges are not legally binding. Furthermore the emergence of the 1997–98 financial crisis has temporarily put off *chaebols'* activities that assist SMEs. It remains to be seen how effectively they will be implemented in the long run. Nevertheless, it is encouraging that the national awareness for cooperation between *chaebols* and SMEs has never been more positive.

An even more encouraging phenomenon is the cooperative movement among SMEs themselves. SMEs are beginning to find advantages in collaborating to solve impending problems by forming associations for joint R&D activities, joint procurements of input materials, joint marketing activities, and so on. The number of such associations have been increasing rapidly, namely 581 associations in 1993 grew to 669 associations in 1996 (August) with the number of member companies totaling 53,781. About half of the associations represent regional companies located away from the concentrated regions like the Seoul-Kyunggi area.

What is most desirable appears to be the formation of a triple alliance (or consortium) between these regional SME associations, regional universities, and regional governments. Pooling the resources that each partner may have in part could create synergy effects; the brainpower of regional universities, coupled with the infrastructure that the regional governments can provide, could reinforce the SMEs' efforts to modernize. To give one example, university labs may be crucial in applying digital technology to the SMEs' production processes. Such cooperation will address the traditionally weak position of SMEs in hiring high-powered engineers who prefer employment in *chaebols.* Furthermore the local government could ameliorate the lack of venture capital supporting SMEs by establishing a special earmarked fund for SMEs. However, such region-specific, tripartite cooperation has yet to be created.

5

National R&D Program
and Government as
Catalyst and Institution
Designer

5.1 Industrialization Policies and Technology Upgrading

South Korea has gone through seven Five-Year Economic Development Plans since 1962. One of the major themes common to all the plans was the need to upgrade technology and the industrial structure in order to improve international competitiveness. Each plan period envisaged a set of priority manufacturing sectors and projects. For instance, during the 1970s development plans targeted iron and steel, cement, fertilizer, chemicals, and machines as priority sectors. Table 5.1 gives an overview of the shifting emphasis and priority since the 1960s.

The record of plan implementation shows that the targets were usually fulfilled or far exceeded in terms of industrial output, export and investment.[1] These achievements have usually been attributed to strategies that promote export. However, as this chapter will show, technology-learning and domestic activities designed to replace imports have also played an important role in upgrading Korea's industrial structure and promoting productivity gains.

Various strategies were employed in the restructuring of industry. Export-promotion, technology-learning, and selective import-substitution policies must all be understood within this larger framework. The shift to an export-oriented policy in the mid-1960s did not mean the discarding of import substitution. Indeed the latter went on along with the export-led strategy. Export expansion and import substitution were not contradictory activities but complemented each other. The expansion of export production required a corresponding increase in demand for imported intermediate inputs, parts and machines. Policy makers and industrialists were quick to notice the opportunities for local production of these export-related imports. But exploiting

Table 5.1
Direction of industrial development and technology strategies

	1960s	1970s	1980s	1990s
Direction of development	Consolidation of industrial base	Industrial restructuring toward heavy chemical industries	Adjustment and upgrading industrial structure	Realization of advanced industrial society
	Selected import substitution			
	Expansion of social overhead capital	Expansion of social overhead capital	Development of system for technology-capability building	To join group of advanced nations in technology
Technology strategies	Established basis for promotion of science and technology	Expansion of S&T education	Nurturing brainpower for high-level S&T development	Continual supply of high brain-power
	Import of advanced technology and technological training	Improvement of imported technologies	Improved application of imported technology	R&D for next-generation technology projects and development of high technology
			Core technology development	
Leading industry sectors	Textile, plywood, cement, fertilizers, electricity, oil refining	Steel (specialty steel), petrochemicals, shipbuilding, construction, shoes, chemical fiber, electronics	Electronics parts, computers, semiconductors, general machines, automobiles	Information industry, advanced materials, bioengineering, systems engineering

Source: Korea Industrial Technology Association, *Industrial Technology White Paper 1986* (in Korean), p. 213.

these opportunities required learning and mastering new technologies (newly imported into Korea). The fast pace at which Korea learned to improve the quality of new products and reduce unit cost enabled industries to add new products to their ever-expanding export lines. The rapid growth in exports brought with it a rapid increase in new companies and new jobs in the economy through the export multiplier effect. This process has gone on continuously during the past three decades and is expected to continue well into the next century.

The policy issues regarding export promotion and import substitution are well documented in the literature, not so the process of technological learning. Learning is not a free good. Learning by doing, by imitation, or by apprenticeship requires substantial investments of money, time, experience, and organizational ingenuity. Earlier chapters have presented evidence (e.g., TFP) stressing learning as the prime engine of growth in Korea. Without rapid learning, export-led growth could easily have ground to a halt because of the heavy competition based on cheap labor in Southeast Asian countries and China. In addition developed countries protect their markets by quotas and other means. How protection is related to learning will be argued below with supporting evidence.

The most serious impetus for a wholesale import-substitution project came in the early 1970s, when rapid export growth brought about chronic trade-deficit problems, especially with Japan. Technological ties with Japan meant that the soaring production of exports required ever-increasing imports of Japanese machinery, intermediate inputs, and parts. At the same time the major markets for Korean exports lay elsewhere, namely in the United States, Southeast Asia, and Europe.

Policy makers decided to correct the trade imbalance in part by fostering production at home to replace imports from Japan and elsewhere. Apparently they realized that a general devaluation of the won alone would not correct the trade imbalance with Japan. Furthermore, orientation toward a new product group provided the opportunity to "deepen the industrial base." In 1973 a "Heavy and Chemical Industry Development Plan" was announced to guide the expansion of heavy industrial sectors for the period 1973 to 1981. A series of projects were formulated in priority sectors, including iron and steel, nonferrous metals, petrochemicals, fertilizer, machinery, electronics, and shipbuilding. These sectors represent Hirschman's "backward-linkage import substitution" to support labor-intensive export sectors in Korea (except shipbuilding). The uninterrupted supply of these products from domestic sources, which were subject to less market volatility than overseas sources, was thought to be crucial for continued export-led growth.

Thus by upgrading the industrial base to include heavy-capital and skill-intensive industries, Korea was able to solve several problems simultaneously: (1) the erosion of comparative advantage in labor-intensive goods due to competition from other developing countries, (2) rapidly rising wages in Korea, and (3) the threat to Korea's future export prospects due to protectionism in industrialized countries. Another imperative was to nurture defense industries for obvious geopolitical reasons (North Korea). Structural change via technological upgrading has been an ongoing process largely pushed by these economic and noneconomic conditions.

In the 1980s import substitution shifted from the "heavy and chemical" sector to "engineering industries." The "engineering industry" is defined as assembly-type manufacturing plus parts production (SITC 381, 382, 282, 284, and 385). It produces capital goods or durable consumer goods (automobiles, color TV sets, home appliances, VTRs, industrial machines, etc.). This shift was necessitated by a deteriorating trade balance.

As in the case of basic industrial materials in earlier periods (e.g., iron and steel, nonferrous metals, petrochemicals, etc.), Korea's trade balance with Japan deteriorated even further during the late 1970s and early 1980s. This was largely due to a heavy dependence on Japanese components and parts for assembly manufacturing. The government initiated programs for "localization" of parts and component production, another wave of backward linkages, à la Hirschman, providing yet another set of opportunities for mastering new technologies.

Table 5.2 provides value-added percentages per ISIC three-digit classification for South Korean manufacturing between 1970 and 1990. The difference between these two years shows relative sectoral advances and lags in value-added structure. A striking fact is that the engineering-intensive sectors gained at the expense of traditional sectors (food, textiles, etc.). The leading sectors include electrical machinery (+11.2 percentage points), transport equipment (+4.0 percentage points), metal products excluding machinery (+2.1 percentage points), iron and steel (+2.1 percentage points), and so on.

A similar pattern of structural changes can be observed also in employment; see table 5.3. The engineering and heavy industry categories gained relatively more employment than other sectors. For instance,

Table 5.2
Sectoral shares of manufacturing output in 1970 and 1990

Sector	1970	Percentage	1990	Percentage	Percentage change, 1970–90
Food	442	8.6	3,200	6.0	−2.6
Beverages	417	8.1	1,010	1.9	−6.2
Tobacco	467	9.1	1,938	3.7	−5.4
Textiles	715	13.9	4,988	9.4	−4.5
Apparel	142	2.8	2,280	4.3	+4.5
Leather	10	0.2	602	1.1	+0.9
Footwear	15	0.3	349	0.7	+0.4
Wood products	165	3.2	347	0.7	−2.5
Furniture	19	0.4	346	0.7	+0.3
Paper products	119	2.3	1,281	2.4	+0.3
Printing	142	2.8	1,201	2.3	−0.5
Industrial chemicals	307	6.0	1,927	3.6	−2.4
Other chemicals	248	4.8	2,542	4.8	0.0
Petroleum refining	366	7.1	1,405	2.6	−4.5
Petroleum and coal products	68	1.3	363	0.7	−0.6
Rubber products	101	2.0	1,638	3.1	+1.1
Plastic products	48	0.9	1,354	2.6	+1.7
Pottery, china	12	0.2	191	0.4	+0.2
Glass products	53	1.0	476	0.9	0.1
Nonmetal minerals	243	4.7	1,687	3.2	−1.5
Iron and steel	181	3.5	2,996	5.6	+2.1
Nonferrous metal	26	0.5	631	1.2	+0.7
Metal fabricated	121	2.3	2,358	4.4	+2.1
Nonelectric machines	91	1.8	3,161	6.0	+4.2
Electric machines	205	4.0	8,088	15.2	+11.2
Transportation equipment	260	5.0	4,793	9.0	+4.0
Professional goods	20	0.4	598	1.1	+0.7
Other manufacturing	149	2.9	1,344	2.5	−0.4
Total	5,152	100.0	53,093	100.0	

Source: UNIDO database.
Note: 1985 million U.S. dollars, value added.

Table 5.3
Sectoral distribution of manufacturing employment in 1970 and 1990 (unit: thousand employees)

Sector	1970	Percentage	1990	Percentage	Percentage change, 1970–90
Food	71.5	8.6	202.0	6.2	−2.4
Beverages	28.3	3.4	32.0	1.0	−2.4
Tobacco	11.0	1.3	10.6	0.3	−1.0
Textiles	203.9	24.7	410.2	12.6	−12.1
Apparel	48.7	5.9	301.6	9.3	+3.4
Leather	3.3	0.4	49.6	1.5	+1.1
Footwear	4.1	0.5	40.3	1.2	+0.7
Wood	34.9	4.2	40.5	1.2	−3.0
Furniture	8.0	1.0	36.4	1.1	+0.1
Paper	18.4	2.2	68.2	2.1	−0.1
Publishing	28.9	3.5	72.0	2.2	−1.3
Industrial chemicals	23.2	2.8	43.7	1.3	−1.5
Other chemicals	25.8	3.1	81.7	2.5	−0.6
Petroleum refining	3.2	0.4	4.8	0.1	−0.3
Petroleum and coal	11.8	1.4	13.4	0.4	−1.0
Rubber	27.1	3.3	212.7	6.6	+3.3
Plastics	8.8	1.1	97.7	3.0	+1.9
Pottery	6.5	0.8	20.6	0.6	−0.2
Glass	8.7	1.1	23.7	0.7	−0.4
Nonmetal minerals	32.5	3.9	79.1	2.4	−1.5
Iron and steel	26.4	3.2	90.7	2.8	−0.4
Nonferrous metal	4.8	0.6	28.3	0.9	+0.3
Fabricated metal	33.7	4.1	172.6	5.3	+1.2
Machinery	25.4	3.1	184.9	5.7	+2.6
Electric machinery equipment	38.9	4.7	506.8	15.6	+10.9
Transport equipment	36.2	4.4	234.2	7.2	+2.8
Professional equipment	5.5	0.7	51.2	1.6	+0.9
Other	47.6	5.8	135.0	4.2	−1.6
Total	827.1	100.0	3,244.5	100.0	

Source: UNIDO database.

the electrical machinery sector increased its employment from 38,900 in 1970 (or 4.7 percent of the total) to 506,800 in 1990 (or 15.6 percent of the total). A large proportion of this increase was owed to the development of electronics industries such as semiconductor chip making. Likewise the transport equipment, general machinery (non-electrical), metal products, and professional equipment sectors gained also relatively more employment. This employment shift along with the record of productivity gains as noted earlier leads one to surmise that a substantial amount of "learning" must have taken place in terms of new skills required in these burgeoning sectors of manufacturing.

It can be argued that the rapid industrial progress achieved during the past three decades owes much to the roles played by the major actors, namely government, private enterprise, and educational institutions. But characteristically the government took the initiative in building research institutes and facilities for training scientists, engineers, and technicians; creating links between industries and universities; and so on. Furthermore the government offered incentives to entice private enterprises into taking technological risks This aspect of policymaking deserves special attention and analysis, particularly the question of how "government failures" were avoided.

Today, however, the South Korean economy seems to be at a crossroads as it faces the challenges of the next century. With the advent of the WTO, borderless competition, the digital revolution, and the information society, many past policy practices and perspectives must be discarded. A glaring example is the need for autonomy of the banking institutions, which have been serving as the control mechanism for resource allocation, according to national development plans.[2] Furthermore, the role of the government in science and technology development appears in need of redefinition in order to meet the challenge of preparing the economy to enter a high-technology era. Below, we examine the way in which professionalism entered into policy making in the past, that is, how think-tank systems as an institutional device were used to solve problems. This review paves the way for diagnosing the problems encountered by the National Research and Development Program and the Government Financed Research Institutes (GFRI). The latter had been the major providers of national R&D infrastructure and were responsible for the National Research and Development Program. However, the GFRI has been criticized lately for inefficiency and lack of direction. At the end of the chapter, a recommendation for organizational reform is offered in order to revitalize the GFRI as a next-generation infrastructure.

5.2   Think-Tank System and Professionalism in Policy Making

The industrialization policies reviewed briefly above were sometimes described in media as "targeting approach" or "picking the winners." This meant that major industrial actors were picked to carry out the policy goals specified quantitatively (so much export by company A, so much by company B, etc.). However, these descriptions concealed the institution-building that went along with the targeting. At a time when there was little experience in taking risks, government-supported research institutions proved to be indispensable. A research institution could collect information, process it, and supply it free or at a nominal cost, and thereby reduce the risks and uncertainties facing an enterprise. Records show that U.S.-trained PhDs were largely recruited to staff these research positions. Through the GFRIs, new ideas were imported from the rest of the world, and high-quality professionalism provided intellectual inputs in policy making. Building such a system of expertise at a time when the knowledge base was virtually nil was itself an innovative idea in the 1960s and early 1970s. To wit, GFRI had two distinct missions. One was to reduce risk for enterprises, the other was to aid policy makers.

This basic idea provided a rationale for the research institutions that proliferated, forming a system of think tanks during the 1960s and 1970s. But at that time such a system of research institutions had to be invented specifically to suit Korean conditions. Furthermore the system had to go through periodic redefinition and reorganization as market conditions (domestic as well as overseas) changed and new challenges appeared. Thus the institutional infrastructure was continuously recrafted during the last three decades to create, nurture, and support the growing market mechanism. This process of institutional development was perhaps more fundamental to Korean industrialization than targeting and "picking winners." This seems to be a worthy hypothesis to pursue. In part, the awareness of the importance of institution-building owes much to the recent experience of the former USSR (or CIS).[3]

Thus, for example, in 1961 the Economic Planning Board (EPB) was founded to formulate, coordinate, and implement industrialization plans. EPB was supported by a think tank, now well-known as the KDI (Korea Development Institute). Since its establishment in 1971, KDI has provided intellectual inputs to policy makers by identifying potential policy options and optimal strategies. KDI has functioned as a learning device at the national level. The knowledge of policy making so created and accumulated through experience (learning-by-doing) formed a unique intellectual asset during each period and laid the basis for development in the next period.[4]

Likewise, in the field of science-and-technology policy, new research institutions had to be put in place so that a surrogate for the nonexistent technology market could be created. Subsequently, when private enterprises gained R&D capabilities and developed sufficiently to become major players in the technology market, the government-financed research institutes could still remain as an S&T infrastructure by evolving into new industry-supporting areas. This appears to be the situation in which the current GFRIs find themselves. They seem to be going through a period of self-examination to redefine their roles as the next-generation infrastructure, as will be explained below.

KIST (Korea Institute of Science and Technology) was established in February 1966, shortly before the Ministry of Science and Technology was created in 1967. In retrospect, this was both a prophetic and symbolic event. At that time no one could foresee that the South Korean economy would be transformed into an economy driven by learning new technology (or climbing the global technology ladder) three decades later. Initially the organizational assistance for designing KIST came from the Battelle Research Institute in the United States. The practice of running the institute on a contract basis rather than a government budget was modelled after that of Battelle. (More on this point later.) The initial construction was financed by the U.S. AID.[5] The first batch of 18 researchers was recruited, all of them holding U.S. PhDs in science or engineering and with five years or more of research experience at U.S. universities or institutes. Since then, the Korean government has been continuously adding specialized R&D institutes to the national network. This is demonstrated in figure 5.1. As of 1990, these institutes were staffed by 10,655 researchers.[6]

The overall contribution of KIST to the process of technology upgrading, though controversial among scholars and critics, should not be underestimated. Some selected aspects of KIST's achievements during the last three decades can be summarized as follows: KIST has (1) played a leading role in industrial technology development through

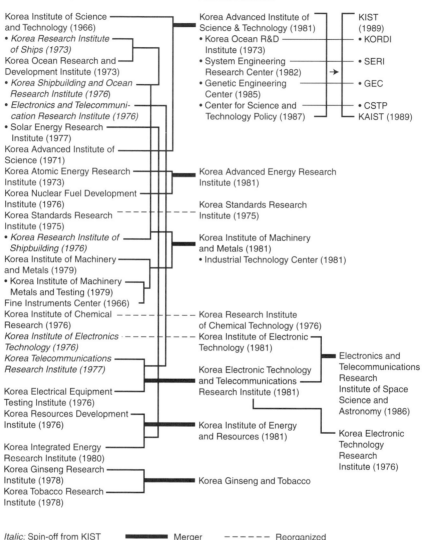

Figure 5.1
Longitudinal development of government-financed research institutes in South Korea.
Source: Dal Hwan Lee, Zong-Tae Bae, and Jinjoo Lee, "Performance and Adaptive Roles of the Government-Supported Research Institute in South Korea," *World Development* 19(1991): 1425.

over 5,600 research projects, (2) established and developed R&D institutions through spinoffs and the dissemination of R&D management systems, (3) trained and placed more than 2,000 highly experienced R&D personnel, (4) acted as the lynch-pin think tank in the national R&D system, supporting the implementation of national R&D policies and the dissemination of state-of-the-art information, (5) offered support to S&T policy makers through policy studies and technical feasibility studies, (6) provided a Korean center for international technical collaboration through cooperative R&D programs, and (7) created a favorable climate for the advancement of science and technology by introducing over 12,000 new technologies to the public.[7] The new technologies mean new product or process knowledge adopted for the first time in Korean manufacturing through invention or import (but mostly the latter adapted to fit the local conditions).

Like the Battelle Research Institute, KIST was designed basically to acquire research money on a contract basis rather than in the form of budget allocations from the government. Thus KIST was able to avoid government interference in R&D activities and personnel management, a crucial factor in its success. However, normally over 90 percent of research funds came from contracts with the government, providing funding stability. Table 5.4 exhibits the steady growth of R&D projects undertaken by KIST during the 1967–89 period. In 1989, for instance, the number of research contracts reached 573 with a total funding of 19.15 billion won (approximately $27.4 million at U.S.$ = approximately 700 won in that year). The sum of money per researcher amounted to 39 million won (approximately U.S.$55,700) in the same year.[8] Compared with Western countries, these numbers may represent a modest level of activities, but KIST's contribution to technological learning in Korea bears great historical significance in opening a new era.

An early event illustrates KIST's worth. In 1971 when POSCO (the Pohang Steel Complex) was being constructed, KIST developed a project to hire a group of Japanese engineers retired from the New Japan Steel Company (Shin-nit-tetsu). They were appointed as senior researchers at the Heavy Industry Research Lab, a unit newly created at KIST, with the task of advising and teaching about raw materials processing (ores), construction and operation of rolling mills, automation, quality control, temperature control, R&D, and so on. Their advisory work, lasting five years (1971–76), was deemed crucial to accelerating the pace of learning technology by Korean workers who did

Table 5.4
Basic statistics of R&D projects undertaken by KIST

Year	Number of projects[a]	Contract Total (billion won)	Amount Per researcher (million won)
1967	5	0.02	3
1968	42	0.07	4
1969	95	0.18	6
1970	152	0.46	11
1971	186	0.89	19
1972	160	1.71	29
1973	166	2.37	34
1974	203	2.79	23
1975	224	3.21	19
1976	251	3.53	20
1977	241	5.02	26
1978	203	7.01	30
1979	172	9.43	31
1980	178	11.18	26
1981	236	6.15	18
1982	135	8.54	23
1983	244	10.13	25
1984	275	13.12	32
1985	330	15.31	31
1986	415	19.14	40
1987	502	20.27	38
1988	624	22.78	37
1989[b]	573	19.15	39

Source: Dal Hwan Lee, Jong-Tae Base, and Jinjoo Lee, "Performance and Adaptive Roles of the Government-Supported Research Institute in South Korea," *World Development* 19 (1991): 1426.
a. Contracts undertaken by KIST's affiliated research institutes are not included. Included are R&D projects undertaken by the academic section from 1981 to 1988.
b. For 1989 contracts of the academic section are excluded. U.S.$1 = approximately 700 won in 1989.

not even have a rudimentary knowledge of steelmaking at the time. The Japanese engineers were treated as "professorial researchers." They were more than willing to transfer their know-how and hard to come by tacit knowledge. In short, KIST played an infrastructure role, serving POSCO's need for technological problem solving. Today POSCO boasts its own research institute, POSTECH, and its technological capability in steelmaking is world-class.[9]

KIST also contributed to policy making by providing technological feasibility studies, especially for the Heavy and Chemical Industry drive of the 1970s. All of the priority sectors included in the plan (automobile, electronics, machinery, shipbuilding, petroleum refinery, steel, and nonferrous metal products) required new imported technologies. KIST's studies played a central role in helping bureaucrats in policy making, since there was no other agency or organization in Korea to match its technological competence. Although KIST itself was then only a fledgling institution, it nevertheless put all its efforts into learning. KIST's study, "Plan for Constructing Pohang Steel Complex, 1969–75," emphasized the basic paradigm of importing and learning state-of-the-art technology (as opposed to "appropriate technology," backyard mill, or short-run profit maximization). This approach proved to be the quickest way to learn to become competitive in the world market.

The structural changes in industry that took place during the 1970s, however, prompted the expectation that demand would soar for information regarding technology transfer, adaptation, negotiation, trouble-shooting on the factory floor, quality control, product development, and so on. KIST alone was not able to handle the expected development. To meet these challenges, the government then decided to establish a set of spinoff research institutes, patterned primarily on the experience of KIST. Thus highly specialized units were born including shipbuilding and marine resources, electronics and telecommunication, atomic energy, machinery and metals. (See table 5.5 for current strength in expenditures, researchers, etc., of each institute. Many of the KIST's seasoned researchers and managers moved to the new institutes.) It should also be borne in mind that KIST and its affiliates (the spinoff institutes) produced trained researchers and managers for private-sector research institutes. (Holders of U.S. PhD degrees at the spinoff institutes went mostly to private universities, lured by social prestige of professorship.) In short, the GFRIs should receive credit for playing an effective role in promoting S&T infrastructure.

Table 5.5
GFRIs status in 1993 (unit: million won)

Institution	Ministry	Number of researchers (PhDs)	Budget
Korea Advanced Institute of Science and Technology	MOST	787 (247)	48,560
System Engineering Research Center	''	357 (22)	26,411
Genetic Engineering Center	''	225 (73)	14,040
Korea R&D Information Center	''	54 (1)	
Science and Technology Policy Institute	''	114 (22)	7,249
Korea Institute of Science and Technology	''	852 (311)	77,444
Korea Standards Research Institute	''	472 (99)	26,175
Korea Astronomy Observatory	''	89 (12)	6,536
Korea Basic Science Center	''	75 (9)	8,399
Korea Research Institute of Machinery and Metal	''	547 (95)	41,104
Korea Aerospace Research Institute	''	127 (33)	10,091
Korea Institute of Nuclear Safety	''	272 (53)	16,916
Korea Atomic Energy Research Institute	''	1,625 (211)	150,851
Korea Atomic Energy Hospital	''	842 (38)	38,938
Nuclear Environment Management Center	''	320 (61)	72,341
Korea Institute of Energy Research	''	347 (83)	17,979
Korea Institute of Geology Mining and Materials	''	457 (112)	22,716
Korea Ocean Research and Development Institute	''	347 (76)	18,978
Korea Electric Technology Research Institute	''	325 (45)	15,093
Korea Research Institute of Chemical Technology	''	405 (110)	24,192
Korea Science and Engineering Foundation	''	120 (1)	74,965
Subtotal	21	8,786 (1,714)	718,978
Korea Ginseng and Tobacco	MOF	351 (101)	14,579
Electrons and Telecommunication Research Institute	MIC	1,747 (234)	112,680
Korea Research Institute of Construction Technology	MOC	186 (28)	6,985
Korea Academy of Industrial Technology	MOTIE	304 (60)	15,168
Korea Electronic Technology Institute	MOTIE	148 (32)	15,925
Korea Food Research Institute	MOAF	199 (64)	7,368
Subtotal	6	2,935 (519)	172,705

Source: MOST.

However, as it turned out, despite contributions from the government-financed research institutes, public criticism against them grew. Ironically the proper function of GFRIs was brought into question because private enterprises were successfully enticed into research activities that strengthened their own international competitiveness. We now turn to a review of this development during the 1980s and 1990s.

5.3   National R&D Program and the Evaluation Problem

In contrast to the policy concerns of export promotion during the 1960s and 1970s, the 1980s saw a shift in policy to *Gisul Ipgook* or "nation building with technology advance." The basic idea was to build upon the achievements of the export-first policy by developing the technological capabilities of industries. The government instituted an "Expanded National Conference for Technology Promotion," which the president convened several times a year. The conference was a symbol of the nationwide campaign of action, analogous to the "Expanded National Conference for Export Promotion" during the Park Chung Hee era. It provided a convenient instrument for consensus building, helpful in mobilizing resources, particularly technology information and new ideas to be shared by policy makers, business executives, bankers, researchers, academics, and journalists.[10]

Beginning in the early 1980s, the government initiated a series of investment programs aimed at strengthening industrial competitiveness through technological innovation. The ongoing programs today include (1) the Special Research and Development Program (SRD) launched by the Ministry of Science and Technology (MOST) in 1982, (2) the Generic Technology Development Program (GTD) started by the Ministry of Trade, Industry, and Energy (MOTIE) in 1987, and (3) the National Telecommunication Research and Development Program (NTC) sponsored by the Ministry of Communication (MOC) in 1992 when ETRI (Electronics and Telecommunication Research Institute) was transferred to the jurisdiction of MOC.[11]

In general, there is an apparent division of labor among the three groups of GFRIs. Those belonging to MOST have engaged mostly in basic and applied research, while those belonging to MOTIE emphasized R&D activities in commercialization phases with more immediate impact on marketability. Those belonging to MOC, notably ETRI, have specialized in information telecommunication technologies. But among them, inevitably there have been interministry turf wars (juris-diction controversies) and fierce competition for attracting R&D re-sources, namely budget allocation. Competition may be useful when it stimulates efforts to win the game by inventing more than one's ri-vals would invent. But it can be harmful if the controversy confuses the basic rules of the game and the basic evaluation criteria. It appears that all of these elements were present. This factor represents at least one of the reasons why some GFRIs have had to change their home-based ministry.[12]

Table 5.5 demonstrates the relative weight of the government-financed research institutes (as of 1993). Note that MOST dominates in terms of total number of institutes, researchers, and allocated budget when compared with MOTIE and MOC. Collectively these GFRIs have accumulated approximately 2,500 PhDs, spending 200 billion won (ap-proximately U.S.$250 million) in 1995. Table 5.6 provides some infor-mation on the specific R&D in which the researchers engaged in a given year. The project topics suggest that since the 1970s, GFRIs have par-tially closed the technological gap with the Western countries.

In one of MOST's publications, a set of quantitative indicators was announced summarizing the outcome of the National Research and Development Program for the 1982 to 1992 period. The ten-year achievements included (1) the number of commercializations com-pleted: 231 technology items; in progress: 286; (2) patents applied: 1,211 (903 domestic and 308 foreign); patents registered: 390 (310 domestic and 80 foreign); papers published: 9,456 (5,050 domestic journals and 4,406 foreign journals); conference papers: 4,687 (2,053 domestic and 2,634 foreign), and technologies exported: 6 items earning licensing fees, a total of U.S.$9.62 million. The total R&D expenditures amounted to 334 billion won for the 1982–87 period, and 834 billion won for the 1988–92 period.[13]

These numbers are impressive, but the problem is how to evaluate their technological and commercial contribution. Was the money effi-ciently spent? Can the performance of GFRIs, the main executor of the National Research and Development Program, be improved? Should GFRIs be rewarded with more research funds in the future? Should they adopt a downsizing strategy for greater efficiency in the future? These questions relate to fundamental concerns about measuring per-formance and appropriate rewards. The debate is ongoing and the jury is still out.

Table 5.6
Highly advanced national projects (unit: $millions)

Category	R&D projects	Period	Technologies to be developed	Investment
Product technology	New drugs and new agrochemicals	1992–1997	2–3 new antibiotics and germicidal agents	2,455
	B-integrated service and digital network (ISDN)	1992–2001	Prototype products of 1-giga ATM	7,237
	HDTV	1990–1994	HDTV technologies for mass production	122
	Next generation vehicle technology	1992–1996	Electric car of 120km/h speed	5,625
Fundamental technology	Next generation semiconductor	1993–1997	Basic and core technology of a super integrated semiconductor	2,442
	Advanced material for information, electronics and energy	1992–2001	30 kinds of new advanced materials	3,398
	Advanced manufacturing system	1992–2001	FMS, CIM, and IMS	5,491
	New functional biomaterial	1992–2001	Process technology of bioactive, new material for commercialization	4,825
	Environmental technology	1992–2001	Core technology	2,894
	New energy technology	1992–2001	Fuel cell system	3,570
	Next generation nuclear reactor	1992–2001	Developing concept and basic design	2,975
Total	11 projects			41,034

Source: MOST, *Science and Technology in Korea*, 1994.

Some critics have pointed out that in 1992, for example, GFRIs employed 2,281 researchers with PhDs, which was 1.6 times the corresponding number for private-sector research institutes. Furthermore GFRIs had 27 percent of the total national R&D expenditures and 18 percent of the total number of researchers. Yet GFRIs' share of patent applications amounted to only 1.9 percent, and patents granted only amounted to 3.6 percent of total Korean patents. In addition only 14.6 percent of R&D projects undertaken by GFRIs have been commercialized.[14]

It should be borne in mind, however, that the GFRIs were basically established not to compete with private enterprises in achieving high scores in R&Ds. GFRIs' purpose is to provide R&D infrastructure so that the private sector can obtain help when needed. Therefore GFRI performance should be evaluated by a different yardstick than that used for private-sector performance. (More on this issue in the sections below.)

Critics went on to point out that the relatively weak performance of GFRIs can be accounted for by deteriorating conditions of work. First, salaries and wages of GFRI researchers have declined to 80 or to 70 percent of those at private-sector research institutes. Second, the seniority system tended to discourage R&D efforts. Third, the bureaucratic requirements for writing interim reports and final reports, coupled with administrative controls exercised by nonexperts in a legalistic manner, tended to vex researchers and waste their time. Fourth, the institute presidents and program directors often cared more about politics (e.g., lobbying or influence peddling) than the welfare and achievements of researchers. Fifth, the goal of the GFRIs along with the evaluation criteria failed to be clearly defined and understood by everyone concerned. Frequent shifts in reorganization and regrouping of GFRIs only made matters worse. Consequently the morale of researchers fell and many of them decided to leave the GFRIs for the private sector or the university.[15]

This development would seem to reflect, in part, the inability of GFRIs to adjust to rapidly changing conditions. The lag in salaries arose largely as a result of the bidding war for high-caliber researchers by the private-sector research institutes through the 1980s when they expanded at great speed. GFRIs were not particularly keen to match the salaries offered by the private sector. Furthermore since 1982, as the research funds of MOST swelled, reflecting its role in carrying out the National Research and Development Program, administrative control has increased. Some of the controls stem from the approach taken by nonspecialists in administering R&D funds by setting up elaborate rules and regulations. This approach was used to absolve the responsible bureaucrats from blame when things went wrong. As a consequence the autonomy of the research institutes and research teams quickly dwindled.

An even more serious problem was the inadequate system of technology evaluation. Because of shallow experience in Korean S&T development, experts who could judge the true value of R&D efforts were scarce. Often, in a very specialized field of technology, there was no one at all or at best only three or four experts in the country. And they were often not willing to render a negative evaluation, reflecting Korean culture's distaste for judging others as failures. Thus, even though a mechanism of peer-group evaluation for research-fund applications was in existence, its operation seldom yielded meaningful evaluations. This state of affairs may be remedied only after substantial experience has been accumulated within the fledgling scientific community. Nevertheless, some strategies could be mulled over to overcome the shortcomings of the existing peer-group evaluation process. For example, including Korean-American scientists and engineers in the peer-group evaluation committees could be considered an option. These issues will be taken up in the last section of this chapter.

5.4 Trade Regime as a Technology Learning Instrument: A Model

This section describes how the government crafted institutional devices in the areas of export and import with an aim toward upgrading technological capabilities of Korean manufacturers. Information flow, incentive structure, and risk-sharing arrangements were built into the trade regime to provide effective motivation for producers to learn new technologies and to innovate. The implication to be drawn here is that R&D activities can also be stimulated with an appropriate set of institutional devices by taking into account Korea-specific cultural, historical elements.

How an export-oriented, outward-looking, industrial strategy is linked with the process of industrial deepening deserves high priority for research.[16] Recently an interesting hypothesis has been advanced stating that NICs in Asia have benefited from foreign buyers, transnational corporations (TNCs), original equipment manufacturer (OEM) arrangements, and licensing deals. These arrangements have provided avenues through which technical specification, training, advice on production and management, even with marketing information, have been made available. Mike Hobday called this an "export-led or export-pull technology development."[17]

Undoubtedly, export-pull technological development played some part. However, more often foreign buyers, OEM arrangements, and TNC operations provided a few opportunities for value adding at the initial stage of acquiring a market niche. The difficult stage in technology learning comes when OEM buyers and TNCs refuse to provide the more sophisticated aspects of a technology to prevent competition. This is often called a "boomerang effect." Thus as an institutional arrangement, the so-called export-pull phenomenon in technology learning can easily stop short of industrial deepening at the lower end of the technology ladder. An ongoing process cannot rely solely on export-pull, though the OEM's positive contribution should be given due credit.

Korea has developed a set of trade-related institutional devices to overcome barriers in accumulating technological capabilities. Below is an attempt to briefly describe the features of such devices, which define also the trade-regime components.

The most notable feature of the trade regime is the well-crafted combination of export promotion schemes and the program of selective import substitution. Commonly it is thought that these two approaches would be contradictory. An import substitution policy would tend to hinder exports because the domestic price rises to the extent that the market is protected. Across-the-boards tariff protection, as practiced in India and Latin American countries provides an example of such a situation. However, the South Korean trade regime appears to have been finely "calibrated" and managed to remove anti-trade effects as well as to enhance technology-learning effects.

Though protective walls have existed, export producers were allowed to import the necessary inputs at the world market price and sell the output abroad at the world market price. Thus Korean exporters were exempt from the usual disadvantages of protective walls. The phenomenal export growth during the 1960s and 1970s, at an annual average growth rate of around 30 to 35 percent, owes partly to the "free-trade" conditions, facing exporters, as in Hong Kong.

Meanwhile the protected domestic market provided a learning ground for those product items selected for nurturing. The case of the automobile industry would help illustrate the learning process in that industry. An automobile consists of 20,000 parts. When the first assembly line was established in Korea in the early to mid 1960s, most of the parts were imported. The domestic content was about 20 to 25 percent. But slowly, increasing numbers of parts have been "locally" produced. The selection criteria for additional parts to be localized included (1) parts with less demanding complexity of technology and engineering resources, (2) parts with large balance-of-payments effects, (3) parts with smaller requirements for capital funds and skilled labor, (4) parts that can be developed in a shorter period of time, (5) parts imported from Japan if such imports exceed 40 percent of the total Korean consumption; and (6) parts with large spillover or linkage effects. By 1985 when finished automobiles were exported, the domestic content rose to over 90 percent.

To decide on the annual target package of parts, the Industrial Policy Deliberation Council meets two or three times a year. The Council consists of representatives from industry, banks, academe, trade associations, engineers, and government officials. They deliberate collectively and agree on the annual package. The result of the collective agreement is made public immediately. This information has great value to individual producers, since the information signals access to bank credits and uncertainty-reduction measures (free information on technology sourcing, tax benefits, etc.).[18]

Based on this information, which defines the next batch of goods to be technologically conquered, producers can begin competition for getting "subsidized credits" for investment in R&D as well as production facilities. Potential producers apply to the subcommittee of the Council to obtain an assistance package. Selection criteria include the producers' potential to become competitive sooner than others, past performance as exhibited by export records, soundness of engineering and management standards, and the like. This process is akin to selecting and nurturing a potential champion in athletic activities. Those selected become eligible to receive assorted assistance for various services as listed in table 5.7.

The items appearing in the table are subject to negotiation between the producer and the officials. There are plenty of opportunities for rent-seeking. The aid package can also work to upgrade technological capabilities of the aid receivers. The existing studies tend to evaluate the overall effect as a positive incentive structure.[19] The localization programs are constantly reviewed and evaluated, such as measuring

Table 5.7
Support schemes to replace imports with local production and to upgrade the industrial base in the Republic of Korea

Type of plan	Industrial base
Financial support schemes	Manufacturing development fund
	Industrial technology improvement fund
	New enterprise creation support fund
	Technology development fund
	Venture-capital fund
	Special fund for small and medium enterprise
	Equipment fund for export and import substitution in raw materials, component parts, lease fund
	Procurement fund for domestically produced machines
Tax benefit schemes	Income tax exemption for foreign engineers
	Exemption of local tax on real estate for constructing research institutes by private enterprises
	Tax exemption for income from technology sales
	Income tax exemption for technology-intensive enterprise initiators
	Special accelerated depreciation allowance for projects using new technology
	Tax credit plus accelerated depreciation for research and development equipment and vocational training equipment
	Reserve funds for research and development accounted as losses
	Tax credit for expenditures on research and development and training
	Tariff reduction (65 to 70 percent) on imports of high-technology industrial equipment

Technology support schemes	Special research and development projects
	Basic technology research and development projects
	Technical guidance on long-term training of researchers, on technical personnel development, on simplifying automation, on invited foreign experts
	Free technological information dissemination
	Free use of expensive test equipment
	Testing of precision equipment and repairs
	Quality seals for domestically produced machines, parts, and raw materials
	Support measures for obtaining foreign quality seals
Miscellaneous support schemes	Comprehensive support package for promising small- and medium-scale suppliers of new products
	System of identifying promising new exportable products (market research) and priority products for import substitution
	Exhibition of domestically produced machines
	Government preference to procure domestically developed new products
	Anti-dumping scheme for newly developed products with domestically developed technology
	Monitoring system to observe impacts of new products
	Fair trade and transaction law
	Exemption of military services requirements for core researchers
	Free consulting service for promotion of localization program

Source: K. R. Lee et al., *Interim Evaluation of Localization Policy and Ways to Improve* (in Korean), Korea Institute for Economics and Technology, Research report 196, April 1990, p. 28.

the extent of localization (local production instead of importing) accomplished and foreign exchanges (U.S.$) saved. Any firms that fail are disqualified from applying for the next round of competition for assistance.

Competitive pressure has also come from a longer–run program of reducing protection. The import liberalization program was nominally begun in 1967 when South Korea joined GATT and shifted from a "positive list system" to a "negative list system."[20] However, the really serious effort began in 1978 when the Committee on Import Liberalization Measures was created and presided over by the Minister of Commerce and Industry. The Committee would meet periodically to decide on the list of products that would be allowed for import without quantitative restrictions. The list would be published with sufficient lead time so that the import-competing industries could be prepared. The Committee declared that this policy would be devised so that it could be used for the purpose of upgrading industrial structure and competitiveness. Table 5.8 lists indicators of import liberalization (latest study available) since 1965.

An evaluation of this import liberalization program, conducted by KDI, suggests that the program indeed had the effect of bracing the domestic producers for upgrading competitiveness and innovation.[21] It would seem that slow and measured import liberalization has functioned as a significant threat component of the whole incentive structure for encouraging innovation and learning.

Another important feature of the incentive structure is the emphasis on importing state-of-the-art technology and mastering it as fast as possible. From experience the policy makers saw that "second-hand" technology become obsolete too soon. Product quality could be achieved and maintained in a competitive overseas market with only the most advanced machines. Nurturing ability to produce high-quality products to be sold in export markets is the guiding principle for choosing "appropriate technology," not the existence of cheap labor dictating labor-intensive technology.

Once a machine, plant, or technology license was purchased, the next step was to reach as soon as possible the maximum output capacity level defined by engineers. This step is consistent with the learning by doing (imitating) hypothesis and not necessarily with the short-run profit-maximization assumption.

There has been a general agreement among bureaucrats and producers that the "success" of technology mastering has to be measured by

Table 5.8
Estimates of overall degree of import liberalization for Korea, 1965–1990 (%)

	Average rate of legal tariff		Inverted total tariff rate, $(1/1 + 2)$	Degree of liberalization from QRs[c]	Overall degree of liberalization
	Regular[a] (1)	Total[b] (2)	(3)		
1965	49.5	52.7	65.5	6.0	35.8
1966	49.5	52.3	65.7	9.3	37.5
1967	49.5	52.6	65.5	52.4	59.0
1968	56.7	58.9	62.9	50.1	56.5
1969	56.7	58.3	63.2	47.1	55.2
1970	56.7	58.5	63.1	46.3	54.7
1971	56.7	57.9	63.3	47.0	55.2
1972	56.7	57.5	63.5	43.4	53.5
1973	48.1	48.2	67.5	44.7	56.1
1974	48.1	48.1	67.5	43.8	55.7
1975	48.1	48.1	67.5	41.6	54.7
1976	48.1	48.1	67.5	44.1	55.8
1977	41.3	41.3	70.8	40.8	55.8
1978	41.3	41.3	70.7	53.2	61.5
1979	34.4	34.4	74.4	56.2	65.3
1980	34.4	34.4	74.4	57.4	65.9
1981	34.4	34.4	74.4	60.7	67.6
1982	34.4	34.4	74.4	62.5	68.5
1983	34.4	34.4	74.4	66.6	70.5
1984	26.7	26.7	78.9	75.0	77.0
1985	26.4	26.4	79.1	78.2	78.7
1986	24.7	24.7	80.2	82.0	81.1
1987	23.9	23.9	80.7	84.1	82.4
1988	22.4	22.4	81.7	86.0	83.9
1989	15.7	15.7	86.4	86.7	86.6
1990	14.1	14.1	87.6	87.5	87.6

Source: Kwang Suk Kim, "Trade and Industrialization Policies in Korea" in G. K. Helleiner, ed., *Trade Policy and Industrialization in Turbulent Times,* London: Routledge, 1994.
a. The average rate of regular tariffs, weighted by the value of 1975 production.
b. Includes the average rate of special tariffs on imports in addition to the regular tariffs for the 1965–1973 period.
c. Represents the degree of import liberalization from QRs (quantitative restrictions) based on both the trade program and special laws.

import needs (e.g., parts or feedstock) replaced by localization, or even better, the amount of exports newly created. It makes sense that world-market acceptance provides the most stringent test of quality and price, and therefore renders a clear yet simple standard of success or failure of technology mastering.

To recapitulate the trade regime's function as an institutional device for building technological capabilities, the following features should be noted:

1. Measures for export promotion helped to reduce or eliminate anti-export biases of selective import substitution measures.

2. Surging export earnings allowed producers to be able to import either new technologies under licensing arrangements or capital goods embodying state-of-the-art technologies, with the aim of gaining competitiveness in the world markets.

3. The trade regime offered two avenues of technological learning. The first avenue was the request for quality upgrades by foreign buyers and OEM patrons, who often provided free consulting services, and the second avenue was the "localization program" whereby domestic content of exportables was augmented via backward linkage serving export activities (parts, feedstock, intermediate inputs, etc.).

In support of the latter argument, there is some evidence indicating that nonexport sector growth has greater correlation with productivity growth than export sector growth; see table 5.9. Although further confirmation may be needed, one could interpret this piece of evidence as showing greater learning effects, and hence productivity growth, in import-replacing industries (i.e., export-supporting linkage industries), compared with the export industries per se.

Other studies have reached similar conclusions. For example, a study summarized: "The speed of technological progress in overall industrial performance in Korea has been measured to be twice as fast as in Japan; 2.6 times as fast in the case of manufacturing; and 5 times as fast in Heavy and Chemical Industries where import replacement by local production has been flourishing."[22] This study compared the period of 1960–70 for Japan with that of 1975–85 for Korea (deemed comparable because heavy industries flourished then in each country, respectively).

Under a trade-regime designed to encourage the upgrading of technological capabilities of enterprises, an able producer can expect a package of assistance tailored for his needs. He can have "free" infor-

Table 5.9
Regression coefficients explaining growth rate of total factor productivity by manufacturing subsectors with export and nonexport production

Classification code	Sector	C	A	B	R^2
3	Manufactures	−7.751 (−1.943)	0.763 (3.603)***	−0.001 (−0.007)	0.54
311/2	Food	−3.573 (−0.59)	0.653 (2.617)**	−0.087 (−1.279)	0.34
313	Beverages	−9.344 (−2.646)*	1.317 (7.087)***	0.075* (2.074)	0.76
314	Tobacco	−4.795 (−1.239)	1.026 (7.642)***	−0.003 (−0.407)	0.79
321	Textiles	1.446 (0.272)	0.869 (3.313)***	−0.294 (−1.688)	0.41
323	Leather	−2.43 (−0.285)	0.12 (5.121)***	−0.021 (−0.163)	0.65
331	Wood and cork	2.438 (0.408)	0.284 (1.564)	−0.262 (−1.684)	0.32
332	Furniture	−7.384 (−1.302)	0.439 (5.339)***	0.116 (2.701)**	0.65
341	Paper products	−11.405 (−2.531)*	1.037 (5.101)***	0.008 (0.957)	0.63
342	Printing	−9.119 (−2.544)*	1.138 (8.062)***	−0.003 (0.189)	0.84
351/2	Industrial and other chemicals	−13.506 (−2.458)*	0.968 (6.713)***	0.096 (1.688)	0.74
353/4	Petroleum refining	−5.834 (−1.053)*	0.197 (1.346)	0.013 (1.511)	0.24
355	Rubber products	−1.173 (−0.272)	0.52 (3.616)**	−0.035 (−0.455)	0.53
361/2/9	Pottery, china	−8.382 (−1.931)	0.685 (3.437)***	0.003 (−0.129)	0.43
371/2	Iron and steel and non ferrous metals	−9.016 (−1.235)	0.584 (2.703)**	−0.011 (−0.178)	0.32
381	Metal products	−5.579 (−1.396)	0.312 (5.403)***	0.115 (−2.411)*	0.66
382	Machinery	−8.753 (−2.177)*	0.52 (6.271)***	−0.08 (−1.303)	0.74
383	Electrical machinery	−13.781 (−1.925)	0.335 (2.206)*	0.253 (2.601)*	0.55
384	Transport equipment	−0.76 (−0.122)	0.516 (2.931)***	0.022 (0.47)	0.43
390	Other manufactures	−2.746 (−0.357)	0.522 (2.267)*	−0.001 (−0.002)	0.29

Source: Youngil Lim, "Industrial Policy and Productivity Gains: South Korean Evidence," *Journal of Economic Development* (Choong-Ang University journal) 18, 1 (June 1993): 76.
Note: Figures in parentheses are *t*-values. Time series 1966–1985 are in 1980 prices. * Significant at 5%; ** significant at 2%; *** significant at 1%.
Regression equation:
$(dT/T) = C + A(dD/D) + B(dX/X)$,
where (dT/T): growth rates of TFP (Solow index), C: constant, (dD/D): growth rates of nonexport production, (dX/X): growth rates of export production.

mation on where he can sell his new products, on what sort of technologies would be available at what price, on what terms he can borrow money (usually at subsidized interest rates), what sort of tax benefits he can claim, and so on. The access to such information alone can help to reduce transactions costs, as well as uncertainties facing the would-be exporter, as compared with the absence of such a service system under the laissez-faire condition.

But the assistance package is not available to everyone who wants it, only to those who pass the screening. The ability indicators for screening purposes include past performance of exports or record of successful "localization" efforts, qualification of engineers hired, quality of plant equipment and management skills. These seem to be what any banker would like to examine before lending money to a potential borrower firm.

The producer, so selected in the examination, is obliged to show evidence of "local production" in exchange for the "rents" from learning fast or mastering new technology. Failure to deliver performance means losing one's chance in the next round of the competition for aid package. The technocrats on the government side also have an incentive for success of the program execution because their promotion depends on its long-run performance record.

The importance of institution has been gaining recognition in recent years. To quote Douglas North, one of the foremost advocates of institutional analysis:[23]

Third World countries are poor because the institutional constraints define a set of pay-off to political/economic activity that do not encourage productive activity. Socialist economies are first beginning to appreciate that the underlying institutional framework is the source of their current poor performance and are attempting to grapple with ways to restructure the institutional framework to redirect incentives that in turn will direct organizations along productivity-increasing paths.

This passage provides an apt view that can explain the productivity difference between North Korea and South Korea largely in terms of systemic incentive differences. Why did North Korea fail in the race of industrialization? Recall that North Korea received a greater sum of industrial assets from the retreating Japanese in 1945 than South Korea. A study estimated that in 1969 North Korea produced U.S.$1.95 billion worth of industrial output while South Korea produced U.S.$1.22 billion in the same year. Per inhabitant, North Korea produced U.S.$139 compared to U.S.$39 for South Korea. Per capita income in North Korea was U.S.$210 compared to U.S.$195 for South Korea in the same year.[24] In 1996 per capita GNP of South Korea was about U.S.$10,000 while the corresponding figure for North Korea was estimated somewhere between U.S.$1,000 to 2,000. (In 1998 per capita GNP of South Korea was about U.S.$6,800, owing to exchange rate depreciation and decline in GNP. It may take three to four years to recover what has been lost. The corresponding North Korean figure is not available.) The productivity difference in manufacturing is reportedly 1 to 6. This compares with 1 to 2 between East Germany and West Germany just before their unification. These cases represent rare historical experimentation dividing up the same ethnic group into two different systems which ultimately lead to different consequences after three decades of an "experimental period." A comparative study of North and South Korea would reveal the importance of incentive structure as well as information flow structure, a research project worth pursuing.

The differential incentive structure between India and South Korea also seems to be capable of explaining the performance of productivity growth. Professor Isher Ahluwalia's TFP growth estimates for India shows a −0.1 percent and −0.6 percent annual average growth for the 1960 to 1966 and the 1967 to 1980 periods, respectively.[25]

How can these negative growth rates of TFP for India be explained? Staffan Jacobsson and Ghayun Alam have compared a selected set of engineering industries (i.e., hydraulic excavators, machining centers, integrated circuits and plate heat exchangers) between India and South Korea. They concluded:[26]

The Indian policy towards its industrial sector, on the other hand, was dominated by a whole set of 'restrictive' instruments which greatly limited the room for manoeuvre of private industry. They included MRTP (Monopoly and Restrictive Trade Practices Act), FERA (Foreign Exchange Regulates Act), industrial licensing policy and the policy vis-à-vis foreign technological collaboration. Indeed, the MRTP legislation aimed at restricting the growth of conglomerates with a superior risk-taking ability, precisely that form of business organization which has led development in Korea. Firm-specific and made-to-measure policies designed to help firms in their learning process seem to have been absent.

To recapitulate my argument, the South Korean achievement of technological capability should be interpreted as the joint work of the government with private enterprises and educational institutions. Technological learning was greatly enhanced by the provision of

infrastructure in various forms. This infrastructure has included research institutes (public and private), educational facilities to produce
engineers and technicians, venture-capital funds (or some surrogates,
e.g., "policy loans") at "below-market rates of interest" to reflect a
long-run horizon for technological learning, and with subsidized
dissemination of techno-commercial information. These institutional
devices proved essential where the market mechanism was absent or
imperfect for information, human capital, and organizational skills.
Overall, the government sector seems to have done its own exercises
of learning (often via a trial and error approach) to build a workable
edifice of infrastructure. The role of the private sector was to take risk,
learn and master new technology, whether imported or invented, and
to expand export and win competition in world markets.[27]

In performing their individual roles, both the government and private sectors have crafted institutional devices in diverse forms. Some
were long-run inventions, others very temporary and makeshift because of the urgency or lack of immediate alternatives. In any event,
institutional devices had to be formulated so as to increase infor-
mational efficiency, to reduce risks and uncertainties and to reduce
transaction costs, so as to entice learning and risk-taking. Reward-per-
formance linkages, and how they are organized, seem crucial for systemic efficiency in learning. This effect has to be analyzed at the firm
level, industry level, and macroeconomic level. Enterprise competitiveness depends on the sum total of these learning activities at all levels.
The total seems to be greater than the sum of micro components because of interfirm and intertemporal externalities in knowledge, human capital, and institutions. This perspective may provide the key
to understanding the phenomenon of learning as well as economywide
dynamic increasing returns observable in South Korea and elsewhere.

5.5   National R&D Program to Strengthen Industry-University-Government Linkages

The campaign to get industry, university, and government to cooperate
on R&D has a long history. For instance, a "Sanhag Hyopdong Jaedan"
(Foundation for Industry-Academe Cooperation) was established in
1974, supported by contributions from Korean foreign traders. The diverse program of the Foundation (lectures, conferences, ad hoc studies
on special issues of cooperative research, etc.) fostered cooperation between industry and academe. This groundwork has served to dispel

the idea that industry and academe cannot be brought together.[28] However, the need for cooperative R&D only became really clear in the 1980s when new technologies emerged as a predominant factor. This section reviews the current need for cooperation in R&D, and suggests some possible strategic options to meet the challenges of the new century.

In the previous sections the complementarity of industry and university were discussed. The industrial sector has money for research but a shortage of intellectual resources, while the university sector has the intellectual resources but little money. In addition GFRIs are facing the need to redefine their vision, mission, and function. Given these conditions, a tripartite complementarity could be designed that would foster synergy through cooperation among industry, university, and GFRIs.

Essentially the problems of GFRIs boil down to the need to devise an incentive system powerful enough to motivate high-caliber researchers. Rewards should be based on achieving research objectives such as the accumulation of patents, papers, training, and the commercialization of inventions in order to raise competitiveness in each technology area, such as the introduction of robotics or the electrical automobiles. Looking at the current incentive system, one finds (1) a low base salary level which is 70 to 80 percent of the salary paid to comparable employees in industry and university, (2) bureaucratic interference and regulations that lead to micromanagement of R&D activities requiring report on expenditures often and in minute detail, and (3) frequent turf wars, reorganization, and regrouping of GFRIs, which disrupts the continuity of R&D programs.

It is generally thought that scientists and engineers are motivated less by financial rewards than by opportunities to demonstrate their research skills and realize their objectives.[29] While this may be often true, one could argue that excellent research facilities combined with high remuneration could lead to even better results. It may be advisable to establish a link between financial rewards and the income-earning capacity of a patent that may come as a result of improved research circumstances. It is noteworthy that at MIT, a professor receives one-third of the licensing income from a patent acquired through his or her research program. Another one-third of the licensing income is earmarked for improving departmental research facilities. This practice could provide GFRI reformers with the strong performance-reward incentive they need in redesigning the Korean system.

In addition to financial rewards, one could offer professorate titles to PhD researchers. The Korean culture values teachers highly; a professorship is regarded as a very high honor. Because of this high status, professorships could be used to draw deserving engineers to the field of education. This option presupposes that GFRIs will strengthen their educational involvement (just as KAIST) to include graduate programs and doctorate programs in engineering. To distinguish their higher degree programs from those of Korean universities, the GFRIs might consider developing a new forward-looking educational agenda such as is explained below.

At present, GFRIs operate a program to retrain researchers from private-sector firms. In cooperation with a university, an employee at a member firm can take formal courses at a university, get practical experience in research at a GFRI, and obtain an advanced degree. But it has been reported that student enrollment has declined for various reasons: (1) lack of advertising, (2) difficulty in attending day courses while working, and (3) a mismatch between the courses offered and the students' needs.

So far this cooperative educational program has been emphasizing the retraining of employees in private companies. Now that a chronic shortage of researchers with PhD and MS degrees is foreseen for the next decade, it may be useful to extend the program to potential employees, namely students who are not yet employed.

A new curriculum could be created to combine research and education. The traditional curriculum leading to a PhD or MS degree consisted mainly of theoretical and hypothesis-testing exercises. The large gap between learned theory and the reality of the factory-floor had to be closed with additional investments of time, effort, and money on the job. In medical schools, there is special training that incorporates clinical research in the curriculum by which students can become familiar with the practice of clinical medicine. In engineering, an equivalent program in the curriculum seems advisable.[30]

In order to integrate research and education, one may consider the merits of graduate schools specialized by industry, such as a graduate school of automotive technology, a graduate school of multimedia technology, a graduate school of iron and steel technology, a graduate school of textile technology, or a graduate school of environmental technology. In this way graduate students could learn an industry-specific combination of technologies (engineering knowledge), along with management, marketing, and decision-making techniques (which can be industry-specific). This nontraditional (potentially controversial) approach would require the creation of new curricula.

GFRIs are in the best position to create such curricula. They have on hand the intellectual resources (over 2,000 PhDs) and the experience in R&D work in both private- and public-sector firms to solve factory-floor problems. They also have experience in retraining research engineers sent to them by firms. If a consensus could be reached, GFRIs could even raise special funds for such curriculum development. They are in a position to produce a new breed of engineers who acquire skills in both theory and practical applications. A special arrangement can be made to set aside a certain percentage (e.g., 20 percent) of government-project funds for providing engineers with additional skills.

Furthermore GFRIs are major contractors; they carry out a large proportion of the national R&D programs that MOST farms out to various institutes and universities. Engineers trained in specific fields of research would carry with them the new knowledge that they have acquired to the places where they will continue to improve it and adapt for local production. Studies have shown that human capital flow can be the most effective instrument of technology transfer from one place (institutes, factories) to another. If carefully planned, GFRI involvement could create a supply of and a demand for special knowledge and human skills (as efficient catalyzers).

Retired engineers represent a powerful storehouse of practical knowledge about factory-floor problems and how they have been solved. As guest lecturers, their theorization of problem-solving techniques could add to the stock of knowledge upon which further technological progress can be constructed. An evolution in manufacturing knowledge thus can be traced, recorded, analyzed, theorized about, and reapplied to further progress in invention and diffusion. Under such a systematized program, retired engineers from Toyota, Matsushita, Sony, Motorola, GM, Samsung, and so on, could be invited to GFRIs to give lectures and clinical demonstrations. GFRI professors and students could team up with these guest lecturers in teaching and researching.

The arrangement by which such a professor would be rewarded would be like that in any other university setting (but with some modifications). The professor's performance evaluation would be based on patents registered, publication, his/her record in training students (teaching and supervision), and professional services provided to industries and the engineering community. The issue of weighting these factors can be studied and debated to reach acceptance among professionals and policy makers (consensus). Here the importance of patent registration is emphasized, particularly in connection with the National R&D Program. Research projects stemming from the National R&D Program carry more priority, and GFRI professors could be selected based on the number of such patents they have registered.

Furthermore researchers who succeed in creating new ideas and new business ventures could be rewarded by stock options. Promotion, social honor, and financial rewards could combine to make a powerful incentive system for Korean engineers. This author believes that MIT has a powerful incentive structure built into its organizational edifice, and that this explains the superb performance of the faculty. MIT has one of the most flexible arrangements in terms of rules and regulations governing professors' research and teaching. For instance, a professor may teach a course, have his or her own research project or program, and own a private engineering or consulting business at the same time. But the MIT evaluation procedure is clear and strict. For tenure, the researcher's peers outside MIT must reach a consensus that the candidate is among the best in the field. GFRIs could adopt a strategy that emulates MIT's incentive structure with a view to becoming world-class, say by the year 2010. Perhaps the measures to redefine GFRI's incentive structure in a fundamental way will boost the falling morale of GFRI researchers. For morale-boosting purposes, flexibility is better than strict rules.[31] Inevitably the issue of flexibility leads to the issue of peer-group evaluation and the definition of excellence.

The practice of peer-group evaluation of personal performance has not been fully instituted in Korean professional organizations and universities, although experiments have been attempted in some quarters. Thus promotion in a university depends on departmental consensus (politics), combined with some sort of seniority system. Research funds are normally distributed more or less equally among the departmental members. When peer-group evaluation was seriously attempted, however, several problems emerged.

Korea has yet to institutionalize a system of refereed journals, an urgent requirement if the Korean scientific and technology communities are to be responsible for creating the infrastructure. GFRIs are well positioned to initiate a referee system in each of their specialty fields. (ETRI appears to have one such system established.) The majority of GFRI researchers hold U.S. PhD degrees, and most have published their research in English-language journals. They themselves could referee the papers submitted. The practice of paper refereeing could also help to build a sense of community in science and engineering which today Western countries enjoy. Recalling how KAIST solved the problem, it may be advisable to make use of publications in foreign journals. But, this approach will pose a language barrier for the majority of non-U.S.-trained scientists and engineers.

A recent study on project evaluation in the National R&D Program has pointed out: "At times, mail peer review is used to guarantee the confidentiality of reviewers. It is verified that external reviewers sometimes lack proper knowledge and expertise about projects in specific high-tech areas. Also such problems inherent in peer review persist, such as the 'old boy' network to protect established fields, leniency effect, halo effect to fund more visible scientists, universities, and institutions, and partiality based on other nontechnical reasons." In part, these problems arose because of a shallow culture in the scientific and technology communities, which have only existed for about twenty years in Korea. The same study commented: "In a nation where the pool of qualified scientists/engineers is small, experts in a particular area are not easily found, and as a result it was nearly impossible to avoid the above-mentioned problems of peer review."[32]

The scarcity of qualified scientists and engineers can be at least partly alleviated if researchers of Korean origin working overseas could be mobilized. The expatriate peers have been providing an important source of technology transfer, such as was seen in the case of Samsung's semiconductors or of Hyundai's automobile engines. In their eagerness to serve the motherland, perhaps these researchers would be happy to act as referees and evaluate the writings of their peers. One way to approach this may be to create a database of expatriate scientists and engineers so that their services can be efficiently utilized. Fortunately the Korean-American Scientists and Engineers Association has reportedly been raising funds for a database project. Such a database could be effectively linked up with a counterpart Korean database to produce an integrated information system, fostering cooperation and creative synergy. The GFRIs as a group, in cooperation with KOSEF and the Korean Federation of Scientists and Engineers Organizations (Kwa-Chong), could initiate such a database project. The Korea Research and Development Information Center (KORDIC) could function as an executive committee office as well as a software lab for this specific purpose.[33]

This state of affairs offers a broad set of challenges to GFRIs, if they are to function as an infrastructure providing support to the Korean S&T community. GFRIs should provide initiative and leadership to build (1) an industry-university-government information center and (2) linkage between the information center and scientific and technological global information networks such as NACSIS (National Center for Science Information Systems, Japan), STN (Scientific and Technical Network, USA) International, and FIZ (Fachinformation Zentrum, Germany). One of the main reasons for the poor cooperation among industry, universities, and GFRIs has been the scarcity of information (read ignorance) about the R&D capabilities of potential partners. GFRIs seem to be best equipped to remedy this situation by launching a program to establish a high-powered information center linked with the global network. A long-term goal in building information networks should be to develop capability for global technology scanning. At the moment no single institution or organization seems to be able to do this in Korea.

Fortunately, however, a modest pilot project for an R&D personnel database was initiated in 1994.[34] The project collected personal data on 4,291 scientists and engineers working at Korean research institutes (government and private) and universities, plus 1,448 researchers of Korean origin working at universities and research institutes in Japan. The purpose in building the database was to facilitate the search for expertise for (1) R&D project performers and evaluators, (2) industry-university-government joint projects, (3) projects needing specialists, and (4) the National Brain Pool system (under construction). The project team has also attempted to develop software for the database operation. The usefulness of the database remains to be proved. The project has yet to include data from other regions of the world, namely, the United States and Europe. It must also develop a system that enables users to judge the quality of researchers by criteria other than their curriculum vitae.

Summing up this section, I have argued that the depressed morale of researchers at GFRIs could be revitalized by redesigning the incentive system and emphasizing GFRIs' educational function. Specifically, industry-specific graduate schools (automobile, information-telecommunication, textile, etc.) could be created as an extension of the GFRIs for advanced degrees in engineering. The teaching faculty could come from the pool of researchers working at GFRIs, and they could be given professorial titles.[35] The professorial title, a coveted form of social recognition in Korean culture, should then be connected to individual performance rather than seniority. The faculty's performance could be gauged by the quantity and quality of papers, patents, pupils, curriculum development, and services rendered to the S&T community. In addition a generous proportion of licensing income from intellectual property returned to the inventor can serve as a powerful incentive.

I have further argued that a system of peer-group evaluation could be institutionalized and strengthened by including Korean scientists and engineers who reside overseas (in the United States, Europe, and Japan). Such an arrangement would help alleviate the relative lack of expertise and objectivity in peer evaluation in Korea. This arrangement involves building networks of S&T information centers domestically and globally. GFRIs collectively can provide a node for industry-university-government linkages in Korea and abroad. A great deal of investment in resources (time, money, efforts, and brains) needs to be devoted to building an information system to meet the challenges of the next century.

5.6   Lessons from the U.S. Cooperation among Industry, Academe, and Government: The Case of Information Technology

This section provides a brief history of different roles played by institutions in developing information technology in the United States. It gives a comparative perspective to the Korean pattern of technology development in which the government is actively involved in selecting as well as financing of R&D projects. The contrast owes much to cultural differences and to the comparatively less competent market institutions in Korea in allocating resources optimally (especially in the case of information technology). Nevertheless, the U.S. pattern of cooperation provides some useful lessons on the potential role of government in Korea.[36]

The history of information technology industry in America is a distinctive example of long-term collaboration among the government, universities, and industry that has generated great economic benefits to its society. The government has been the biggest research funding source of computer and telecommunication technologies as well as an important customer of information technology products. It also has built the infrastructure of industry and education whenever the market alone did not properly serve the public interest. NSF and NIH provide apt examples. The more important tactics of U.S. government is perhaps its "masterful inactivity,"[37] which has ensured the vitality of the private industry. Universities, especially elite research universities such as MIT and Stanford, have taken the lion's share of federal funds directed to electronics and computer technologies. Such universities have also created fertile pools of talented researchers, engineers, and entrepreneurs. Information technology firms as well as user firms of their products have developed new ways of doing business better suited to exploit the vast potential of the new technology.

In 1945 Vannevar Bush, a leading scientist who headed the U.S. government's wartime Office of Scientific Research and Development, argued that the government support of science would benefit society by means of its contribution to the economy and national security because "science is the endless frontier." Information technology turned out to be the most salient case for his argument. The information warfare escaped from futurists' reverie[38] to become a reality in the Gulf War in 1992[39] and to enter the regular curriculum in military education.[40] America soon became the world's only superpower by its superb lead in information technology and also by the collapse of the Soviet Union.

The economic impact of information technology is more visible than the impact on military technology. According to the International Data Corporation, three-quarters of the $100 billion worth of packaged software sold in 1996 were made in America. The U.S. software sector employs 2 million people, which exceeds in number the combined figure of all major industrialized countries. Although Japan is catching up in computer hardware production through its manufacturing prowess, the leading computer hardware manufacturers are still American firms such as IBM, HP, Intel, and Compaq. Many observers believe that the 1990s' revival of the American economy from the decade-long worries due to Japanese and German challenges is largely due to its strong position in the information technology industry.

Many observers reckon that since the end of the Vietnam War the American federal government has taken an increasingly active role in various aspects of society. Support of scientific research is one of the key areas of increasing government involvement.[41] (See table 5.10.) According to Mazuzan, a historian at National Science Foundation, this was largely due to the intense effort during the Second World War: "Not only was government support of scientific endeavors sharply escalated, but the relationships among government agencies, universities, private foundations, and industry were altered in ways that disallowed a return to prewar times."[42]

Table 5.10
U.S. federal R&D obligations, 1955–1995 (unit: $millions, current)

Year	Total	National defense	Health	Space technology	Percentage of GNP	Percentage of defense
1955	2,533	2,151			0.63	84.92
1956	2,988	2,535			0.70	84.84
1957	3,932	3,327			0.88	84.61
1958	4,570	3,801			1.01	83.17
1959	6,694	5,556			1.35	83.00
1960	7,522	6,107			1.47	81.19
1961	9,059	7,005			1.70	77.33
1962	10,290	7,238			1.80	70.34
1963	12,495	7,764			2.07	62.14
1964	14,225	7,829			2.20	55.04
1965	14,614	7,342			2.08	50.24
1966	15,320	7,536			1.99	49.19
1967	16,529	8,566	915	4,778	2.03	51.82
1968	15,921	8,275	1,021	4,304	1.79	51.98
1969	15,641	8,356	1,088	3,799	1.63	53.42
1970	15,339	7,981	1,084	3,606	1.52	52.03
1971	15,543	8,110	1,288	3,048	1.42	52.18
1972	16,496	8,902	1,547	2,932	1.37	53.96
1973	16,800	9,002	1,585	2,824	1.24	53.58
1974	17,410	9,016	2,069	2,702	1.19	51.79
1975	19,039	9,679	2,170	2,764	1.20	50.84
1976	20,780	10,430	2,351	3,130	1.18	50.19
1977	23,450	11,864	2,629	2,832	1.19	50.59
1978	25,976	12,899	2,968	2,939	1.16	49.66
1979	28,208	13,791	3,401	3,136	1.13	48.89
1980	29,739	14,946	3,694	2,738	1.10	50.26
1981	33,735	18,413	3,871	3,111	1.11	54.58
1982	36,115	22,070	3,869	2,584	1.15	61.11
1983	38,768	24,936	4,298	2,134	1.14	64.32
1984	44,214	29,287	4,779	2,300	1.17	66.24
1985	49,887	33,698	5,418	2,725	1.24	67.55
1986	53,249	36,926	5,565	2,894	1.25	69.35
1987	57,069	39,152	6,556	3,398	1.26	68.60
1988	59,106	40,099	7,076	3,683	1.21	67.84
1989	62,115	40,665	7,773	4,555	1.18	65.47
1990	63,781	39,925	8,308	5,765	1.15	62.60
1991	65,898	39,328	9,226	6,511	1.15	59.68
1992	68,398	40,061	10,055	6,744	1.14	58.57
1993	65,603	41,249	10,280	6,988	1.03	62.88
1994	67,371	38,020	10,936	7,212	1.00	56.43
1995	69,147	39,496	11,417	7,665	0.98	57.12

Source: National Science Foundation/SRS.

Among universities, MIT stands out as a main beneficiary of the growing government wartime and postwar support. For example, in the 1940s and 1950s MIT laboratories received $117 million of $330 million funds from the Office of Scientific Research and Development.[43] Even as of 1996 MIT's research funds depend heavily on the federal government. More than $600 million federal research funds were directed to MIT (and its affiliate Lincoln Laboratory, which is mostly contracted for military projects). The federal funds comprise 85 percent of MIT's total research budget (table 5.11).

In addition to research funding, the federal government has been the main customer of the early electronics firms sprouting up along route 128, a major Massachusetts highway near MIT which is where many high-technology firms now reside. These infant information technology firms secured $6 billion of defense contracts during the 1950s, more than the annual $10 billion during the 1960s. Half the sales of the firms went to the federal government purchases.[44] Although Silicon Valley firms did not get as much support as Massachusetts firms did, postwar federal funds directed to the early players of information technology marked a watershed in the development of West Cost electronics firms as well. For example, Hewlett-Packard Company, founded in 1937 at

Table 5.11
Research Sponsorship of MIT in fiscal 1996 (unit: $thousands)

Organization	Campus	Lincoln Laboratory	Combined	Percentage
U.S. Department of Defense	$59,997	$280,952	$340,949	48.16
U.S. Department of Energy	$69,588		$69,588	9.83
U.S. DHHS	$58,211		$58,211	8.22
NASA	$39,190	$2,158	$41,348	5.84
NSF	$35,837	$70	$35,907	5.07
Other federal	$8,721	$48,457	$57,178	8.08
Federal government subtotal	$271,544	$331,637	$603,181	85.20
Industry	$67,164		$67,164	9.49
Other nonprofit	$25,926	$4,055	$29,981	4.23
Other sponsors	$3,372	$2,603	$5,975	0.84
State, local, and foreign Governments	$1,652		$1,652	0.23
Other sources subtotal	$98,114	$6,658	$104,772	14.80
Total	$369,658	$338,295	$707,953	100

Source: MIT Facts (World Wide Web MIT Home Page), 1997.

Palo Alto, took off during the Second World War. Its sales then went up to $75,000 in 1945 from $37,000 in 1941.[45] The two regions, Massachusetts' route 128 and the Silicon Valley, became the two focal points of information technology firms. Federal research funds and defense procurement provide milk and honey for the infant high-technology firms.

The development of the Internet is another striking example of how government research funds and infrastructure building paved a way to a new high-technology industry. The Internet grew out of the defense project ARPANET.[46] MIT's J. C. R. Licklider, who was the first to suggest computer networking interaction, became the first head of the computer research program at DARPA[47] in October 1962. A great many computers were assembled for the ARPANET project right after the new protocol TCP/IP became the defense standard in 1980. The Internet with TCP/IP protocol gained momentum further when National Science Foundation adopted the protocol of the NSFNET. NSFNET, developed and maintained by NSF funds, quickly grew to combine computers of a much wider research community including government research labs and universities. During the last ten years the Internet has become commercialized, and almost all major companies and people around the globe have joined in using this new means of communication. NSF's funding to maintain NSFNET made it attractive to researchers and university students in the United States. Today NSF still subsidizes use of the Internet by the American research community. Table 5.12 shows the NSF's information technology funds in 1996.

Table 5.12
NSF's information technology spending (unit: $millions)

Field	FY 1994	FY 1995	FY 1996
Computer and computation research	39.1	40.26	42.91
Information, robotics, and intelligent systems	29.58	32.28	35.13
Microelectronics information processing systems	23.54	25.83	28.14
Advanced scientific computing	74.61	79.21	84.06
Networking and communications research and infrastructure	49.94	56.46	59.56
Cross-disciplinary activities	22.75	24.23	25.77
Total	$239.52	$258.27	$275.57

Source: National Science Foundation.

The role of universities in the development of information technology industry has been crucial. The early history involving MIT and Stanford demonstrates how university research can benefit industries. A recent survey[48] reports that MIT graduates and faculty members have founded 4,000 firms generating $232 billion revenue and employing over one million people. These figures are higher than the GDP of Thailand. Information Technology firms—electronics manufacturing and software—comprise more than 60 percent of these firms (table 5.13).

Early on, while MIT relied heavily on federal funds in research, Stanford University developed a close link with the industry. The first big company in Silicon Valley was the Hewlett-Packard Corporation, founded in 1937. The founding episode of HP foreshadowed Stanford's role in the development of Silicon Valley. Frederick Terman, an MIT-educated electrical engineering professor at Stanford, encouraged his graduate students, William Hewlett and David Packard, to commercialize an audio-oscillator that Hewlett developed while working on his master's thesis. Professor Terman even lent $528 to start producing machines.[49] HP led the development of the Silicon Valley; its sales in 1996 amounted to $38 billion, which ranked it as the 16th largest U.S. firm according to the Fortune 500.

Saxenian summarizes Stanford's role in the early stages of Silicon Valley:

Three institutional innovations during the 1950s reflect the relationships that Terman pioneered in the region. First, Stanford established the Stanford research Institute to conduct defense-related research and to assist West Coast businesses. . . . Second, Stanford opened its classrooms to local companies through the Honors Cooperative Program. The university encouraged engineers at electronics companies to enroll in graduate courses directly or through a specialized televised instructional network which brought Stanford courses into company classrooms. . . . Third, Terman promoted the development of the Stanford Industrial Park. . . . By 1961 [Stanford Industrial Park] had grown to 652 acres and was home to 25 companies that together employed 11,000 people.[50]

The Center for the Continuing Study of the Californian Economy estimates that Silicon Valley's 2 million people produce around $65 billion in value-added terms—which approximates that of Chile's GDP in 1996.[51]

The fast-growing information technology sector, which was due to the widespread use of personal computers and the Internet, has con-

Table 5.13
MIT-related companies, 1996

Industry	Companies	Percentage of total	Employment (thousands)	Percentage of total	Sales ($billions)	Percentage of total
Total	2,884	100	1,117	100	231	100
Electronics	379	13.10	635	56.90	129.2	55.90
Machinery	78	2.70	39.1	3.50	7	3.00
Chemicals, materials	64	2.20	17.8	1.60	3.8	1.60
Aerospace	19	0.70	89.8	8.00	18.2	7.90
Other manufacturing	229	7.90	112.3	10.10	36.3	15.70
Manufacturing subtotal	769	27	894	80	195	84.10
Software	365	12.70	63.1	5.70	9.6	4.20
Drugs, biotechnology, medical	199	6.90	23.9	2.10	5.1	2.20
Energy, utilities	58	2.00	7.2	0.60	1.7	0.70
Publishing, schools	36	1.20	6.1	0.50	1	0.40
Architecture	299	10.40	16.8	1.50	2.7	1.20
Engineering consulting	346	12.00	23.5	2.10	3.3	1.40
Management consulting	243	8.40	12.2	1.10	1.7	0.70
Finance	195	5.80	14.7	1.30	7.2	3.10
Law, business services	122	4.20	39.3	3.50	1.5	0.70
Other	252	8.70	16	1.40	2.8	1.20

Source: *MIT: The Impact of Innovation*, Boston: BankBoston, 1997.

Table 5.14
Automobile versus information technology industry

	Sales, 1996 ($billions)	Employees (thousands)	Market value, 3/97 ($billions)
General Motors	164.1	647.0	43.0
Ford	147.0	345.0	38.0
Chrysler	61.4	114.0	22.0
Total	372.5	1,106.0	103.0
Intel	20.8	49.0	116.0
Microsoft	8.7	21.0	120.0
Cisco	4.1	10.0	34.0
Total	33.6	80.0	270.0

Source: Compustat.

tributed to the vast wealth of the U.S. economy. Note in table 5.14 the striking contrast between the old smoke stack industries and the new information technology industries. The market worth of Microsoft, which employs only 21,000 people, is more than the combined worth of the big three car companies who employ over one million. While output and employment numbers of car companies are more than ten times the size of three information technology companies, in terms of market value these information technology companies are twice as large as the entire car industry. Implied in the higher market value to sales ratio is the huge growth potential of the information technology industry.

Perhaps, the more important innovation in the information technology industry is not technological but organizational. We will examine three broad categories of organizational innovation: (1) organizational innovations of the information technology firms, (2) the industry innovation of the information technology sector, and (3) organizational innovations of intensive information technology user firms.

Many observers document striking differences between leading information technology firms and conventional bureaucratic organizations. But only a few have noticed that successful information technology firms are in many ways similar to successful firms of other industries. The leading information technology firms have not only transformed the business activities but also conserved many of important former innovations that occurred elsewhere. For example, some hardware manufacturers such as HP and Motorola successfully and creatively adopted the Japanese-style quality management and lean production system.[52] Dell computer adopted the direct-mail-order innovation of the retail industry and creatively applied it to personal computer manufacturing and sales.[53] Microsoft and Intel, two of the most successful companies in the information technology sector, have developed unique marketing strategies, human resource management systems, and new ways of using time-based competition.[54] Although these two companies have developed unique business strategies, they share many features with other successful knowledge-intensive firms such as law firms, management consultants, hospitals, and bio-tech firms.

The tremendous increase of computer power has been influential both within the information technology sector and without, in the profound transformation that information technology has inspired across almost all industries. First, recent studies have documented much higher marginal products of information technology capital than of conventional capital.[55] The market valuation of information technology is also higher.[56] Second, heavy users of information technology have transformed their organization styles. They are now flatter, more networked, more cooperative, and less bureaucratic.[57] Not only the providers of information technology but also the users of it have been changing their way of doing business to exploit the huge potential of information technology.

Silicon Valley provides an interesting picture of life in the information technology sector. It consists of a collection of small thriving firms and a flexible labor market. These characteristics of the region imply that in the information economy the scale economy is not contained within a firm. The concept of scale-and-scope economy should be applied at the industry level or the regional level. A collection of focused small and large firms can comprise a thriving industrial region that benefits from a scale economy such as has been demonstrated at Silicon Valley.

A striking characteristic of Silicon Valley is the extremely flexible markets of capital and labor. Employees not only move around firms; they sometimes do not even change parking lots. Firms go through ever shorter life cycles: They are created, they fail, and they are recreated.[58] "Tolerance of failure" and "tolerance of treachery"[59] may be vital to the well-being of the information technology industry worldwide.

Saxenian gives an account of some other cultural characteristics of Silicon Valley.[60] Unlike the secretive style of conventional firms or the

East Coast information technology firms and engineers, the Silicon Valley engineers help one another. It is a case of fierce competition and productive collaboration that go hand in hand among the firms. The Silicon Valley firms tend to be very focused; they maximize scale economies ("even beyond their firm's fuzzy boundary") and exploit the scope economies of the region.

The firms in this region value diversity and variety. They are almost obsessed with the "cool ideas" that emerge out of diversity. Lots of Indian, Chinese, and other foreign immigrant engineers work for these firms. The region's well-developed venture capitalists of course play crucial roles. They not only identify and fund potential ventures but also provide valuable management skills that start-up engineering firms often lack. (This mechanism is lacking in Korea. Even Japan has not thought of this approach.) The federal and California state governments have no role in the day to day business of the region, which keeps intact the vitality of the industry and the region.

The information technology revolution in the United States is founded on many success stories. The early initiatives and ongoing research funds from the government provided the incentives and financing that researchers and start-up firms need to survive. Universities outfitted the modern workforce with new knowledge and perhaps made it the most important productive element of the modern economy. Industry of course has done its part in technological and organizational innovations. If one element of this collaboration were missing, there would be no information technology revolution in the United States or anywhere in the world.

What emerges from this brief review is the value of market flexibility both for capital and for labor. Flexibility is a feature of competition as well as cooperation in the information technology market. The traditional notion of each firm having a boundary is changing constantly as flexibility enables firms to manage scale and scope economies and meet continual market shifts with new ideas. These circumstances have been enhanced by a government that is also flexible. The U.S. government has opted to be active in providing financial support but inactive in meddling in the workings of the market. This is something for Korean policy makers to mull over.

6

Summary and Conclusions

Korean firms have learned new (mostly imported) technologies quickly. They have mastered new ways of organizing enterprises to transform knowledge into productivity and productivity into competitiveness. *Chaebols* have been in the forefront of this development. The Korean educational system has played a crucial role by supplying an increasing number of highly educated engineers and technicians, thanks to foreign universities, particularly U.S. universities, which contributed by training Korean students in cutting-edge technologies. But an excessive supply of university graduates has led to graduate unemployment coupled with a mismatch of skills. Meanwhile, the quality of graduates has suffered, particularly in engineering, as a result of inadequate laboratory equipment.

The Korean government has played its part in upgrading the technological capabilities of firms by creating a science and technology infrastructure. Examples include government-financed research institutes such as KIST and its spin-offs, educational facilities for science and engineering such as KAIST, financial facilities to support ventures, information services, and institutional devices for risk-sharing. This cooperation among business, educational institutions, and government has laid the foundation of a market-oriented political economy, expediting Korea's climb up the technological ladder. Consistently government, universities, and industries have cooperated in building human capabilities (skill development), in organizing them with an appropriate incentive structure, and thus in enhancing technological learning individually and organizationally.

The contributions of government have not been free of problems. One just has to note that two former presidents are jailed on corruption charges, long hours are wasted in traffic jams, smog and polluted rivers have upset the ecological balance, and bridges and buildings have collapsed (e.g., Sung-su bridge and Sam-poong department store) due to faulty engineering and maintenance. Critics point out that these negative happenings stem from the corruption inherent in any government-business symbiosis. For example, the susceptibility of government bureaucrats and politicians to "kickbacks" undermines the value of government contracts (e.g., bridge building) for the business side since bribe money comes from contract funds. Consequently costs are cut by using substandard materials, which in the case of a bridge-building project may cause the bridge to collapse.

Nevertheless, the economic system has been evolving consistently during the last three decades. There has been a gradual movement toward a more market-oriented, decentralized system and increasing linkages to the global economy. These linkages have provided channels through which Korean firms can import and master new technologies. *Chaebols* have taken the lead (at the micro level of the economy) in creating linkages and broadening business opportunities abroad.

In the process myriad institutional devices have been invented, tested, and changed. This tendency toward self-reorganization, whose purpose was to develop an effective incentive structure, has provided a driving force that has made "technological learning" possible and quick. In consequence the technology content of Korean manufactures and exports has been rising at a speed unmatched by any other country. In short, learning to do new things (though by imitating) has gone on, and learning is expected to continue in coming decades. The government has become an entrepreneurial agent that invents and crafts new institutional devices continually to meet new needs arising at the macro level of the economy. This function should not be confused with "market intervention" or "market repression."

This concluding chapter addresses two questions: What are the lessons that the past experience provides for the future? Can the Korean experience furnish a tool for science and technology diplomacy? These are far-reaching questions, and the answers can only be speculative. Nevertheless, they are worth asking if only because similar questions are asked so frequently both in Korea and elsewhere.

6.1 Lessons for the Future: New Challenges

An important issue concerns the role of government.[1] Since the start of Korean industrialization in the 1960s and 1970s, the government took a leadership role in planning, developing, and upgrading the industrial structure. A selective protection approach provided the means by which newly emerging industries could learn technologies. Korea's current export capability is proof that this learning strategy was successful.

It is well recognized, however, that the role of government needs to evolve so that it does not retain outmoded methods. First, Korean industries have grown up; they no longer need spoon-fed types of protection. Second, reliance on market mechanisms for industrial adjustment is less costly than governmental industrial restructuring, such as trimming of *chaebols'* power. Third, Korea's advanced economic status (e.g., OECD membership) in the era of WTO has rendered many forms of government intervention obsolete, shackling, or even illegal. The need to liberalize the financial sector provides a case in point. Entrepreneurs have been clamoring for interest rates to be lowered by letting foreign funds flow in more freely. This would greatly reduce the financial disadvantages currently facing Korean manufacturers.

Nevertheless, the government has not finished its role as catalyst and builder of infrastructure for the high-tech sectors. Having reached the mid-tech level on the "global technology ladder," Korean industries are now poised to enter into the high-tech areas. This means that issues relating to a whole new set of technologies must be grappled with, particularly with respect to information and telecommunications. These issues include the shortening product life cycle, lean production (in contrast to Fordism), heavy, high-risk R&D investment requirements, technology fusion, multiple-skilling of the workforce, networking on a global scale, and the like. Open competition requires that Korean industries learn to manage these problems from a global perspective. With few exceptions, the private enterprise sector in general is ill-equipped to meet the requirements of global operation. To cite several examples, there is a lack of information on technology development abroad, on opportunities for joint ventures, and on marketing. The government must work with private enterprises in order to construct an appropriate and diverse science and technology infrastructure to help them overcome these problems.

Government-Financed Research Institutes

Obviously the raison d'être of GFRIs is to provide infrastructure, and the point has been made here that the most needed infrastructure is an arrangement enhancing industry-academe-government cooperation. This means that GFRIs must enter into R&D activities that the private sector has chosen not to undertake for various reasons. Certain R&D projects carry large external benefits, high stakes coupled with excessively high risks and uncertainties, or time horizons that are too long (though desirable for other reasons) for private enterprise. GFRIs are empowered to become a center for developing the scientific basis for such technologies.

Further such R&D projects could involve pooling the complementary resources of industries, universities, and GFRIs themselves. GFRIs have an advantage in that they already have the seasoned manpower (over 2,000 PhDs), specialized laboratory equipment, and research experience reaching back several decades. These R&D resources could be re-deployed to improve the existing infrastructure and to meet the challenges of high technology. The morale of discouraged researchers at GFRIs could be raised by redefining their roles and by giving them new tasks. These are discussed in the following order: (1) combining research with teaching, (2) developing new journals, (3) building a comprehensive national center for a science and technology database, and (4) providing global technology scanning.

Teaching has not been a primary concern of KIST-spin-off GFRIs, although they have provided some opportunities for company employees to be retrained and also produced some doctorates and masters under a cooperative teaching arrangement with universities. Little recognition and reward is given for training engineers. (KAIST is an exception, having started with the specific mission of producing engineers with PhDs.) Their primary concern has been to do research on a contractual basis with government agencies and private enterprises.

A proposal is advanced here to strengthen the teaching role of GFRIs and to integrate it with research. In other words, research is to be done concurrently with teaching. Equal weight can be given to teaching and research (as in the case of KAIST). Students get trained for graduate degrees in engineering while doing research to get frontline knowledge together with professor-researchers from GFRIs (much as in clinical medicine).

This arrangement may be designed so as to help solve several problems at once. First, recall that manpower projections for the next decade show an acute shortage of researchers with advanced degrees, particularly in electronics and the information-telecommunication industries. These future needs offer a challenge that GFRIs have to grapple with. GFRIs should be well equipped to produce a doctorate in engineering, for instance, and provide hands-on experience in design as well as basic theoretical knowledge.[2] Students would be required to obtain patents in their major fields as a condition for a doctoral degree. In addition they would need to publish an article in an established international journal of engineering.

Upon graduation, the engineer would carry the technological knowledge and design skills with him to the company employing him. It has been shown that the transfer of personnel offers the most effective method of technology transfer between factories, and even between the research unit and production lines within a company.[3] This arrangement would represent an improvement over the past practice of universities producing PhDs in engineering with theoretical training but lacking practical experience or concern for factory-level problems. Compared with universities, GFRIs are better equipped to train high-quality engineers because they have been engaged in research for private enterprises for decades.

Second, the teaching staff at GFRIs (particularly the KIST spin-offs) should be given academic titles such as professor, associate professor, or assistant professor. KAIST provides a model for this purpose. Of course academic titles should be conferred on a highly selective, peer-reviewed basis. This would make the well-recognized Korean respect for academic titles a means of rewarding performance. Such an arrangement would enhance the underdeveloped reward system for scientists and engineers in Korea, especially in GFRIs. Korea deserves an improved system of rewards. The creation of such a system based on performance could prove a wise investment in the creation of knowledge-based national wealth. It is worth noting that "approximately 3,000 prizes in the sciences were available in North America alone in the 1990s. This is five times the number awarded 20 years earlier."[4]

Performance criteria for professor-researchers at the GFRIs should include the publication of papers, patent registrations, teaching evaluations, and public services (emphasizing contributions to cooperative projects involving industries, universities and government). It is particularly desirable that promotions and salary increases be linked to such quantifiable (objective) performance, along with peer-group (subjective) evaluation. This combination of "objective and subjective" approaches has proved in U.S. universities to be more useful (less controversial) than any single-component approach. (Alternatively, one could also emulate the practice of the best U.S. universities, e.g.,

Harvard, where tenure is based on the best six pieces of published work. This approach honors only creativity, not the number of pages published.)

The inclusion of patent registration in performance evaluation, though not practiced in U.S. universities, emphasizes that R&D at GFRIs should deal more closely with problems on the factory floor. Patent registrations could be placed on a par with published papers, if the GFRIs so wish. The problem of how specific performance should be weighted must be solved by peer consensus.

Furthermore the GFRIs may recruit retired engineers from private enterprises, in addition to university professors, for joint appointments (temporary or permanent). This arrangement would be useful in enhancing linkages between the three major spheres (industry, university, and government). Retired engineers renowned for excellent innovative contributions could offer students motivation from their lifetime experiences (as is done in Japan).

University professors may be allowed to get joint appointments with GFRIs and possibly carry out joint research at GFRIs. In other words, GFRIs as a system should facilitate human flow within industries and universities. Conventionally professors as well as researchers have not been allowed to have any kind of outside occupation because of a fear of venality, corruption, or "intellectual prostitution." But times have changed. Competition for excellence between universities could prove to be better at preventing corruption than any set of rigid rules.

New Journals

The free flow of ideas and thoughts could be emphasized by periodic conferences on industry-university-government cooperation programs. Since the central role of this cooperative movement is to be played by GFRIs, the logical home of the journal (or journals) and the managing editor may be located at GFRIs. Initially most of the referees should come from the research staff of GFRIs, although outside experts can participate in refereeing on a rotational basis. The journal(s) provide a forum to debate, judge, and evaluate the merits of research results. Certainly publication in the journal(s) constitutes a form of recognition for researchers.

Journals can provide a long-term foundation for building the much needed community of science and engineering in Korea. An essential component in building such a community is the institution of credible peer-group evaluation. On no account should peers be expected to render entirely perfect, objective, value-free, apolitical evaluation; these are difficult criteria to uphold even in the United States and Europe.[5] Nevertheless, there seems to be no better substitute, and at its inception, the inclusion of "foreign peers" on the editorial board may be desirable. Korean-American scientists and engineers could prove invaluable here, considering the shortage of experts in some areas as well as the language problem for other nationals.

National Database

The campaign for industry-university-government cooperation can be buttressed by a national database center covering the R&D activities of these three spheres. Ignorance about what others are doing poses an important barrier to cooperation. It has been reported that only about 20 out of the 234 academic associations in science and engineering fields have established R&D databases with information on R&D personnel and research results.[6] Reportedly MOST had been pushing a "Seven-Year Plan for Constructing a Database for Academic Associations" as a part of the national project for building an information highway, but the plan was aborted due to a lack of cooperation among government ministries. The absence of a database means that vast amounts of research in the form of reports and dissertations are wasted. The lack of an information network has also been the cause of inefficient allocation of research funds, and duplication of research in industries, universities, and GFRIs.

Collectively GFRIs may take the initiative and formulate a long-term (e.g., ten-year) program for building a national center for a science and engineering database. The center should cover information on all R&D personnel, research results in different forms (papers, patents, reports, dissertations, conference proceedings, etc.), records of technology assessment, policy analyses, and so on. The database system should connect industries, universities, and GFRIs. The value of such a database system would be virtually limitless. Because it is a public good, it is imperative that GFRIs (rather than industries or universities) be in charge of its construction and management.

Global technology scanning offers an additional challenge to the Korean R&D system. Technology scanning involving other countries will be in great demand as Korean industries become more globalized. The competitive advantage of possessing such scanning capabilities needs no elaboration.[7] The revolution in digital technology has made it possible to think about developing scanning capability as an infrastructure. An individual company, a university, or a single government agency may not be able to afford to build the facility. Early investment on a massive scale appears warranted. Learning this technology could well take the next ten years and involve software, hardware, and expert scanning operators.

Corporate Organization

It has been noted that the *chaebol* groups have led the way in introducing new technologies to Korean industry. They have accumulated technological knowledge, human capital, and organizational skills more rapidly than non-*chaebol* companies. Their performance is most likely to continue into the foreseeable future. For instance, *chaebols* are expected to lead in absorbing high-tech knowledge into the production process such as flexible manufacturing systems, computer-integrated manufacturing, computer-aided design, and robotics as well as organizational changes that will provide a driving force in raising productivity.

Looking into the future on the matter of human capital, one may expect the levels of education and skill development among manufacturing employees to continue to rise. A multiple-skilled labor force will emerge in response to the demands placed by new production technologies. Investment in retraining over the workers' lifetime of employment will add to the accumulation of human capital. Consequently a 7 to 8 percent growth in labor productivity is a rather conservative estimate for the next five to ten years. The "intelligent factory" is more likely to win the competitive race.

Decentralization of decision making can be envisaged as a major trend among *chaebol* groups. Already some leading *chaebols* (e.g., Samsung, Daewoo, Lucky-Goldstar) have adopted a small group system, meaning that a few vertically related member companies form subgroups and act independently in hiring, investing, and divesting decisions. The new arrangement gives flexibility to the "chairman of the small group" in making decisions. Some *zaibatsu* in Japan have adopted this arrangement (e.g., Hitachi). This is reminiscent of Peter Drucker's prediction concerning the future of "flotillas." This arrangement gives a freer hand in decision making to the member companies within the constraints imposed by the *chaebol*'s overall view. Whether this trend will lead to further decentralization and complete independence remains to be seen.

Further the government has been urging *chaebols* to trim their size by shedding less efficient member companies. Lessons should be learned, the government says, from the examples of AT&T, Ford, and IBM, all of which lost out to more adroit and nimble competitors. The government has been asserting that *chaebols* have grown too big to be efficient competitors, having been nurtured with subsidies and protection. Furthermore the sheer size of *chaebols* is viewed as harmful to fair income distribution and also to the development of SMEs. This admonition represents a turnaround from the past practice of encouraging *chaebols'* growth through diversification and through mergers and acquisition.

Opponents argue that there is no specific need for the government to enforce the "downsizing" of *chaebols*. Opening up Korean markets to international competition would bring about restructuring as a matter of course, if indeed size hinders productivity growth and competitiveness.

In the long run the debate should be settled on the basis of technological capability building. Opinions abound, but the following view is worth noting: "All in all, the Korean experience suggests that diversification is not associated with inefficiency, when in fact the obverse is true. Diversification—related or unrelated—will work if proper attention is paid to the development of the human resources needed to sustain it. As such the adoption of policies intent on restructuring the *Chaebols* based on the pattern of the American diversified firm alone may be largely misplaced."[8] In short, one could argue that the important criterion for judging efficiency should be not just the size of an enterprise but its ability to master new technology.

More specifically, the point I want to emphasize is expressed in the following statement: *"The extremely high degree of concentration in the electronics industry is the single factor that can ensure Korea's international success in the industrial sectors chosen. In these, success will go to large integrated companies capable of financing the massive investments necessary to commercialize the new technologies and operate successfully in international markets. The large conglomerates are the best chance Korea has to break out of its dependence on foreign technology.''*[9]

An equally important long-term issue concerns the question of defining labor participation in the decision-making process and also in reward sharing. Korean capitalism is in the process of being created, meaning that myriad institutional devices are being designed and tested. The form and extent of labor participation make a difference in determining the pace of technology upgrading. It is proposed here that stock options need to be made available to all employees, including managers at all levels in the hierarchy, R&D personnel, as well as production-line workers. There are many stock option variations, but they need to be tested in order to find the scheme that best motivates employees to learn, both individually and collectively.

One possible scenario, just to illustrate the point made above, is that awards for useful suggestions could be in the form of stock (with voting rights) in addition to regular bonuses, promotions, and salary increases. Awards for excellent group performances could also be made in stock. The amount of stock given for different types of employee performance should be defined clearly. In other words, the rules of the game should be well defined and known to everyone concerned.

The ultimate goal of an enterprise is to satisfy consumers as well as to provide a secure workplace for employees, a respectable income, and *boram*—a Korean word for a sense of satisfaction and achievement attendant to doing something meaningful. The *boram* as a reward variable could be exploited to enhance motivation. For instance, the company could provide opportunities for employees to improve their skill levels throughout their working life. This is consistent with the Confucian value of respecting learning. Institution building within an enterprise (for that matter in any organization) requires a skillful combination of such tangible and nontangible reward variables linked to performance. Thus a distinctive organizational culture is being created at Samsung, Hyundai, Daewoo, L-G, and others. This aspect of institution building (incentive-reward structure) offers a fruitful area for future research (e.g., in comparative socioeconomics).

Richard Nelson advanced a similar idea to explain international differences in competitiveness: ''The co-evolution of technology and institutions is a fascinating subject. . . . There clearly have been major national differences in how the institutions needed to support particular evolving technologies themselves evolved. Perhaps in the study of the co-evolution of technology and institutions we will begin to develop a serious theory of how national comparative advantage comes into being, or is lost. . . ."[10]

Universities

As pointed out in chapter 3, universities face the challenge of raising the quality of both professors and students. The challenge involves reforming the incentive structure. One way is to link faculty performance to rewards such as tenure, promotion, salary increases, flexibility in teaching loads, and frequency of sabbaticals. The system of measuring and evaluating faculty performance has not been well established in Korea compared to advanced industrial countries such as the United States, England, and Germany.

In principle, the performance of university faculties can be evaluated in terms of excellence in research, publication, teaching, and community services. It is, however, up to the individual university (or department) to define the quality standard and relative weight given these component items. A minimum standard can be defined for each rank (assistant professor, associate professor, full professor, etc.). For instance, tenure can be decided on at the end of either the assistant professor or associate professor level, depending on the criteria a university adopts. In the mechanical engineering department at MIT, for instance, tenure requires that ten outside letters of recommendation unanimously confirm that the faculty member in question is among the world's best in his/her field of specialization.

Conventionally in the Korean university system lifetime employment is conferred de facto at the time of initial employment. Then the seniority system almost automatically promotes one to full professorship. It is no wonder that Korean professors have had an abysmally low publication record. Fortunately in numerous universities reforms are being tested in a serious manner.

If a university with an engineering college wishes to emphasize applied aspects of research, patent rights acquired by a faculty could be added as a performance indicator. Patent income (through licensing fees) could be shared between the faculty and the university, adding a potent monetary incentive to the performance-reward system. For this purpose the university should establish an office along with a set of rules to manage the patent rights earned by faculty members. Many American universities have successfully managed patent rights to enrich their university endowments for furthering research and teaching. Examples include MIT, Harvard, Stanford, CalTech, Columbia, and so on. Korean universities could certainly learn from these experiences.

It is desirable to institute flexibility in university rules and regulations regarding joint appointments. A professor could be allowed to do research and teaching at an enterprise-owned R&D institute or at a GFRI, say, on a half-time basis (temporarily or permanently). MIT has very flexible rules for faculty appointment. For instance, a senior lecturer (e.g., Professor Richard H. Lyon, a world renowned expert on noise and vibration) teaches one course every semester at MIT and at the same time owns a research firm of which he is also the president. MIT is well aware that the free flow of people with ideas facilitates the rapid diffusion of technology.

The above dictum is also true internationally. Generally, Korean universities have yet to understand the advantages of hiring foreign professors as regular teaching staff. The necessity of doing so seems to have been recognized by the Seoul National University faculty when the school announced in 1996 its intention to hire foreign professors up to 10 percent of the total teaching faculty. Other universities should be encouraged to do likewise. Foreign professors on campus can be a powerful antidote to the inbreeding that has plagued Korean universities in the past.

As for the problem of raising the quality of graduates, the KAIST model has proved effective, providing lessons for other universities. Recall that PhD candidates at KAIST are expected to publish an article in an internationally recognized journal. The incentive package for the degree include an exemption from the military duty, free tuition plus room and board, instruction given by top-notch professors, excellent laboratory facilities, and so on. The fierce competition for entrance among aspirants enables KAIST to choose the best students. In short, a university's pursuit of excellence has to be translated into a set of attractive rewards that encourage the student's performance and culminate in a degree such as a doctorate in engineering. Each university should invent its own incentive package compatible with available resources (money, strategic nonmonetary assets, comparative regional advantages, etc.). Ultimately competition for good students will decide who the winner will be. Fortunately in recent years an increasing number of universities have begun to think in strategic terms. For example, Ajou University has embarked on an all-out campaign to become one of the nation's top five universities by the year 2000.

6.2   Korean Experience as a Tool for Science and Technology Diplomacy

The Republic of Korea joined OECD in 1996. Korean policy makers now face the challenge of figuring out what Korea's proper role should be in OECD in the twenty-first century. What can Korea offer to the world community? Korea received much aid when she suffered abject poverty and hopelessness during the late 1940s and 1950s.[11] Now the country has to shift from a receiver to a giver of aid. Perhaps Korea can share with other developing countries its experience of industrialization through learning. What lessons can the Korean experience offer?

Debate has been going on for some time about whether the Korean experience of rapid growth (or the so-called East-Asian miracle) can be replicated.[12] Though a consensus has yet to be reached, there appears to be increasing recognition that the problems of market failure and imperfection must be dealt with in developing countries. Korea has invented and managed its own approach to deal with the problems. The perspective adopted in this book offers a conceptual framework that can be used in thinking about the goals and means of aid giving.

Suppose that the goal of aiding a country (with few natural resources) is to help the industrial sector to learn, build, and upgrade its industrial base. Korea has ample experience to draw upon. Korea should be prepared to give cooperative assistance to raise the level of technological knowledge, human capital, and institutional-organizational skills. Of course, such an aid-giving operation requires careful study of existing conditions in the aid-receiving country. Institutional-organizational devices need to be studied with utmost care, since this is a politically sensitive area that is still little understood.

An aid program with a learning perspective should emphasize human capital formation. It may be possible to formulate a cooperative program whereby managers, R&D personnel, and engineers would be invited to come to Korea for training. Foreign students could also be invited to work on their degrees. The Korean experience has proved that "human bridges" (e.g., the Koreans trained in the United States) pay long-term dividends.[13] Well-trained, well-organized, and well-motivated human resources provide the foundation for wealth and new business opportunities.

The most suitable agency to formulate and carry out the program of science and technology cooperation appears to be the Science and Technology Policy Institute (STEPI). This agency has evolved to play

Box 6.1

Science and Technology Policy Institute (STEPI)

This institute was established in January 1987 under the jurisdiction of KAIST. Now it is under MOST. STEPI has three purposes. First, the institute collects and disseminates information useful for R&D management (for business and government) as well as for science and technology policy formulation. Second, the institute evaluates government research projects (proposals and research results) in order to enhance the overall efficiency of national research programs. Third, the institute provides the intellectual basis for scholarly research on technological innovation, scientific progress, and policy formulation.

The main function of the institute consists of (1) formulation of policy alternatives for the system of scientific and technological innovation, (2) planning, administration, and evaluation of national research programs as well as training and education for research management techniques, and (3) research on strategy of international cooperation for science and technology development and implementation of cooperative projects.

As of January 1997 the institute has 168 employees, 48 of whom have PhDs. Seventy-five of them are researchers, 10 are engineers, 32 are technicians, and the rest are administrators. The total budget for 1996 amounts to 10,989 million won (approximately U.S.$13.7 million).

During 1987 to 1996 the institute carried out altogether 273 projects. The summary follows:

Research area	Number of projects	Main content of projects
Long-term strategy planning	37	Long-term S&T development plan toward year 2010 Scenario and strategies for technological innovation in major industries
National system of innovation	36	S&T development system of OECD member countries Regional system of technological innovation
Enhancing R&D productivity	56	National R&D budget and policy targets Roles and functions of GFRIs
Advancement of S&T support system	31	R&D support system and new international economic order S&T related laws and reformulation
Globalization of science and technology	52	Trends of S&T policies in major countries Strategies for S&T globalization
Upgrading of S&T infrastructure	61	Construction of S&T information flow system Policy measures for S&T population

an important role in formulating and managing national science and technology policy. It was experimental in 1984 as a Technology Assessment Center attached to KAIST. It is now a think tank under MOST with the following mission: (1) To conduct research on a national system of innovation and technology as well as on the formulation of policy alternatives, (2) to plan, manage, and assess national R&D projects, and also to run education programs on R&D management, and (3) to conduct research on strategies for international cooperation in science and technology and to implement cooperation projects.

The agency is a Korean invention with a unique interdisciplinary approach involving natural science, engineering, economics, sociology, business management, public administration, and international relations. The knowledge accumulated in STEPI can provide good educational materials for students from other countries. It is here recommended that STEPI expand its educational program to grant advanced degrees in technology management. This educational program could be combined with the research program, resulting in new curriculum development.

These proposals may seem "unrealistic" to some skeptics. But they are based on the thesis that productivity growth stemming from learning can bring about dynamic increasing returns in the form of new business opportunities for all. This perception counters the static view expressed by the trade pessimists. They claim that NICs' experience cannot be replicated because markets of advanced industrial countries cannot receive unlimited floods of labor-intensive goods.[14] But the reality among Asian NICs has proved otherwise. There is already a second tier of NICs in the Asia-Pacific region, expanding mutual trade volumes. In learning new (imported) technologies, they have created and expanded each others' markets. Korean industry should be aiming for a positive-sum game by helping other developing countries to learn new technologies. The advent of the information-telecommunication revolution can be expected to intensify the positive-sum game effect in the decades to come.

Appendix A
Indicators of
Technological Capabilities
in South Korea

A.1   Number of Research Institutes and Researchers in South Korea, 1964–1996

Year	R&D performing institution		Number of researchers	
	Total number	Private companies	Total number	Private companies
1964	87	13	1,906	n.a.
1965	105	22	2,765	n.a.
1966	108	22	2,962	n.a.
1967	223	98	4,061	n.a.
1968	273	100	5,024	n.a.
1969	280	104	5,337	n.a.
1970	297	107	5,628	1,159
1971	305	118	5,320	925
1972	319	133	5,599	1,149
1973	368	167	6,065	1,405
1974	456	242	6,314	2,552
1975	553	303	10,275	2,655
1977	626	278	11,661	3,258
1978	647	291	14,749	4,304
1979	641	305	15,771	4,405
1980	647	321	18,434	7,165
1981	662	323	20,718	7,165
1982	860	554	28,448	9,959
1983	1,080	742	32,117	12,586
1984	1,143	782	37,103	15,914
1985	1,291	928	41,473	18,996
1986	1,682	1,321	47,042	22,915
1987	1,856	1,478	52,783	26,104
1988	2,821	1,633	56,545	28,299
1989	2,077	1,689	66,220	35,167
1990	2,105	1,718	70,503	38,737
1991	2,352	1,943	76,252	45,043
1992	3,106	2,657	88,764	51,074
1993	3,318	2,864	98,767	54,078
1994	2,640	2,179	117,446	59,281
1995	2,587	2,152	128,315	68,625
1996	2,856	2,435	132,023	71,193

Source: MOST, *Science and Technology Yearbook* (annual).

A.2   R&D Expenditures in South Korea, 1963–1996 (unit: 100 million won; %)

Year	Total	Government	Nongovernment
1963	12	—	—
1964	14	96.4	3.6
1965	21	89.9	10.1
1966	32	89.9	10.1
1967	48	83.6	16.4
1968	67	85.2	14.8
1969	98	81.8	18.2
1970	105	71.3	28.7
1971	107	72.2	27.8
1972	120	68.1	31.9
1973	156	55.6	44.4
1974	382	65.7	34.3
1975	427	66.7	33.3
1976	609	64.8	35.2
1977	1,083	47.7	52.3
1978	1,524	48.8	51.2
1979	1,740	54.5	45.5
1980	2,117	51.6	48.4
1981	2,931	43.6	56.4
1982	4,577	41.3	58.7
1983	6,217	27.5	72.5
1984	8,339	21.4	78.6
1985	11,552	19.5	80.5
1986	15,233	19.1	80.9
1987	18,780	20.4	79.6
1988	23,747	17.7	82.3
1989	28,173	20.4	79.6
1990	33,499	19.4	80.6
1991	41,584	19.6	80.4
1992	49,890	17.6	82.4
1993	61,530	16.9	83.1
1994	78,947	15.9	84.1
1995	94,406	18.9	81.1
1996	108,780	17.4	82.6

Source: MOST, *Science and Technology Yearbook* (annual).

A.3   Indicators of Technological Capability in South Korea, 1963– 1995 (unit: numbers)

Year	Technology imports	Patents applied		Patents granted		Capital goods imported ($million)	Export items (CCCN 8-digits[a])
		Total	Korean nationals	Total	Korean nationals		
1963	3	n.a.	n.a.	n.a.	n.a.	n.a.	119
1964	1	908	n.a.	n.a.	n.a.	n.a.	142
1965	4	1,018	n.a.	n.a.	n.a.	n.a.	350
1966	18	1,060	n.a.	n.a.	n.a.	172	445
1967	36	1,177	n.a.	n.a.	n.a.	310	513
1968	51	1,463	n.a.	n.a.	n.a.	533	650
1969	59	1,699	n.a.	317	n.a.	593	822
1970	92	1,846	n.a.	266	n.a.	590	952
1971	47	1,906	n.a.	229	n.a.	685	983
1972	53	1,995	n.a.	218	n.a.	762	1,002
1973	67	2,389	n.a.	199	n.a.	1,159	1,059
1974	88	4,455	n.a.	322	n.a.	1,849	n.a.
1975	99	2,914	n.a.	442	n.a.	1,909	n.a.
1976	127	3,261	n.a.	479	n.a.	2,427	n.a.
1977	168	3,139	1,177	274	104	3,008	n.a.
1978	297	4,015	994	427	133	5,080	n.a.
1979	291	4,722	1,034	1,419	258	6,314	n.a.
1980	222	5,070	1,241	1,632	186	5,125	n.a.
1981	247	5,303	1,319	1,808	232	6,158	4,356
1982	308	5,924	1,556	2,609	274	6,233	4,401
1983	362	6,394	1,559	2,433	245	7,851	4,434
1984	437	8,633	2,014	2,365	297	10,106	4,773
1985	454	10,587	2,703	2,268	349	11,079	4,850
1986	517	12,759	3,641	1,894	458	11,340	5,142
1987	637	17,062	4,871	2,330	596	14,552	5,270
1988	751	20,501	5,696	2,174	575	19,033	
1989	763	23,315	7,021	3,972	1,181	22,370	
1990	738	25,820	9,082	7,762	2,554	25,545	
1991	582	28,132	13,253	8,690	2,553	30,092	
1992	533	31,073	15,952	10,502	3,570	30,580	
1993	707	36,491	21,459	11,446	4,545	30,603	
1994	430	45,712	38,564	11,683	5,774	40,429	
1995	236	78,499	n.a.	12,512	n.a.	53,555	

Source: MOST and MOTIE.
a. Note: The use of CCCN classification was discontinued in 1988.

Appendix B
Regression of Total Factor Productivity Function with R&D and Education as Determinants in South Korea

B.1 Data Description

TL (total factor productivity)	Level estimation (1980 = 100); source same as table 2.4
RDR (R&D investment)	The ratio of the R&D investment to output; source same as above
Ed	Average education years; source same as table 3.2
RDR(x)	RDR lagged by x year

B.2 Fixed Effect Model

$$\ln(TL_{it}) = I * C_i + b1_{it} * RDR(1)_{it} + b2_{it} * RDR(2)_{it} + b3_{it} * RDR(3)_{it} + b4_{it} * Ed_{it} + e_{it}$$

Sample (adjusted)	1982–1992; regression for pooled data of cross section and time series
Included observations	11 after adjusting endpoints
Total panel observations	340

Variable	Coefficient	Standard error	t-statistic	Probability
RDR(1)?	0.020350	0.010393	1.957965	0.0510
RDR(2)?	0.033464	0.010827	3.090928	0.0021
RDR(3)?	0.047362	0.009946	4.762100	0.0000
ED?	0.057167	0.004938	5.877600	0.0000

Fixed Effects (for 36 manufacturing subsectors as classified in table 2.4)

1–C 4.316957

2–C 4.191522

4–C 4.279916

5–C 4.342714

6–C 4.349215

7–C 4.339751

8–C 4.359398

9–C 4.319176

10–C 4.307041

11–C 4.384885

12–C 4.245163

13–C 4.277594

14–C 4.108623

15–C 4.321110

16–C 4.385879

17–C 4.314970

18–C 4.458964

19–C 4.415343

20–C 4.223764

21–C 4.263987

22–C 4.311988

23–C 4.373500

24–C 4.316791

25–C 4.414372

26–C 4.466719

27–C 4.371274

28–C 4.346564

29–C 4.318096

30–C 4.033595

31–C 4.416907

32–C 4.415400

33–C 4.426065

34–C 4.417554

35–C 4.337746

36–C 4.382723

R-squared	0.785972	Mean dependent variable	4.718407
Adjusted R-squared	0.758952	SD dependent variable	0.089714
SE of regression	0.044046	Sum squared residual	0.583966
F-statistic	368.4535	Durbin-Watson statistic	0.486487
Prob(F-statistic)	0.000000		

B.3 Pooled Regression

$$TL_{it} = C + b_{it} * RDR_{it} + C_{it} * Ed_{it} + e_{it}$$

Sample (adjusted)   1980–1992 pooled data

Included observations   13 after adjusting endpoints

Total panel observations   455

Variable	Coefficient	Standard error	t-statistic	Probability
C	88.13851	3.989047	22.09513	0.0000
RDR?	3.571725	0.371054	9.625898	0.0000
ED?	1.514806	0.384923	3.935347	0.0001

R-squared	0.258506	Mean dependent variable	109.7768
Adjusted R-squared	0.255225	SD dependent variable	10.19493
SE of regression	8.798261	Sum squared residual	34989.05
F-statistic	78.78993	Durbin-Watson statistic	0.151236
Prob(F-statistic)	0.000000		

B.4 Fixed Effect Model (or the Least Squares Dummy Variable Model)

$$TL_{it} = I * a_i + b_{it} * RDR_{it} + C_{it} * Ed_{it} + e_{it}$$

Sample (adjusted)   1980-1992

Included observations   13 after adjusting endpoints

Total panel observations   455

Variable	Coefficient	Standard error	t-statistic	Probability
RDR?	3.754822	0.431831	8.695117	0.0000
ED?	6.306429	0.458309	13.76022	0.0000

Fixed Effects

1–C 38.35935
2–C 23.12730
4–C 38.47976
5–C 44.35437
6–C 45.07283
7–C 46.33767
8–C 47.01850
9–C 41.35278
10–C 39.53775
11–C 37.12279
12–C 25.86731
13–C 24.13828
14–C 13.72598
15–C 45.59959
16–C 44.70680
17–C 33.99978
18–C 56.14558
19–C 43.75678
20–C 32.98493
21–C 31.41352
22–C 35.84871
23–C 39.17893
24–C 32.05449
25–C 39.81756
26–C 44.73910
27–C 29.51106

28–C 27.40260
29–C 22.87260
30–C 24.63260
31–C 38.52483
32–C 36.30483
33–C 37.13310
34–C 37.13714
35–C 28.98860
36–C 44.66515

R-squared	0.691061	Mean dependent variable	109.7768
Adjusted R-squared	0.664453	SD dependent variable	10.19493
SE of regression	5.905554	Sum squared residual	14577.99
F-statistic	935.0164	Durbin-Watson statistic	0.712530
Prob(F-statistic)	0.000000		

B.5 Pooled Regression

$$\ln(TL_{it}) - C + b_{it} * RDR_{it} + C_{it} * Ed_{it} + e_{it}$$

Sample (adjusted)   1980–1992
Included observations   13 after adjusting endpoints
Total panel observations   455

Variable	Coefficient	Standard error	t-statistic	Probability
C	4.506661	0.035042	128.6090	0.0000
RDR?	0.032429	0.003259	9.948922	0.0000
ED?	0.012935	0.003381	3.825534	0.0001

R-squared	0.266313	Mean dependent variable	4.694326
Adjusted R-squared	0.263067	SD dependent variable	0.090032
SE of regression	0.077288	Sum squared residual	2.699980
F-statistic	82.03323	Durbin-Watson statistic	0.157246
Prob(F-statistic)	0.000000		

B.6 Fixed Effect Model (or the Least Squares Dummy Variable Model)

$$\ln(TL_{it}) = I * a_i + b_{it} * RDR_{it} + C_{it} * Ed_{it} + e_{it}$$

Sample (adjusted)　　　　　1980–1992

Included observations　　　13 after adjusting endpoints

Total panel observations　455

Variable	Coefficient	Standard error	t-statistic	Probability
RDR?	0.033342	0.003694	9.025475	0.0000
D?	0.057167	0.003921	14.58063	0.0000

Fixed Effects

1–C 4.050562

2–C 3.905483

4–C 4.050139

5–C 4.103667

6–C 4.109795

7–C 4.120890

8–C 4.128879

9–C 4.076516

10–C 4.060994

11–C 4.033266

12–C 3.935759

13–C 3.921574

14–C 3.818029

15–C 4.115565

16–C 4.105814

17–C 4.010295

18–C 4.204794

19–C 4.093344

20–C 3.996232

21–C 3.985957

22–C 4.027329
23–C 4.057235
24–C 3.994354
25–C 4.057014
26–C 4.096047
27–C 3.969305
28–C 3.952162
29–C 3.910615
30–C 3.927275
31–C 4.048537
32–C 4.027296
33–C 4.035408
34–C 4.035225
35–C 3.965778
36–C 4.107292

R-squared	0.710082	Mean dependent variable	4.694326
Adjusted R-squared	0.685113	SD dependent variable	0.090032
SE of regression	0.050521	Sum squared residual	1.066904
F-statistic	1023.786	Durbin-Watson statistic	0.783401
Prob(F-statistic)	0.000000		

B.7   Pooled Regression

$$\ln(TL_{it}) = C + b_{it} * \ln(RDR_{it}) + C_{it} * \ln(Ed_{it}) + e_{it}$$

Pooled LS // dependent variable is LTL?
Sample (adjusted)   1980–1992
Included observations   13 after adjusting endpoints
Total panel observations   455

Variable	Coefficient	Standard error	t-statistic	Probability
C	4.383997	0.079021	55.47863	0.0000
LRDR?	0.052935	0.004205	12.58912	0.0000
LED?	0.129382	0.033364	3.877891	0.0001

R-squared	0.340979	Mean dependent variable	4.694326
Adjusted R-squared	0.338063	SD dependent variable	0.090032
SE of regression	0.073250	Sum squared residual	2.425207
F-statistic	116.9330	Durbin-Watson statistic	0.237845
Prob(F-statistic)	0.000000		

B.8   Fixed Effect Model (or the Least Squares Dummy Variable Model)

$$\ln(TL_{it}) = I * a_i + b_{it} * \ln(RDR_{it}) + C_{it} * \ln(Ed_{it}) + e_{it}$$

Sample (adjusted)	1980–1992
Included observations	13 after adjusting endpoints
Total panel observations	455

Variable	Coefficient	Standard error	t-statistic	Probability
LRDR?	0.036356	0.005160	7.045476	0.0000
LED?	0.605029	0.044449	13.61177	0.0000

Fixed Effects

1–C 3.272618

2–C 3.130275

4–C 3.268675

5–C 3.322204

6–C 3.328332

7–C 3.344913

8–C 3.348925

9–C 3.301291

10–C 3.278095

11–C 3.256260

12–C 3.156610

13–C 3.150299

14–C 3.076516

15–C 3.352183

16–C 3.330124
17–C 3.234124
18–C 3.432146
19–C 3.316299
20–C 3.213349
21–C 3.214135
22–C 3.244699
23–C 3.280312
24–C 3.216589
25–C 3.279250
26–C 3.318282
27–C 3.225182
28–C 3.208040
29–C 3.166493
30–C 3.183152
31–C 3.275979
32–C 3.254738
33–C 3.263752
34–C 3.262668
35–C 3.207566
36–C 3.324375

R-squared	0.687182	Mean dependent variable	4.694326
Adjusted R-squared	0.660241	SD dependent variable	0.090032
SE of regression	0.052479	Sum squared residual	1.151175
F-statistic	918.2406	Durbin-Watson statistics	0.686121
Prob(F-statistic)	0.000000		

Appendix C
Regression of Wage
Function with Education,
Age, and Sex as
Determinants in South
Korea

Table C.1

Year	C	b1	b2	b3	b4	b5	b6	R^2
1980	9.599808	0.065787	0.068659	−0.00081	0.330049	0.003142	0.002174	0.661898
	(429.6836)	(95.74721)	(45.68838)	(−36.9824)	(60.86013)	(35.66213)	(30.10163)	
1982	9.870909	0.068422	0.056087	−0.00063	0.329994	0.025923	0.104376	0.67249
	(436.7595)	(97.025)	(36.61426)	(−29.3079)	(60.88603)	(31.86923)	(42.17192)	
1984	10.03395	0.071103	0.056368	−0.00062	0.325762	0.027865	0.089724	0.69486
	(442.3727)	(102.1113)	(37.04722)	(−29.1023)	(62.50393)	(39.26252)	(38.82315)	
1986	10.30205	0.067251	0.058391	−0.00064	0.279283	0.028566	0.073523	0.662997
	(475.3463)	(101.7682)	(41.39389)	(−33.7111)	(47.00929)	(49.61562)	(33.95668)	
1988	10.82413	0.066171	0.040344	−0.00047	0.296222	0.036203	0.075046	0.676137
	(517.0457)	(97.0655)	(30.14756)	(−25.2713)	(64.30213)	(60.02539)	(34.55479)	
1990	11.24572	0.060022	0.039878	−0.00048	0.280876	0.037671	0.046437	0.588203
	(568.0256)	(99.21289)	(35.78037)	(−33.3283)	(67.08882)	(85.69458)	(42.16824)	
1992	11.57377	0.06122	0.035038	−0.0004	0.28251	0.026598	0.058313	0.673278
	(659.9032)	(110.5124)	(34.28113)	(−30.1881)	(79.27925)	(66.10693)	(54.80806)	
1994	11.91983	0.050163	0.032834	−0.00036	0.349749	0.020628	0.072231	0.530786
	(476.492)	(67.52824)	(22.51166)	(−19.306)	(68.82044)	(42.36698)	(48.27469)	

Data Source: KLI (Korea Labor Institute), Occupational Wage Survey Samples

Samples size:

1980	1982	1984	1986	1988	1990	1992	1994
30,551	30,743	31,147	31,003	30,872	47,005	40,982	42,328

Note: Regression equation:

$$\ln \text{Wage} = C + b1\ \text{EDUYEAR} + b2\ \text{AGE} + b3\ (\text{AGE})^2 + b4\ \text{DSEX} + b5\ \text{TENYY} + b6\ \text{CARR}$$

where EDUYEAR = educational year attained (6, 9, 12, 14, 16 years), AGE = real age, DSEX = sex dummy (male = 1), TENYY = tenure year, and CARR = career year. Figures in parentheses are *t*-values.

Table C.2

Year	C	b1	b2	b3	b4	b5	R^2
1980	9.469864 (338.8176)	0.067578 (89.93597)	0.013799 (15.98802)	0.078334 (49.09899)	-0.0008 (-34.3139)	0.320965 (55.56791)	0.61460
1982	9.656723 (334.2851)	0.069376 (87.62819)	0.014168 (18.42222)	0.08294 (51.73255)	-0.00084 (-36.4362)	0.318107 (53.81341)	0.61042
1984	9.7807 (336.4492)	0.071082 (89.6989)	0.012347 (19.70207)	0.08369 (52.73805)	-0.00082 (-36.0025)	0.316527 (55.42291)	0.63364
1986	9.922559 (418.7251)	0.069159 (90.89629)	0.009342 (14.4868)	0.09048 (61.27404)	-0.0009 (-43.7602)	0.25334 (38.30303)	0.58143
1988	10.49079 (431.7239)	0.07036 (85.00718)	0.007001 (11.58844)	0.057656 (45.83925)	-0.00065 (-31.0867)	0.310179 (57.80122)	0.56013
1990	10.60414 (465.3269)	0.070764 (97.18884)	-0.00384 (-6.28988)	0.078609 (63.179)	-0.00082 (-50.2431)	0.315959 (64.15099)	0.42597
1992	10.92413 (539.592)	0.066585 (96.38793)	0.002056 (5.113628)	0.03023 (72.1025)	-0.00084 (-56.5244)	0.306119 (71.75755)	0.53205
1994	11.08882 (423.0371)	0.055862 (64.43191)	-0.00011 (-0.25485)	0.090262 (63.25671)	-0.00093 (-49.7348)	0.356083 (63.37986)	0.42672

Data Source: KLI (Korea Labor Institute), Occupational Wage Survey Samples

Samples size:

	1980	1982	1984	1986	1988	1990	1992	1994
	30,551	30,743	31,147	31,003	30,872	47,005	40,982	42,328

Note: Regression equation:

$$\ln \text{Wage} = C + b1\ \text{EDUYEAR} + b2\ \text{EDUYEAR} * \text{DSE} + b3\ \text{AGE} + b4\ (\text{Age})^2 + b5\ \text{DSEX}$$

where EDUYEAR = educational year attained (6, 9, 12, 14, 16 years), AGE = real age, DSEX = sex dummy (male = 1), DSE = scientists and engineer dummy (according to OCC number: DSE = 1 during 1980 ~ 1992 if 000 < OCC < 110; in 1994: 200 ≤ OCC < 230 or 300 ≤ OCC < 330). Figures in parentheses are t-values.

Notes

Chapter 1

1. Bela Balassa, "Exports and Economic Growth: Further Evidence," *Journal of Development Economics* (June 1978): 181–89. Anne O. Krueger, "Asian Trade and Growth Lessons," *American Economic Review* (May 1990): 108–12. Deepak Lal, *The Poverty of Development Economics*, London: Institute of Economic Affairs, 1983.

2. In 1993 the World Bank published *The East Asian Miracle: Economic Growth and Public Policy* (Oxford University Press, 1993). In this book the Bank revised its stance, admitting that the role of government in the Asian NICs has played a positive role in repairing market failures and imperfections. Earlier some neoclassical economists even held that had the government been less interventionist, the South Korean economy would have grown even faster than it did. The pure logic of economics could lead to such a far-fetched conclusion unless tempered by more down-to-earth realism. The presupposition that an efficient market mechanism was in existence seems misleading, as the recent experience of the former USSR and Poland demonstrate.

3. An outstanding case of successful import substitution is the Pohang Steel Complex. Quick learning of steelmaking technology provides the explanation, not resource endowments. J. L. Enos and W. H. Park studied the speed of learning in the iron and steel industry of Korea. See their *The Adoption and Diffusion of Imported Technology: The Case of Korea* (London: Croom Helm, 1988, ch. 7).

4. Howard Pack and Larry E. Westphal, "Industrial Strategy and Technological Change: Theory versus Reality," *Journal of Development Economics* 22 (June 1986): 87–128. Henry Bruton, "Import Substitution," *Handbook of Development Economics*, vol. 2, ed. by H. Chenery and T. N. Srinivasan, New York: Elsevier Science Publisher, 1989. Linsu Kim, *Imitation to Innovation: The Dynamics of Korea's Technological Learning*, Boston: Harvard Business School Press, 1997. Jin-Ju Lee, *Policy Issues and Technological Innovation Process in Industrial Sectors* (in Korean), Seoul: Korea Advanced Institute of Science and Technology, 1986. Christopher Freeman, *Technology Policy and Economic Performance: Lessons from Japan*, London: Pinter, 1987. Giovanni Dosi et al., *The Economics of Technical Change and International Trade*, London: Harvester Wheatsheaf, 1990. Giovanni Dosi, "Sources, Procedures, and Microeconomic Effects of Innovation," *Journal of Economic Literature* 26 (September 1988): 1120–71. For an energy-centered input-output analysis and technological changes, though with little institutional implications, see Haider A. Kahn, *Technology, Energy, and Development: The South Korean Transition*, Lyme, NH: Edward Elger Publishing, Inc., 1997.

5. Pack and Westphal, *op. cit.*, p. 91.

6. Alice Amsden, *Asia's Next Giant: South Korea and Late Industrialization*, Oxford: Oxford University Press, 1989; Takashi Hikino and Alice H. Amsden, "Staying behind, Stumbling back, Sneaking up, Soaring ahead," *Convergence of Productivity: Cross-National Studies and Historical Evidence*, ed. by William J. Baumol, Richard R. Nelson, and Edward N. Wolff, New York: Oxford University Press, 1994, pp. 285–315; Shahid Alam, *Government and Markets in Economic Development Strategies: Lessons from Korea, Taiwan, and Japan*, New York: Praeger, 1989. Chalmers Johnson, "Political institutions and economic performance: The government-business relationship in Japan, South Korea, and Taiwan Province," *Asian Economic Development—Present and Future*, ed. by R. A. Scalapino et al. Berkeley: Institute of East Asian Studies, University of California, 1985. Chung H. Lee, "The Government, Financing System, and Large Private Enterprises in the Economic Development of South Korea," *World Development* 20 (February 1992): 187–98. Douglas C. North, *Institutions, Institutional Change and Economic Performance*, Cambridge: Cambridge University Press, 1990.

7. This approach was originated by Robert Solow, "Technical Change and the Aggregate Production Function," *Review of Economics and Statistics* 39 (1957): 319–30.

8. Richard R. Nelson, "Why Do Firms Differ, and How Does It Matter?" *Strategic Management Journal* (Winter 1991): 61–74. William Lazonick, *Competitive Advantage on the Shop Floor*, Cambridge: Harvard University Press, 1990. Masahiko Aoki and Ronald Dore (eds.), *The Japanese Firm—Sources of Competitive Strength*, Oxford: Oxford University Press, 1994. Giovanni Dosi, David Teece, and Sidney Winter, "Toward a Theory of Corporate Coherence: Preliminary Remarks," *Technology and the Enterprise in Historical Perspective*, ed. by G. Dosi, R. Gianetti, and A. Toninelli, Oxford: Oxford University Press, 1992. Terry L. Besser, *Team Toyota—Transplanting the Toyota Culture to the Camry Plant in Kentucky*, Albany: State University of New York Press, 1996.

9. Douglas C. North, *Institutions, Institutional Change and Economic Performance*, New York: Cambridge University Press, 1990, p. 135. See also Lewis M. Branscomb, "Social Capital: The Key Element in Science-Based Development," *Annals of the New York Academy of Sciences* 798 (1996): 1–8.

10. "If the hallmark of appreciative theory is story-telling that is close to the empirical nitty-gritty, the hallmark of formal theorizing is an abstract structure set up to enable one to explore, find and check, logical connections." This passage is quoted from Jan Fagerberg, "Technology and International Differences in Growth Rates," *Journal of Economic Literature* (September 1994): 1155.

11. It should be recalled that, when the Japanese occupation ended in 1945, North Korea had inherited most of the industrial facilities (mines, smelting, electricity, chemicals, etc.) while South Korea was practically an agrarian economy based mainly on rice production. North Korea was ahead of South Korea in heavy industries until the mid-1970s.

12. See Theodore Groves et al., "Autonomy and Incentives in Chinese State Enterprises," *Quarterly Journal of Economics* 108 (February 1994).

13. An example of information flow system illustrates the importance of institutional device in Japan. "Matsushita Electric (94,000 employees) handles 4 million suggestions per year, and Toyota Motors (57,000 employees) 2 million suggestions per year. In 1990 about 700 companies with a total of 2 million employees handled 62 million suggestions; 600 companies paid in total 14 billion yen in reward, while 480 gained in total 480 billion yen from adopted suggestions." Quoted from Robert J. Ballon, "Foreign vs. Japanese Products," *Journal of Japanese Trade and Industry*, no. 5 (1996): 46. See also Masahiko Aoki, *Information, Incentives, and Bargaining in the Japanese Economy*, New York: Cambridge Uni-

versity Press, 1989; Fumio Kodama, *Analyzing Japanese High Technologies: The Techno-paradigm Shift*, London: Pinter, 1991; Lewis M. Branscomb and Fumio Kodama, *Japanese Innovation Strategy—Technical Support for Business Visions*, Cambridge: Harvard University Press for the Kennedy School of Government, 1993; Masahiko Aoki and Ronald Dore (eds.), *The Japanese Firm—Sources of Competitive Strength*, Oxford: Oxford University Press, 1994.

14. The need for comparative studies with other countries' experiences would seem self-evident, particularly for policy insights. But that will require many more studies, a challenge for the future. An apt example of comparative study is given by Robert Wade, "How Infrastructure Agencies Motivate Staff: Canal Irrigation in India and the Republic of Korea," Ashok Mody (ed.), "Infrastructure Strategies in East Asia—the Untold Story," EDI Learning Resources Series, World Bank 1997, pp. 109–27.

15. Martin Feltstein argues that the IMF package for Korea contains some reform recommendations for structural changes of long-term nature that are not really urgent to solve the current "cash flow" crisis facing the economy. Thus the package, if implemented fully, can incur excessive costs in the form of unemployment, loss of output, and adverse impact on export performance. See Feltstein, Refocusing the IMF, *Foreign Affairs* (March–April 1998): 20–33. See also Steven Radelet and Jeffrey D. Sachs, "The East Asian Financial Crisis: Diagnosis, Remedies, Prospects," *Brookings Papers on Economic Activity* no. 1 (1998): 49–64; Duck-Woo Nam, "IMF's High Interest Rate Policy at Issue," *Korea Focus* (March–April 1998): 107–12; Ha-Joon Chang, "Korea: The Misunderstood Crisis," *World Development* 26 (1998): 1555–61.

Chapter 2

1. See Lewis M. Branscomb and Young-Hwan Choi (eds.), *Korea at the Turning Point: Innovation-Based Strategies for Development*, Westport, CT: Praeger, 1996.

2. In 1985 the U.S. dollar was worth about 890 won.

3. See, for instance, World Bank, *The East Asian Miracle: Economic Growth and Public Policy*, New York: Oxford University Press for the World Bank, 1993; K. Gannicott, "The Economics of Education in Asian-Pacific Developing Countries," *Asian-Pacific Economic Literature* (March 1990): 41–64; Harry T. Oshima, "Human Resources in East Asia's Secular Growth," *Economic Development and Cultural Change* (April 1988).

4. Namely $\ln Q = \ln A + a \ln K + (1 - a) \ln L$, in a natural log form, where Q is the quantity of output, A is the level of technology, K is capital, L is labor, a is the capital share of output, $(1 - a)$ is the labor share of output. The function, in the form of growth rates implies that $(dA/A) = (dQ/Q) - a(dK/K) - (1 - a)(dL/L)$, where (dA/A) is the growth rate of the technical level, (dQ/Q) is the growth rate of output, (dK/K) is the growth rate of capital, and (dL/L) is the growth rate of labor. See Robert Solow, "Technical Change and the Aggregate Production Function," *Review of Economics and Statistics* 39 (August 1957): 214–31.

5. Sung-Duk Hong and Jung-Ho Kim, *Long Term Changes in Total Factor Productivity of Manufacturing: 1967–93* (in Korean), Seoul: Korea Development Institute, June 1996.

6. The author's own estimate for the same subsector shows a higher annual average TFP growth rate, namely, 0.0 percent for 1971–75, 5.8 percent for 1976–80, and 8.7 percent for 1981–85. The difference between the author's estimates and those reviewed above appears to stem from different methods of data preparation, periodization, and a

difference in the production function adopted. For instance, in the estimates reviewed above, the researchers used a three-year moving average for data used in their calculation. They also used a production function with intermediate input materials as an input, while mine disregarded intermediate inputs. See Youngil Lim, "Industrial Policy, Trade and Productivity Gains: South Korean Evidence," *Journal of Economic Development* (Chung-Ang University Journal) 18 (June 1993): 67.

7. Ji Hong Kim, "Korean Industrial Policy in the 1970s: The Heavy and Chemical Industry Drive," *KDI Working Paper 9015,* Seoul, July 1990. Some economists have re-evaluated the HCI program positively. The entire program is regarded as initiating a catch-up phase of the Korean industry. For this view, see R. M. Auty, "The Macro Impacts of Korea's Heavy Industry Drive Re-evaluated," *Journal of Development Studies* 29 (October 1992): 24–48.

8. Staffan Jacobsson, "The Length of the Infant Industry Period: Evidence from the Engineering Industry in South Korea," *World Development* 21 (1993): 407–19.

9. See POSCO, *A 20 Year History of Pohang Steel Company* (in Korean), Pohang, Korea: POSCO, 1989, pp. 135–37.

10. See his "Output and Labor Productivity, R&D Expenditure and Catch-up Scenarios: A Comparison of the U.S., Japanese, and Korean Manufacturing Sectors," in Korea Economic Research Institute, *Technology Innovation and Industrial Technology Policy,* Seoul: KERI, 1994, p. 27.

11. See his "The Tyranny of Numbers: Confronting the Statistical Realities of the East Asian Growth Experience," *Quarterly Journal of Economics* 110 (August 1995): 641–80.

12. Ibid., p. 670.

13. Laurits R. Christensen and Diane Cummings, "Real Product, Real Factor Input, and Productivity in the Republic of Korea, 1960–1973," *Journal of Development Economics* 8 (1981): 285–302. David Dollar, "Convergence of South Korean Productivity on West German Levels, 1966–88," *World Development* 19(1990): 263–73. David Dollar and Kenneth Sokoloff, "Patterns of Productivity Growth in South Korean Manufacturing Industries, 1963–1979," *Journal of Development Economics* 33 (1990): 309–27. Kwang-suk Kim and Joon-kyung Park, *Sources of Economic Growth in Korea 1963–1982,* Seoul: Korea Development Institute, 1985. Jene K. Kwon, "Capital Utilization: Economies of Scale and Technical Change in the Growth of Total Factor Productivity—An Explanation of South Korean Manufacturing Growth," *Journal of Development Economics* 24 (1986): 75–89. Heewha Moon, Byung-Tahk Jo, Ihn-ho Whang, and Kyung-buhm Kim, *Total Factor Productivity in Korea: An Analysis of 27 Manufacturing Industries* (in Korean), Seoul: Korea Productivity Center, 1991. Hak-kil Pyo and Ho-young Kwon, "Estimation of Real Factor Input and Factor Productivity in the Korean Private Sector," *Korean Economic Journal* 30 (1991): 147–94. Hak-kil Pyo, Byung-ho Kong, Ho-young Kwon, and Eun-ja Kim, *An Analysis of the Causes of Growth and Productivity by Industry for the Republic of Korea, 1970–1990* (in Korean), Seoul: Korean Economic Research Institute, 1993. Arnold Harberger shows an estimate of TFP for Korea: 2.38 percent per year (1971–1991), one of the highest among a sample of 32 countries. See his, "A Vision of Growth Process," *American Economic Review* 88 (1998): 25.

14. This author prefers not to adjust labor quality by education because education and training contribute to learning new technology, thereby enhancing productivity. Estimates of TFP as an index of learning for catching up should subsume the effect of education.

15. A detailed estimate of engineers, technicians, and craftsmen needed over the five-

year period was then prepared. In 1961, according to the plan document (page 26), 2,610 students graduated with bachelor's degree in science and engineering.

16. Chuk Kyo Kim and Byung Taek Cho, *R&D, Market Structure and Productivity* (in Korean), KDI, September 1989; Jin Kyu Chang et al., *Analysis of R&D Investment and Spillover Effects* (in Korean), STEPI, January 1994. R&D capital stock comprises the sum of investments in machines, equipment, land and building for R&D purposes in addition to expenditures for patent fees, salaries of researchers, technology consulting services, and the like. The concept suffers from the problems of depreciation and other measurement difficulties.

17. A. Jaffe, "Technological Opportunity and Spillovers of R&D: Evidence from Firms' Patents, Profits and Market Value," *American Economic Review* 76 (1986): 984–1001.

18. A high social rate of return on R&D capital over the private rate of return has also been reported in the U.S. electrical-electronic machinery industries. See Jeffrey I. Bernstein and M. Ishaq Nadiri, "Interindustry R&D Spillovers, Rates of Return, and Production in High-Tech Industries," *American Economic Review* 78 (1988): 429–34.

19. See his "Effects of Technology Development by Private Enterprise and the Government: Implications for Technology Policy" (in Korean), Korea Economic Research Institute, Seoul, 1995.

20. See, for instance, Chyuk Kyo Kim and Byung Taek Cho, *R&D, Market Structure and Productivity* (in Korean), KDI, September 1989, p. 86.

21. William J. Baumol, Sue Anne Batey Blackman, and Edward N. Wolff, *Productivity and American Leadership: The Long View*, Cambridge: MIT Press, 1989, p. 204.

22. George Psacharopoulos, "Education and Development: A Review," *World Bank Research Observer* (January 1988): 99–116.

23. At the time of liberation from Japanese occupation (1945), Korea's achievements in education were rather meager. According to one source, in 1944, 86.6 percent of Korean population had no schooling whatsoever (i.e., were illiterate), and only 11.3 percent of the population had 1 to 6 years of education, and 1.8 percent had 7 to 12 years of education. Only 0.1 percent had a college education or more. See Chang-young Jung, "Human Resources in the Korean Economic Development," Yonsei University, Seoul (mimeo), March 1977, p. 5; the paper was presented at the Multi-disciplinary Conference on South Korean Industrialization, which was held at the University of Hawaii, June 14–17, 1977. A massive investment in education was made between 1945 and the early 1960s, when the industrialization drive was launched. On national debate for educational policy, see Michael J. Seth, "Education, State and Society in South Korea, 1948–1960," PhD dissertation, University of Hawaii, 1994. See the next chapter for more on this.

24. This finding would seem highly suggestive since an extensive study using worldwide cross-country data reported a high correlation between the proportion of high school enrollment and real GDP growth rate. The study by Baumol et al. confirms: "Finally, the calculation's results turned out to be far stronger, consistent, and statistically significant when the education variable employed was that related to secondary education rather than to primary or higher education. In other words, the calculation firmly supported Professor Lewis's thesis, . . . that education does matter a good deal for a nation's economic growth, and that what matters most is the share of the population with secondary education." W. Baumol et al., op. cit., p. 206.

25. Kang-Shik Choi, "Investment in Education, Technological Change, and the Structure of Wage Differentials in Developing Countries: The Case of Korea," PhD dissertation,

Yale University, New Haven, 1993. For a normative evaluation of wage income and distribution in South Korea, see David L. Lindauer et al. (eds.), *The Strains of Economic Growth: Labor Unrest and Social Dissatisfaction in Korea,* Cambridge: Harvard Institute for International Development, 1997.

26. George Psacharopoulos, "Returns to Investment in Education: A Global Update," *World Development* 22 (1994): 1325. The Korean case contradicts this conclusion. See Jin-Hwa Jung, *Educational Expansion and Economic Returns to College Education in Korea,* Seoul: Korea Institute for Industrial Economics and Trade, 1996, p. 37.

27. This phenomenon was analyzed in Youngil Lim, "Capital, Labor and Skill Contents of Trade: South Korea," *Southern Economic Journal* 42 (January 1976).

28. Lester C. Thurow, *The Future of Capitalism: How Today's Economic Forces Shape Tomorrow's World,* New York: Morrow, 1996, p. 74.

29. Hyundai, Daewoo, and Kia, the three major automobile makers, announced last year (1996) that each one of them planned to become one of the world's ten big producers. In 1998, Kia dropped out of the race. The track records of Hyundai and Daewoo give some weight to their announcements. Despite the financial setback during 1997–98, their long-term goals remain the same.

30. "By appreciative theorizing, I mean the descriptions and explanations of what is going on that economists put forth when they are paying considerable attention to the details of the subject matter. While less abstract than formal theorizing, this attempted description of what is going on certainly is a form of theorizing, albeit theorizing relatively close to the empirical subject matter." Quoted from Richard R. Nelson, *The Sources of Economic Growth,* Cambridge: Harvard University Press, 1996, p. 5.

Chapter 3

1. Noel F. McGinn et al., *Education and Development in Korea,* Cambridge: Harvard University Press, 1980, pp. 81–82.

2. Kunmo Chung, "Science and Technology and Development of Korea: Phase-one Report, Korea Science and Technology Policy Instruments Project," Seoul: Korea Advanced Institute of Science and Technology, 1973, p. 21.

3. Robert J. Keller, "The Role of Government in the Reform of Higher Education," *Innovation in Higher Education,* ed. by Tae Sun Park (in Korean), Seoul: Yonsei University Press, 1973, p. 210.

4. For a scholarly examination of Japanese economic policy, see Sang Chul Suh, *Growth and Structural Change in the Korean Economy 1919–1940,* Cambridge: Harvard University Press, 1978.

5. It should be noted that the Korean independence movement had a strong cultural impact as it resisted the Japanese policy of making Koreans second-class Japanese. Korean language and education provided the arena for the ideological struggle against the Japanese policy makers in Korea. For an excellent study of this issue, see Michael Robinson, *Cultural Nationalism in Colonial Korea, 1920–1925,* Seattle: University of Washington Press, 1988, ch. 3.

6. One could argue that there is a certain parallel between the vacuum in institution building that resulted from the 35-year Japanese occupation of Korea and that resulting from the 10-year cultural revolution in China.

7. Jong Chol Kim, *Education and Development: Some Essays and Thoughts on Korean Education*, Seoul: Seoul National University Press, 1985, ch. 3.

8. Some even observe that "Korea has maintained one of the world's most competitive educational systems, in which access to higher education is determined by a uniform standard. With few exceptions, access is determined by the applicant's score on a national exam—unlike in Western countries where multiple standards such as family background, extracurricular activities, alumni connections, and leadership skills are considered. . . . Such an environment of equal status with fair competition created great potential for vertical mobility in society: the general public was given almost equal opportunity and strong incentives to move up the 'status ladder' by investing in human capital or by entrepreneurial activities." Quoted from Joon-Kyung Kim et al., "The Role of Government in Promoting Industrialization and Human Capital Accumulation in Korea," in *Growth Theories in Light of the East Asian Experience*, ed. by Takatoshi Ito and Anne O. Krueger, Chicago: University of Chicago Press, 1995, p. 183.

9. McGinn, op. cit., p. 240.

10. The Philippines has invested heavily in university education, producing proportionately more graduates than Korea throughout the 1970s and 1980s. See Jee-Peng Tan and Alian Mingat, *Education in Asia: A Comparative Study of Cost and Financing*, Washington: World Bank, 1992; also Hiromitsu Muta (ed.), *Educated Unemployment in Asia*, Tokyo: Asian Productivity Organization, 1990.

11. See Michael P. Todaro, "A Model of Labor Migration and Urban Unemployment in Less Developed Countries," *American Economic Review* 59 (March 1969): 138–48.

12. Changwon Lee, "Social Capital, Social Closure, and Human Capital Development: The Case of Managerial Workers in Korean *Chaebol*," PhD dissertation, University of Chicago, March 1994.

13. Theodore W. Schultz, *Restoring Economic Equilibrium, Human Capital in the Modernizing Economy*, Oxford: Basil Blackwell, 1990, p. 79.

14. See Paul Krugman, "The Myth of Asia's Miracle," *Foreign Affairs* 73 (November–December 1994): 62–78.

15. Hak K. Pyo, "A Time-Series Test of the Endogenous Growth Model with Human Capital," in *Growth Theories in Light of the East Asian Experience*, ed. by Takatoshi Ito and Anne O. Krueger, Chicago: University of Chicago Press, 1995, p. 236, table 9.3.

16. See Gur Ofer, "Soviet Economic Growth: 1928–1985," *Journal of Economic Literature* 25 (December 1987): 1778.

17. See David Dollar, "Convergence of South Korean Productivity on West German Levels, 1966–78," *World Development* 19 (1991): 263–73.

18. See Vikram Nehru and Ashok Dhareshwar, "New Estimates of Total Factor Productivity Growth for Developing and Industrial Countries," Policy Research Working Paper 1313, World Bank, Washington, DC (June 1994), p. 1. Their regression shows that only human capital and no other variables could explain intercountry variations of TFP growth covering 83 countries.

19. See, for example, Orley Ashenfelter and Alan Krueger, "Estimates of the Economic Return to Schooling from a New Sample of Twins," *American Economic Review* 84 (December 1994). The authors concluded "that increased schooling increases average wage rates by about 12–16 percent per year completed. This is larger than most estimates in the

prior literature." See also Jeff Grogger and Eric Eide, "Changes in College Skills and the Rise in the College Wage Premium," *Journal of Human Resources* 30 (1996): 280–310.

20. This phenomenon stands in contrast to the experience of the American labor market during the 1980s. "The college wage premium for new labor market entrants rose sharply during the 1980s. . . . The trend away from low-skill subjects such as education and toward high-skill subjects such as engineering accounts for one-fourth of the rise in the male college wage premium." Grogger and Eide, op. cit., p. 280.

21. One recent study would appear to corroborate with this proposition. See Kang-Shik Choi, "The Impact of Shifts in Supply of College Graduates: Repercussion of Educational Reform in Korea," *Economics of Education Review* 15 (1996): 1–9. ". . . we examined the hypothesis that technology changes are more complementary with highly educated workers than with less educated workers. The results imply that technology changes in Korea increased the relative demand for more educated workers, especially for college educated workers." (op. cit., p. 8)

22. Se-il Park, "Labor Market Consequences of Higher Education Expansion (II)," *Korea Development Review,* KDI journal (in Korean), (1983): 28.

23. Se-il Park, "Labor Issues in Korea's Future," *World Development* 16 (1988): 99–119.

24. In Japan the "unit cost" per student in sciences and engineering is reported to be twice that in humanities and social sciences. For instance, in 1988 the doctoral program's per unit cost was $1,811 and $985, respectively, and the master program's per unit cost was $1,267 and $689, respectively. The difference was largely due to the salaries of chaired professors. The unit cost of chairs was $13,124 for humanities and social sciences and $51,331 for sciences and engineering in the same year. See Morikazu Ushiogi, "Graduate Education and Research Organization in Japan," in *The Research Foundations of Graduate Education, Germany, Britain, France, United States, Japan,* ed. by Burton R. Clark, Berkeley: University of California Press, 1993, p. 318.

25. The following observations pertain to the period up to 1993 when university presidents began to introduce some serious reforms that challenged the then dominant perception and inertia. The last three years have seen the burgeoning of new thinking on the need for radical changes to the curriculum and tenure policy of higher education in Korea.

26. In the American university system, promotion is closely connected to a faculty member's publication history in refereed journals. Hence the teaching function is often neglected, although students' evaluations of teaching are a factor in the promotion procedure.

27. Korean researchers published 3,910 papers in 1994 in S&T (SCI) journals. This figure is seen to be low when it is divided by the 42,700 researchers in colleges and universities then. The average publication figure would be further lowered if researchers in government R&D Institutes (15,465 in 1994) were to be included in the calculation.

28. According to a report, the figure for laboratory expenditures on science and engineering students averaged 57,000 won (approximately $70) per student in 1993 at private universities and 150,000 won (approximately $187) per student at public universities. See "Toward Activation of S&T Universities: An Urgent Need for Specialization" (in Korean), *Jonja Shinmun* (*Electronics Daily News*), October 8, 1996.

29. "Final Report: Consultation / Evaluation of the Programs in Engineering and Science at the Korea Advanced Institute of Science and Technology," submitted to KAIST by

Leslie F. Benmark (Evaluation Team chair) et al., New York: Accreditation Board for Engineering and Technology, 1993, p. 3.

30. For detailed history, see KAIST, *20-Year History of Korea Advanced Institute of Science and Technology 1971–1991* (in Korean), KAIST, 1992.

31. *Ibid.,* p. 274.

32. This practice has not yet been adopted by other higher learning institutions. One of the difficulties in introducing this practice is the resistance from the older faculty members in the various departments.

33. ABET Report, op. cit., p. 6.

34. This compares with the university share of 13.5 percent for Japan (1993 figure), 11.9 percent for the United States (1994 figure), and 17.5 percent for Germany (1993 figure).

35. The long-range need for cooperation between the two sectors is self-evident. The stories of Silicon Valley in California and route 128 in Massachusetts have demonstrated the mutual benefits to universities and industries.

36. The research park idea started in 1951 at Stanford University. A prototype research park was established on 660 acres of land; it ended up housing over eighty companies. Thus Silicon Valley was already primed to thrive in the 1970s and the 1980s. Reportedly, some 50 research parks were established in the United States by the mid 1980s. For some interesting examples of innovative alliances between universities and industries, see David R. Powers et al., "Higher Education in Partnership with Industry," *Opportunities and Strategies for Training, Research, and Economic Development,* San Francisco: Jossey-Bass, 1988, ch. 3.

37. Korean research parks could learn from American examples, since in the past American universities faced similar problems: "An inherent tension nevertheless existed between the commercial activities into which universities ventured and the disinterested pursuit of teaching and learning for which they ineluctably stood. . . . In its more prevalent form, it consisted of acquiescence in practices that rubbed against the academic grain—secrecy or noncooperation in research; attempts to exclude foreign firms from technology transfer; suspicion of the misuse of graduate students; diversion of faculty time and effort from teaching and research. Universities learned from a succession of embarrassments to contain many of these problems." Robert L. Geiger, "Research and Relevant Knowledge," *American Research Universities Since World War II,* New York: Oxford University Press, 1993, p. 320. To avoid these problems, the planners and administrators of university research parks formulated a number of alternative institutional devices. The efficiency of a university research park depended on how skillfully such conflicts are handled.

38. For details, see KOSEF, "Science and Engineering Research Center 1995," Taejon: Korea Science and Engineering Foundation, 1995.

39. The basic goals and approaches are drawn from the National Science Foundation's (USA) ERC Program, which was launched in 1984. A detailed account of the program is given in General Accounting Office of the United States, "Engineering Research Centers: NSF Program Management and Industry Sponsorship," GAO/RCED-88-177, Washington, DC, 1988.

40. "Successful Outcome of KOSEF's Center of Excellence Program," *Hanguk Kyungje Shinmun (Korea Economic Daily)* April 4, 1996.

41. Theodore Schultz advances the idea of the positive effect of experts on the rest of human capital. "These effects spill over from one person to another. People at each skill level are more productive in high than low human capital environments. Human capital enhances the productivity of both labor and physical capital." Quoted from his *Restoring Economic Equilibrium—Human Capital in the Modernizing Economy*, Oxford: Basil Blackwell, 1990, p. 215. The Samsung case does not confirm exactly Schultz's assertion because the Stanford PhD holders descended from high (United States) to low human capital environments (Korea). Nevertheless, one could detect powerful human capital externalities in the Samsung case.

42. See Fumio Kodama, *Analyzing Japanese High Technology, The Techno Paradigm Shift*, London: Pinter, 1991, p. 121.

Chapter 4

1. Korean *chaebols* adopted the Japanese institutional form but with important differences. "Despite some differences in management styles such as Japanese groupism and bottom-up decision-making versus Korean autocratic dynamism and top-down decision-making, Koreans have successfully adapted the Japanese systems in their own way. The top-down decision-making system was probably necessary for Korea to catch up with advanced technologies in a short period of time in a less expensive manner." Quoted from Hiroshi Kakazu, "Industrial Technology Capabilities and Policies in Selected Asian Developing Countries," *Asian Development Bank Economic Staff Paper*, no. 46, Manila, June 1990, pp. 21–22. See also Chan Sup Chang, "Comparative Analysis of Management Systems: Korea, Japan, and the United States," *Korea Management Review* 13 (1983): 77–98; Sangjin Yoo and Sang M. Lee, "Management Style and Practice of Korean *Chaebols*," *California Management Review* 24 (Summer 1987): 95–110; and Chan Sup Chang and Nahn Joo Chang, *The Korean Management System: Cultural, Political, Economic Foundations*, Westport, CT: Quorum Books, 1994, ch. 9 ("Office of Planning and Control: Think Tanks of Organization") and ch. 10 ("The Korean Management System and Management Systems of Japan and the United States"). Further see Alice Amsden, "Project Execution Capability, Organizational Know-how, and Conglomerate Corporate Growth in Late Industrialization," *Industrial and Corporate Change* 3 (1994), and also her, "Scientific Publications, Patents and Technological Capabilities in Late Industrializing Countries," *Technology Analysis and Strategic Management* (1997). Hahn Been Lee points out that army officers, trained in modern techniques of military management, have contributed to enhancing organizational skills of firms and government agencies in the 1950s and 1960s. See his *Korea: Time, Change, and Administration*, Honolulu: East-West Center Press, 1968, ch. 8.

2. This concept differs from "economies of scale or advantages of mass production." See Byong Ho Gong, *Rise and Fall of Korean Enterprise* (in Korean), Seoul: Myong-Jin Publishing, 1995, pp. 147–54.

3. Some *chaebols* with greater potential for expanding exports have been allowed to establish general trading companies in order to exploit their ability to gather marketing information in the global market—another institutional device borrowed from Japan. See Dong-Sung Cho, *The General Trading Company, Concept and Strategy*, Lexington, MA: Lexington Books, D.C. Heath, 1987.

4. See his "A Study of Technology Diffusion at Enterprise Level with Special Reference to Machinery Sectors" (in Korean), Seoul: Korea Economic Research Institute, April 1988.

5. This also explains the absence of all forms of insurance, such as life, disaster, damage, or even automobile insurance during the 1950s and 1960s.

6. For such an interpretation, see Yoon Je Cho, "Finance and Development: The Korean Approach," *Oxford Review of Economic Policy* 5 (Winter 1989).

7. Op. cit., pp. 142–44. Other studies note strong leadership on the part of the owner-managers, which enabled the firms to change quickly, responding to the changes in environments. See Yoo-kun Shin et al., *The Management Characteristics of Korea's Large Enterprises* (in Korean), Seoul: Sae-Kyung-Sa, 1995, pp. 423–28.

8. For historical details, see Won Chul Oh, *Industrialization in Korean Style: An Engineering Approach* (in Korean), vol. 1, Seoul: KIA Economic Research Institute, 1995, pp. 177–79.

9. The adverse impact of the 1979–80 recession upon the economy should not be confused with the neoclassical economists' criticism of the HCI program. The latter argue, for instance, that "the HCI promotion drive of 1973–79 scarred the Korean economy for years. It created excess capacities in some unprofitable industries, while depleting investment funds that would have otherwise been available to other export industries. Distortions in the domestic capital market were also severe, since preferential loans below market rates became a major instrument in promoting the HCIs." Quote from Chong-Hyun Nam, "The Role of Trade and Exchange Rate Policy in Korea's Growth," in *Growth Theories in Light of the East Asian Experience*, ed. by Takatoshi Ito and Anne O. Krueger, East Asia Seminar on Economics, vol. 4, National Bureau of Economic Research, Cambridge, MA, 1995, p. 162. This writer maintains that the criticism should be evaluated against a backdrop of the benefits, namely early opportunities for technological learning.

10. A group of economists has begun to pay more attention to the importance of firm-level learning, a departure from the previous neglect of what goes on in the "black box" or inside a firm. See, for instance, R. R. Nelson, "Why Firms Differ, and How Does It Matter?" *Strategic Management Journal* 12 (Winter 1991): 61–74; see also Alfred D. Chandler, "Organizational Capabilities and the Economic History of the Industrial Enterprise," *Journal of Economic Perspectives* 6 (Summer 1992): pp. 79–100.

11. See Samsung Semiconductor and Telecommunications, Inc., *A Ten-Year History of Samsung Semiconductor and Telecommunications* (in Korean), Seoul: Samsung Semiconductor and Telecom., Inc., 1987.

12. This event seems to lend support to the proposition that human capital flows prove to be the most effective means for technology transfer and learning.

13. For more details, see *A 50-Year History of Samsung* (in Korean), published by Samsung Planning Office, 1988, pp. 498–505.

14. See an interview article, "The Ambition and Might of Samsung Electronics," *Shindong-A Magazine*, October 1995, pp. 370–79.

15. It is clearly the case of more given to those who already have some.

16. Samsung's salaries more than match any competitor's by at least 5 percent. Other *chaebol* groups appear to be greatly challenged. But so far, they have not followed the Samsung example, such as instituting an eight-hour work day schedule.

17. A study of Korean *chaebols* advances the view that they represent a unique form of capitalism, blending Korean family values based on Confucianism, the military

command traditions inherited from the Japanese occupation as well as the Korean war, and Western organizational techniques. See Roger L. Janelli and Dawnhee Yim, *Making of Capitalism—The Social and Cultural Construction of a South Korean Conglomerate,* Stanford: Stanford University Press, 1993. An evaluation of the training program for new employees appears on pages 140–44.

18. Jun and Han, op. cit., pp. 96–100. See also, Jung-Woong Suh, *Samsung Group—Ordinary Salaryman* (in Korean), Seoul: Sung-Jung Publishing, 1987. In a memoir form, the author describes vividly the internal organization and the motivation, loyalty and competition of employees.

19. Young Rak Choi, "Dynamic Techno-management Capability—The Case of Samsung Semiconductor Sector in Korea," PhD dissertation, Roskilde University (Denmark), 1994, p. 136.

20. Tamio Hattori, a Japanese expert on Korean *chaebols,* has pointed out that this separation between R&D engineers and line-workers constitutes a culture-based weakness of Korean enterprises. See his *Korea's Management and Chaebols Seen from a Japanese Perspective,* trans. by Ryu, Han Sung, et al., Seoul: Hwa-Pyung-Sa Publishing, 1991, pp. 363–72.

21. See, for example, George Stalk Jr., "Time—The Next Source of Competitive Advantage," *Harvard Business Review* (July–August 1988): 41–51.

22. "Under a competency multiplier process, teams made up of highly competent members outperform other teams even beyond what their individual abilities would predict. The multiplicative effects of individual abilities are particularly important when the team's work is complex, uncertain, and interdependent. Highly able team members can solve nonroutine problems and teach those solutions to one another. . . . These members contribute valuable nonoverlapping skills and cancel one another's errors, so team interaction bestows extra benefits on team performance." Quoted from Sara Kiesler et al., "Coordination as Linkage: The Case of Software Development Teams," in *Organizational Linkages: Understanding Productivity Paradox,* ed. by Douglas H. Harris et al., Washington: National Academy of Science, 1994, p. 219.

23. The final section of this chapter considers possible forms the internal organizational structure of *chaebols* could take.

24. SMEs are defined in Korean statistics as firms having less than 300 permanent employees; small if less than 20 permanent employees (i.e., in manufacturing).

25. For an account of government policy favoring large enterprises in the 1960s and 1970s, see Youngil Lim, *Government Policy and Private Enterprise: Korean Experience in Industrialization,* Institute of Asian Studies, Berkeley: University of California, 1981, ch. 3.

26. In the name of protecting labor, Indian labor law prohibits firing of employees. However, in return, insolvent firms may request government subsidies or even let the government take over "sick industries." The government has collected 158,000 such sick firms by 1988, providing a source of government budget deficits. See UNIDO, *Industry and Development Global Report,* 1989 / 90, p. 71. The perversity of this incentive system should be pointed out. In effect, when an inefficient firm is subsidized, it is given a "reward for inefficiency." This is in marked contrast to the Korean practice of subsidizing firms according to export performance.

27. For a theory of the *keiretsu* system, see Ken-ichi Imai and Hiroyuki Itami, "Interpenetration of Organization and Market: Japan's Firm and Market in Comparison with

the U.S.," *International Journal of Industrial Organization* 2 (December 1984). More recently, Japanese are moving toward less exclusivity in their relationships, and SMEs have gradually acquired broader access to technology, in part thanks to information technology. See D. Hugh Whittaker, "SMEs, Entry Barriers, and Strategic Alliances," in *The Japanese Firm: Sources of Competitive Strength,* ed. by Masahiko Aoki and Ronald Dore, Oxford: Oxford University Press, 1994, pp. 209–32.

Chapter 5

1. In the First Five-Year Plan (1962–1966) exports were targeted to increase from $54.8 million in 1962 to $135.6 million in 1966, but actually a whopping $250.3 million was achieved in 1966. In the Second Five-Year Plan (1967–1971), exports were targeted to increase from $300 million in 1967 to $550 million in 1971, but actually $1,067.6 million was achieved in 1971. In the Third Five-Year Plan (1972–1976), exports were targeted to increase from $1,584 million in 1972 to $3,510 million in 1976, but actually $7,715 million was achieved in 1976. Similar orders of overfulfillment were reported for investment and output targets. See Youngil Lim, *Government Policy and Private Enterprise: Korean Experience in Industrialization,* Berkeley: University of California Institute of East Asian Studies, 1981, pp. 9–13.

2. Today the legacy of government control is hindering industrial competitiveness because of high interest rates and the inefficiencies inherent in the control policy. For an interesting policy analysis, see Dongchul Cho and Youngsun Koh, "Liberalization of Capital Flows in Korea: Big-Bang or Gradualism?" National Bureau of Economic Research Working Paper Series 5824, Cambridge, MA, 1996.

3. For example, the lack of a developed banking system wrought havoc to the Russian economy which underwent a Big-Bang type of reformation. Market mechanisms can grow and mature only gradually; they cannot be created overnight.

4. This asset could prove useful when and if Korea takes a leadership role in its foreign policy to help industrialize developing countries and eliminate their poverty. For an evaluation of the Economic Planning Board (reorganized into the Ministry of Economics and Finance in 1995) and KDI, see Man-Hee Lee, *Has the EPB Created a Miracle?* (in Korean) Seoul: Haedodee Publishing, 1993; Byung-Sun Choi, "Institutionalizing a Liberal Economic Order in Korea: The Strategic Management of Economic Change," PhD dissertation, Graduate School of Arts and Sciences, Harvard University, 1987.

5. The idea for establishing KIST is said to have resulted from a meeting between Lyndon Johnson and Park Chung Hee in 1965.

6. On the occasion of the thirtieth anniversary of KIST, February 10, 1996, a newspaper article reported that KIST undertook 6,184 R&D projects; published 4,239 papers; applied for intellectual property rights to 1,783 items; commercialized 695 items of technology developed by KIST; earned 19 billion won in income from licensing fees involving 183 items of technology owned by KIST; and spun off 11 affiliated research institutes. See "Science and Technology Think-Tank: KIST Commemorates 30th Anniversary," *Jonja Shinmun* (*Electronics Daily*), February 12, 1996.

7. This summary evaluation is quoted from Dal Hwan Lee, Zong-Tae Bae, and Jinjoo Lee, "Performance and Adaptive Roles of the Government-Supported Research Institute in South Korea," *World Development* 19 (1991).

8. The U.S. average in 1989 amounted to U.S.$148,300 per researcher. Germany averaged

U.S.$201,100 in 1989 and Japan averaged U.S.$195,000 (1992 figure). Quoted from MOST, *Report on the Survey of Research and Development in Science and Technology*, 1994, p. 64.

9. Hyung Sup Choi, *Research Institute Where Lights Never Go Out: Choi Hyung Sup Memoir* (in Korean), Seoul: Chosun Daily News Publishing, 1995, p. 81.

10. This ritualistic policy instrument is culture-specific with little applicability to other countries. In Korea, one could argue, it is useful in generating and disseminating information, and also in rewarding achievers with social recognition. For hundreds of years artisans had been looked down upon, and engineers had suffered from this cultural tradition. The conference contributed toward changing the Korean outlook.

11. ETRI, initially established in 1976 under MOST's jurisdiction, was transferred to MOC in 1992.

12. For an insightful history, see OECD, *Reviews of National Science and Technology Policy, Republic of Korea*, Paris, 1996, also Young-Ho Nam, "Change in Roles of Korean Government-Supported Research Institute: Mission Analysis from Their Inception up to Present," paper presented at the First Korea-ASEAN workshop sponsored by STEPI, Seoul, April 7–8, 1994; see also Dal Hwan Lee, Zong-Tae Bae, and Jinjoo Lee, "Performance and Adaptive Roles of the Government-Supported Research Institute in South Korea," *World Development* 19 (1991).

13. MOST, *We Have Accomplished These Tasks* (in Korean), Seoul: MOST, October 1992, p. 42.

14. KITA, *Industrial Technology White Paper 1993* (in Korean), Seoul: KITA, 1993, pp. 73–77.

15. Those PhDs who grumbled and left GFRIs numbered 138 in 1992, 126 in 1993, 115 in 1994, and 131 in 1995 (up to August). *Korea Economic Weekly*, December 11, 1996, p. 11. In a sense, however, those who left the GFRIs may be seen as being beneficial to technology (or skill) diffusion within the country. They carried with them technological expertise as well as R&D management techniques to the private sector.

16. Robert E. Lucas has attempted to build a model to explain the growth performance of Korea as compared with the Philippines by linking the effect of learning spillover with trade and product diversification. But the model fails to consider the organizational variable which seems crucial to explain the difference in performance. See his "Making a Miracle," *Econometrica* 61 (March 1993): 251–72.

17. See his "Export-led Technology Development in the Four Dragons: The Case of Electronics," *Journal of Development Studies* (October 1994): 333–61. A similar view has also been expressed by Larry Westphal. See L. E. Westphal, Y. W. Rhee, and G. Pursell, "Korean Industrial Competence: Where It Came From," World Bank Staff Working Paper 469, July 1981, p. 72.

18. For instance, during the 1986–87 period, the localization program has succeeded in achieving U.S.$1,360 million worth of import replacement plus U.S.$700 million worth of export creation owing to 727 of product items which have been localized. See Korea Industrial Technology Association, *Industrial Technology White Paper* (in Korean), 1988, p. 30.

19. See, for example, K. R. Lee et al., *Interim Evaluation of Localization Policy and Ways to Improve* (in Korean), Seoul: Korea Institute for Industrial Economics and Trade (KIET), April 1990.

20. A negative list system means that any commodity not listed could be imported without being subject to quantitative restrictions. A positive list system means that only those listed could be imported, and all others would be subject to quantitative restrictions.

21. See Soogil Young, "Import Liberalization and Industrial Adjustment," KDI Working Paper 8613, Seoul: Korea Development Institute, December 1986.

22. Min, Kyung Whee, *The Changes of Input-Output Structure in Korean Industries: A Comparison with Japan* (in Korean), Research Series 93-08, Seoul: Korea Institute for Industrial Economics and Technology, 1993, p. 154.

23. Quoted from Douglas North, *Institutions, Institutional Change and Economic Performance*, Cambridge: Cambridge University Press, 1990, p. 110.

24. See Joungwon A. Kim, *Divided Korea—The Politics of Development 1945–1972*, Cambridge: Harvard University Press, 1976, p. 339.

25. See I. J. Ahluwalia, "Industrial Growth in India: Performance and Prospects," *Journal of Development Economics* 23–24 (1986): 4.

26. Quoted from Staffan Jacobson and Ghayur Alam, *Liberalization and Industrial Development in the Third World: A Comparison of the Indian and South Korean Engineering Industries*, New Delhi: Sage Publications India, 1994, p. 233.

27. This finding seems consistent with the main theme of Michael Porter, *The Competitive Advantage of Nations*, New York: Free Press, 1990. He concludes that the competitiveness of an enterprise depends, among others, on the support system of the economy including technological infrastructure.

28. See The Industry-Academe Cooperation Foundation, *A Ten-Year History (1974–1984)* (in Korean), Seoul, 1984

29. James M. Watson and Peter F. Meiksins, "What Do Engineers Want? Work Values, Job Rewards, and Job Satisfaction," *Science, Technology, and Human Values* 16 (Spring 1991): 140–72; see also C. Orpen, "Individual Needs, Organizational Rewards, and Job Satisfaction among Professional Engineers," *IEEE Transactions on Engineering Management* 32 (1985): 177–80.

30. Fortunately this problem appears to have been recognized by the Minister of Trade and Industry, who in 1996 announced the establishment of a graduate school for information and communication. But the research component has yet to be added or elaborated on.

31. In 1996 it was reported that a professor was given an appointment by a university and an off-campus research institute simultaneously. This is rather slow progress. Until the mid 1990s it had been thought that an industry appointment would hinder a professor's teaching responsibilities and hence it was prohibited by law. This way of thinking is changing but slowly.

32. Quoted from Mushin Lee, Byoungho Son, and Kiyong Om, "Evaluation of National R&D Projects in Korea," *Research Policy* 25 (1996): 807. Even in the United States, where the peer-review system is firmly established, debates still go on as to whether it is an impartial, objective, and therefore reliable, system. Some argue that a peer-group evaluation system serves the interests of mainstream groups, political pork-barrel stake holders, and the like, with no accountability to broader social issues. See Daryl E. Chubin and

Edward J. Hackett, *Peerless Science: Peer Review and U.S. Science Policy*, Albany: State University of New York Press, 1990, ch. 2.

33. A survey reports that only one academic association out of 234 associations in Korea has a database with information on R&D human resources located overseas. The survey recommends that KIST should formulate a seven-year plan for database construction involving at least 70 important academic associations in Korea. See STEPI, *Informationalization of Academic Associations: A Survey and Policy Options for Dissemination* (in Korean), Seoul, July 1995, pp. 17 and 27.

34. Ki-ho Lee, Young-ho Yang, and Kang-ryol Son, *Database of Science and Technology Manpower: Its Construction and Operation Scheme* (in Korean), Seoul: KIST and R&D Information Center, January 1995.

35. "To improve the relatively low social prestige of laboratory researchers, the proposal to bestow professor status on researchers that meet certain qualifications should be given serious consideration." Quoted from Young-Hwan Choi and Boong-Kyu Lee, "The Importance and Needs of Public Laboratories," in *Korea at the Turning Point—Innovation-Based Strategies for Development*, ed. by Lewis M. Branscomb and Young-Hwan Choi, Westport, CT: Praeger, 1996, p. 156.

36. This section has been co-authored by Youngil Lim and Shinkyu Yang. For public policy on building capabilities in the information sector of Korea, see James F. Larson, *The Telecommunications Revolution in Korea*, Oxford: Oxford University Press, 1995.

37. See "A Survey of Silicon Valley," *The Economist* 342, March 29, 1997, p. 12.

38. See A. Toffler and H. Toffler, *War and Anti-war: Survival at the Dawn of the 21st Century*, Boston: Little, Brown, 1993.

39. See E. Mann, "Desert Storm: The First Information War?" *Airpower Journal* 8 (Winter 1994).

40. See J. Fitzsimonds and J. v. Jol, "Revolutions in Military Affairs," *Joint Force Quarterly* (Spring 1994).

41. See H. Dupree, *Science in the Federal Government: A History of Policies and Activities*. Baltimore: Johns Hopkins University Press, 1986.

42. See G. T. Mazuzan, "A Brief History," *NSF General Publication* no. 88-16, 1994.

43. See S. Rosegrant and D. R. Rampe, *Route 128: Lessons from Boston's High-Tech Community*, New York: Basic Books, 1992.

44. See R. C. Estall, "The Electronic Products Industry of New England," *Economic Geography* 39 (1963): 189–216.

45. See D. Packard, *The HP Way: How Bill Hewlett and I Built Our Company*, New York: HarperBusiness, 1996.

46. See Barry M. Leiner, Vinton G. Cerf, et al., *A Brief History of the Internet*, Reston, Virginia, Internet Society, 1997.

47. Defense Advanced Research Project Agency, a private agency connected to the Department of Defense charged with long-range research to develop capabilities not currently available to the military services. The name has been altered several times from DARPA to ARPA. The ARPANET project started with the name Advanced Research Project Agency. DARPA is the current name, but it was returned from ARPA in 1996.

48. See W. M. Ayers and BankBoston, *MIT: The Impact of Innovation.* Boston: BankBoston, 1997.

49. See D. Packard, *The HP Way: How Bill Hewlett and I Built Our Company,* New York: HarperBusiness, 1996.

50. See Annalee Saxenian, *Regional Advantage,* Cambridge: Harvard University Press, 1994.

51. See "A Survey of Silicon Valley," *The Economist* 342, March 29, 1997.

52. See B. P. Shapiro and L. B. Levine, *Hewlett-Packard: Manufacturing Productivity Division (A), (B), and (C),* Boston: Harvard Business School, 1987.

53. See D. Narayandas and V. K. Rangan, *Dell Computer Corp.* Boston: Harvard Business School, 1995.

54. See M. A. Cusumano, and R. W. Selby, *Microsoft Secrets: How the World's Most Powerful Software Company Creates Technology, Shapes Markets, and Manages People.* London: HarperCollins, 1996; A. S. Grove, *Only the Paranoid Survive: How to Exploit the Crisis Points That Challenge Every Company and Career,* New York: Currency Doubleday, 1996.

55. See E. Brynjolfsson and L. Hitt, "Paradox Lost? Firm-Level Evidence on the Returns of Information Systems Spending," *Management Science* 42 (1996): 541–58; and E. Brynjolfsson and S. Yang, "Information Technology and Productivity: A Review of the Literature," *Advances in Computers* 43 (1996): 179–215.

56. See S. Yang and E. Brynjolfsson, "Market Valuation of Computer Capital," MIT Sloan School Working Paper, 1997.

57. See E. Brynjolfsson and L. Hitt, "Information Technology and Internal Firm Organization: An Exploratory Analysis," MIT Sloan School of Management, 1997; T. W. Malone, "Is Empowerment Just a Fad?" *Sloan Management Review* 38 (1996): 23–35.

58. See H. Bahrami and S. Evans, "Flexible Recycling," *California Management Review* 37 (1995): 62–89.

59. See "A Survey of Silicon Valley," *The Economist* 342, March 29, 1997, p. 6.

60. See Annalee Saxenian, *Regional Advantage,* Cambridge: Harvard University Press, 1994.

Chapter 6

1. See, for instance, World Bank, *The East Asian Miracle: Economic Growth and Public Policy,* Washington: World Bank, 1993; "Symposium on the World Bank's The East Asian Miracle: Economic Growth and Public Policy," *World Development* 23 (April 1994). In the preceding chapters of this book, we observed South Korea's accumulation of knowledge, skills, and institutional assets. The role of the entrepreneurial government, as opposed to a predatory one, over the last three decades has been to nudge the country toward a less imperfect market economy. For South Korea the Walrasian perfect market represents only a special (and extreme) case of the imperfect–perfect spectra of market architectures.

2. Recall that training in design skills is a weakness of KAIST.

3. "Interviews also confirmed problems of intrafirm information transfer—getting results from the R&D component of the organization into commercial use. Two key factors contributing to this problem are that (1) much technical knowledge is tacit and cannot

easily be transferred from R&D to production without the transfer of key people; and (2) bringing a new idea into commercial practice requires a great deal of commitment and perseverance. Thus, frequently, the best way to commercialize R&D results is to transfer the inventor. This explains the success of many new small companies in which an inventor leaves a large company or university in order to have more flexibility in commercializing research ideas and realizing financial rewards." Quoted from Steven Ballard et al., *Innovation through Technical and Scientific Information: Government and Industry Cooperation,* New York: Quorum Books, 1989, p. 178.

4. Paula Stephan, "The Economics of Science," *The Journal of Economic Literature* 34 (September 1996): 1201.

5. These views and issues are discussed critically in Daryl E. Chubin and Edward J. Hackett (eds.), *Peerless Science: Peer Review and U.S. Science Policy,* Albany: State University of New York Press, 1990.

6. Sang Ryong Kim, "Science and Technology Database, Urgently Needed," *Jonja Shinmun* (Electronic Times), January 25, 1979, p. 2.

7. Japanese companies are known to use global scanning techniques when they want to find out whether, and where and at what price, a certain technology will be available for developing a new product.

8. Gerardo R. Ungson, Richard M. Steers, and Seung-Ho Park, *Korean Enterprise: The Quest for Globalization,* Boston: Harvard Business School Press, 1997, p. 81.

9. Martin Bloom, *Technological Change in the Korean Electronics Industry,* Paris: OECD, 1992, p. 120.

10. Quoted from Richard Nelson, *The Sources of Economic Growth,* Cambridge: Harvard University Press, 1996, p. 118.

11. "In 1948, Charles Helmick, Deputy of the Military Government of U.S. Occupation Forces in South Korea, reported to Washington: Korea can never attain a high standard of living. There are virtually no Koreans with the technical training and experience required to take advantage of Korea's resources and make improvements over its rice economy status. When U.S. occupation forces withdraw and stop sending in supplies that South Korea needs, its full economy will be reduced to a bull cart economy, and some nine million non-food producers will not be able to survive." Quoted from Yong-Teh Lee and Lewis M. Branscomb, "Korean Information Technology: Status and Policy Implications," Lewis M. Branscomb and Young-Hwan Choi, op. cit., p. 242. For a perspective on the backwardness of pre-capitalist South Korea in the 1950s, see Yong Sam Cho, *Disguised Unemployment in Underdeveloped Areas, with Special Reference to South Korean Agriculture,* Berkeley: University of California Press, 1963.

12. See, for example, Joseph E. Stiglitz, "Some Lessons from the East Asian Miracle," *World Bank Research Observer* 11 (August 1996): 151–77; Alice H. Amsden, "Late Industrialization: Can More Countries Make It?" in *Political Economy for the 21st Century: Contemporary Views on the Trend of Economics,* ed. by Charles J. Whalen, New York: Armonk, M.E. Sharpe, Inc., 1996, pp. 245–61; William R. Cline, "Can the East Asian Model of Development be Generalized?" *World Development* 10(1982): 81–90.

13. It is no exaggeration to say that the burgeoning Korean trade in electronics-related goods with the United States is built upon the numerous contributions that U.S. trained Korean engineers have made.

14. William Cline, op. cit.

Name Index

Subject Index